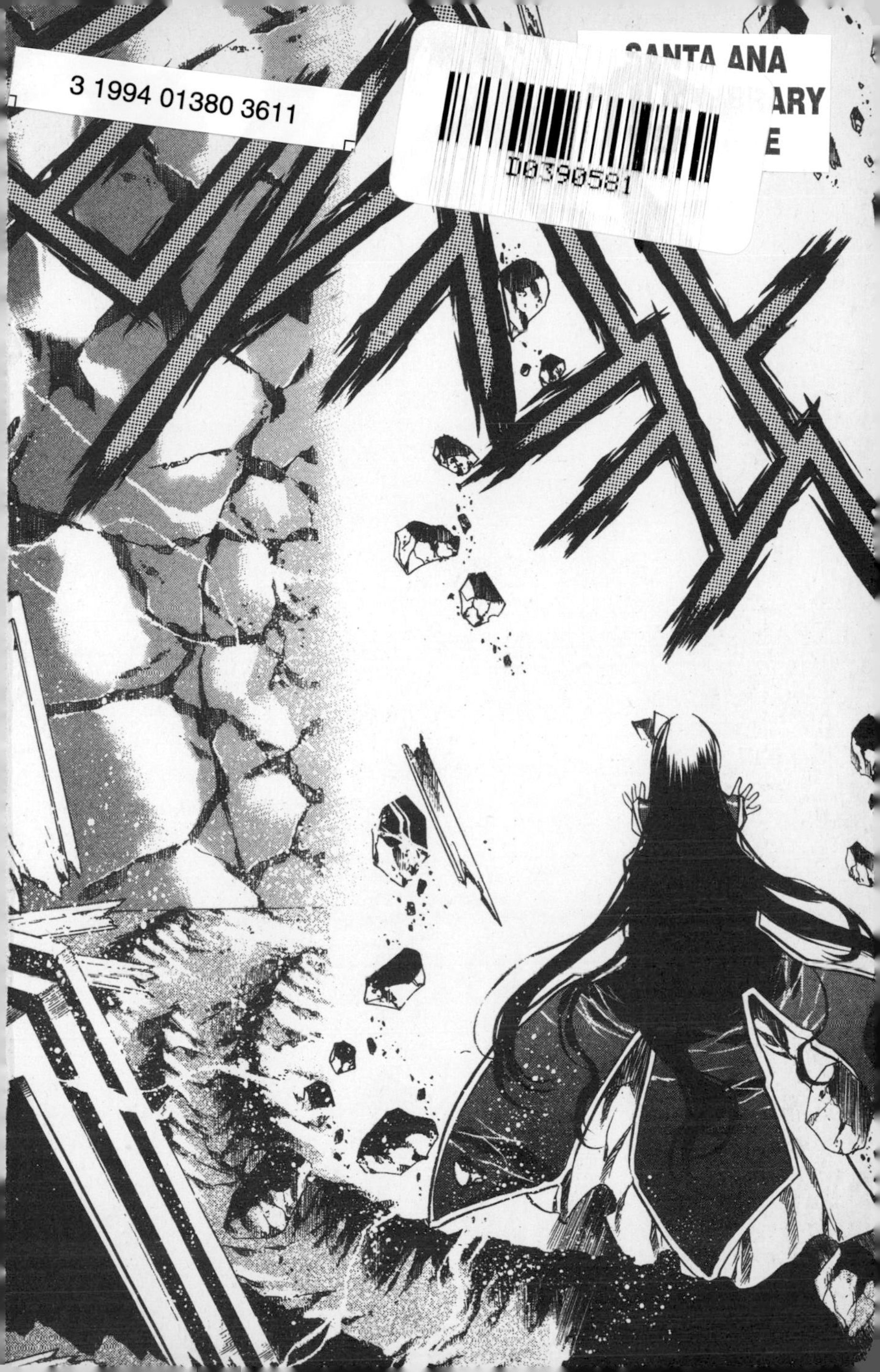

CHRONICLES OF THE CURSED SWORD

Volume 8

Story by
YEO BEOP-RYONG
Art by
PARK HUI-JIN

TOKYOPOP

HAMBURG // LONDON // LOS ANGELES // TOKYO

Chronicles Of The Cursed Sword Vol. 8
written by Yeo Beop-Ryong
illustrated by Park Hui-Jin

Translation - Yongju Ryu
English Adaptation - Matt Varosky
Copy Editor - Christine Schilling
Retouch and Lettering - Abelardo Bigting
Production Artist - Louis Csontos
Cover Design - Gary Shum

Editor - Bryce P. Coleman
Digital Imaging Manager - Chris Buford
Pre-Press Manager - Antonio DePietro
Production Managers - Jennifer Miller and Mutsumi Miyazaki
Art Director - Matt Alford
Managing Editor - Jill Freshney
VP of Production - Ron Klamert
President and C.O.O. - John Parker
Publisher and C.E.O. - Stuart Levy

A  Manga

TOKYOPOP Inc.
5900 Wilshire Blvd. Suite 2000
Los Angeles, CA 90036

E-mail: info@TOKYOPOP.com
Come visit us online at www.TOKYOPOP.com

ISBN: 1-59182-425-7

First TOKYOPOP printing: September 2004
10 9 8 7 6 5 4 3 2 1
Printed in the USA

Chronicles

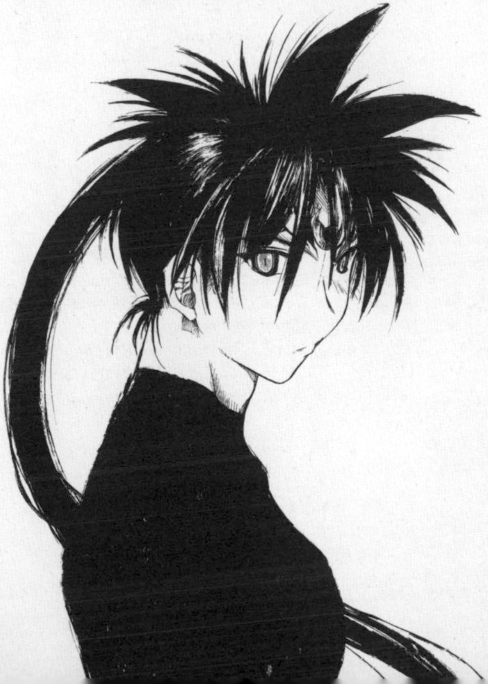

CHRONICLES OF THE CURSED SWORD

the cast of characters

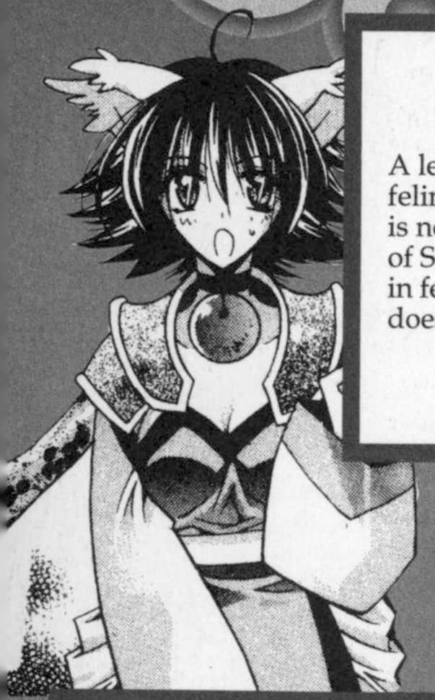

MINGLING

A lesser demon with feline qualities, Mingling is now the loyal follower of Shyao Lin. She lives in fear of Rey, who still doesn't trust her.

THE PASA SWORD

A living sword that hungers for demon blood. It grants its user incredible power, but at a great cost—it can take over the user's body and, in time, his soul.

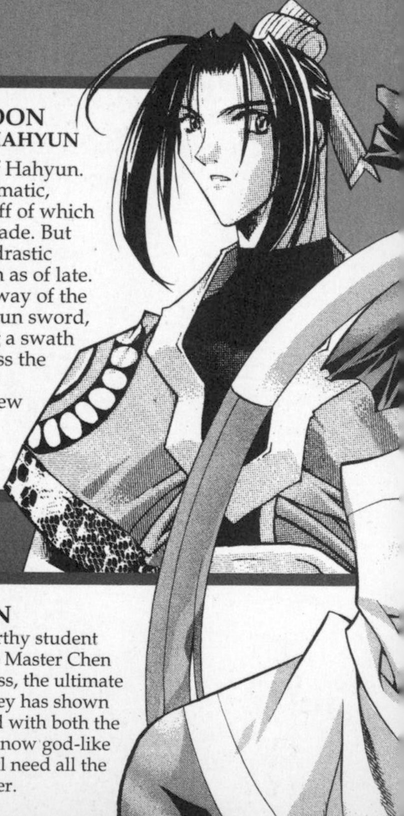

JARYOON
KING OF HAHYUN

Jaryoon – King of Hahyun. Noble and charismatic, Jaryoon is the stuff of which great kings are made. But there has been a drastic change in Jaryoon as of late. Now under the sway of the spirit of the PaChun sword, Jaryoon is cutting a swath of humanity across the countryside as he searches for his new prey…Rey.

SHYAO LIN

A sorceress, previously Rey's traveling companion and greatest ally. Shyao has recently discovered that she is, in fact, one of the Eight Sages of the Azure Pavilion, sent to gather information in the Human Realm. Much to her dismay, she has been told that she must now kill Rey Yan.

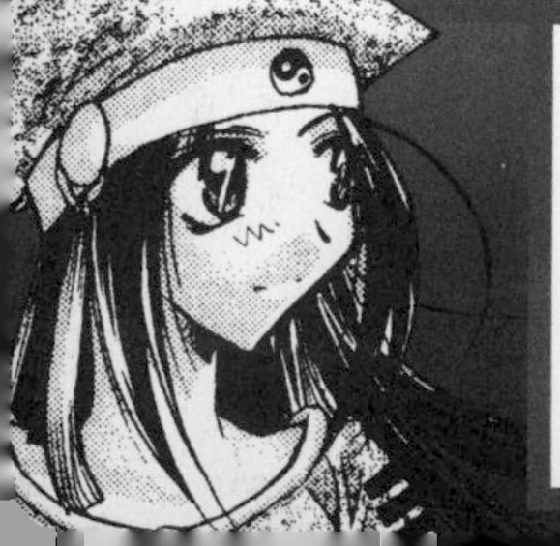

REY YAN

Rey has proven to be a worthy student of the wise and diminutive Master Chen Kaihu. At the Mujin Fortress, the ultimate warrior testing grounds, Rey has shown his martial arts mettle. And with both the possessed Jaryoon and the now god-like Shyao after his blood—he'll need all the survival skills he can muster.

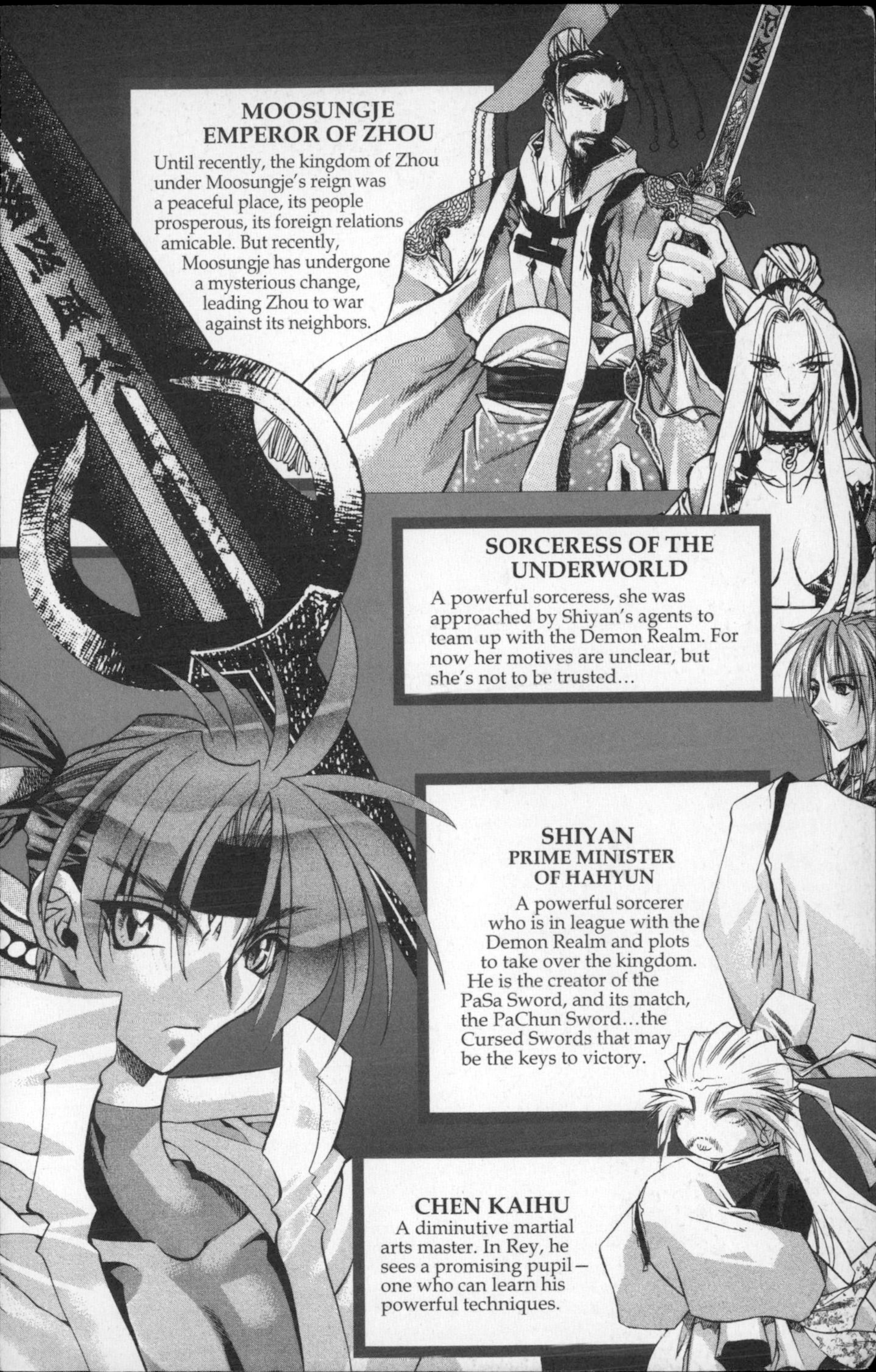
MOOSUNGJE
EMPEROR OF ZHOU
Until recently, the kingdom of Zhou under Moosungje's reign was a peaceful place, its people prosperous, its foreign relations amicable. But recently, Moosungje has undergone a mysterious change, leading Zhou to war against its neighbors.
SORCERESS OF THE UNDERWORLD
A powerful sorceress, she was approached by Shiyan's agents to team up with the Demon Realm. For now her motives are unclear, but she's not to be trusted...
SHIYAN
PRIME MINISTER OF HAHYUN
A powerful sorcerer who is in league with the Demon Realm and plots to take over the kingdom. He is the creator of the PaSa Sword, and its match, the PaChun Sword...the Cursed Swords that may be the keys to victory.
CHEN KAIHU
A diminutive martial arts master. In Rey, he sees a promising pupil—one who can learn his powerful techniques.

CHRONICLES OF THE CURSED SWORD

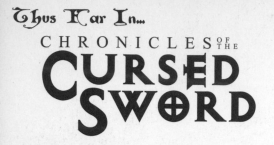

It is told that in eons past, the Emperor of the Heavenly Realm banished his only heir to the Demon Realm. This was the beginning of a centuries-long struggle between the Heavenly Realm and the Demon Emperor—an epic war that would shake the Earth and spill the blood of countless humans and demons alike.

Two mystical swords are the keys that keep the Demon Emperor at bay— the Pa-Sa sword, which feeds upon the blood of slain demons, and its dark mate, the Pa-Chun sword, which thirsts for human blood.

A young warrior, Rey Yan, has been possessed by the spirit of the PaSa sword, while the once-noble King Jaryoon has fallen under the influence of the PaChun. Pitted against each other by unseen forces and hunted by both enemies and former allies, the two unsuspecting pawns are now all that stands between the world of men and a hell on earth...

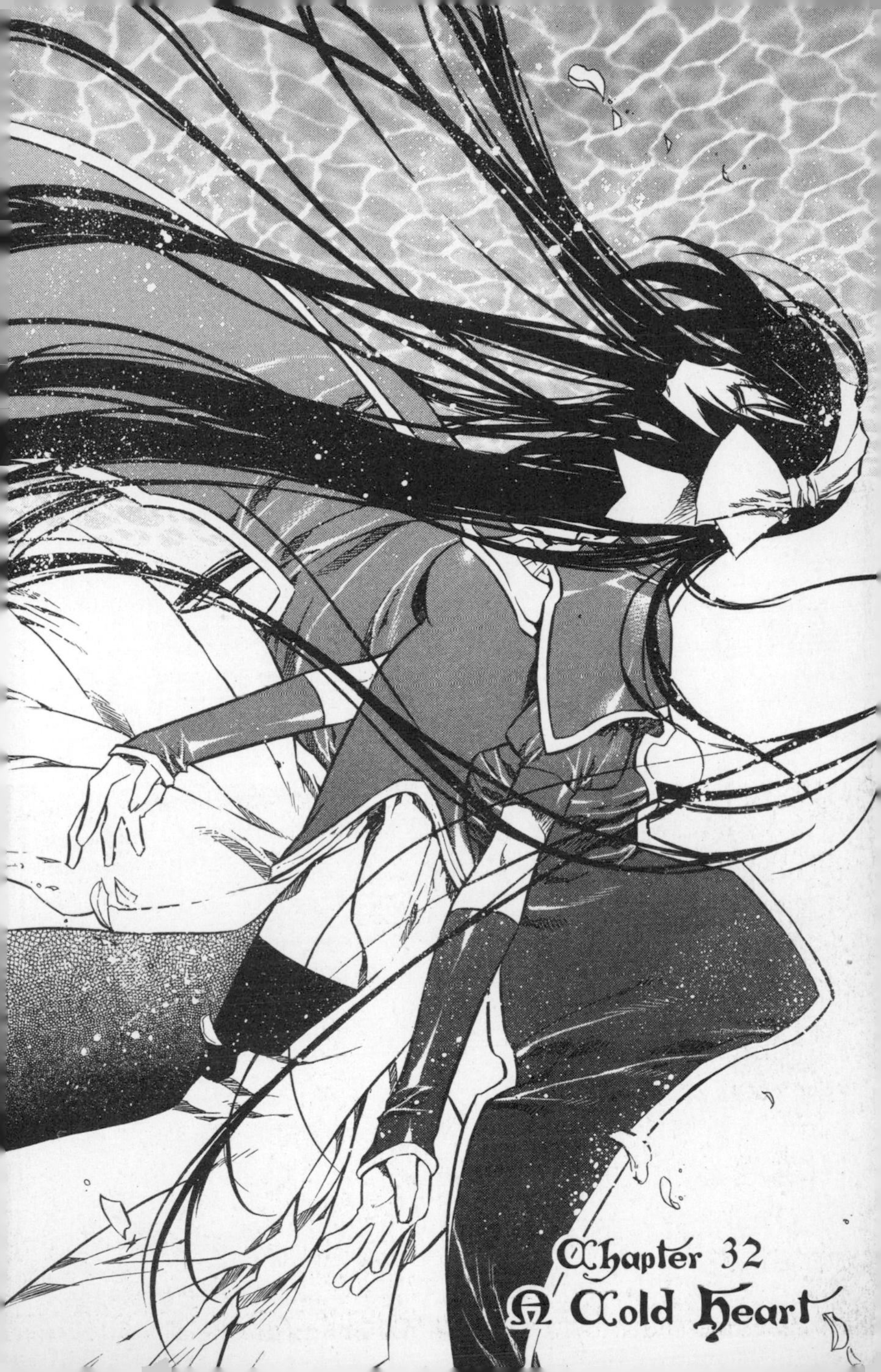
Chapter 32
A Cold Heart

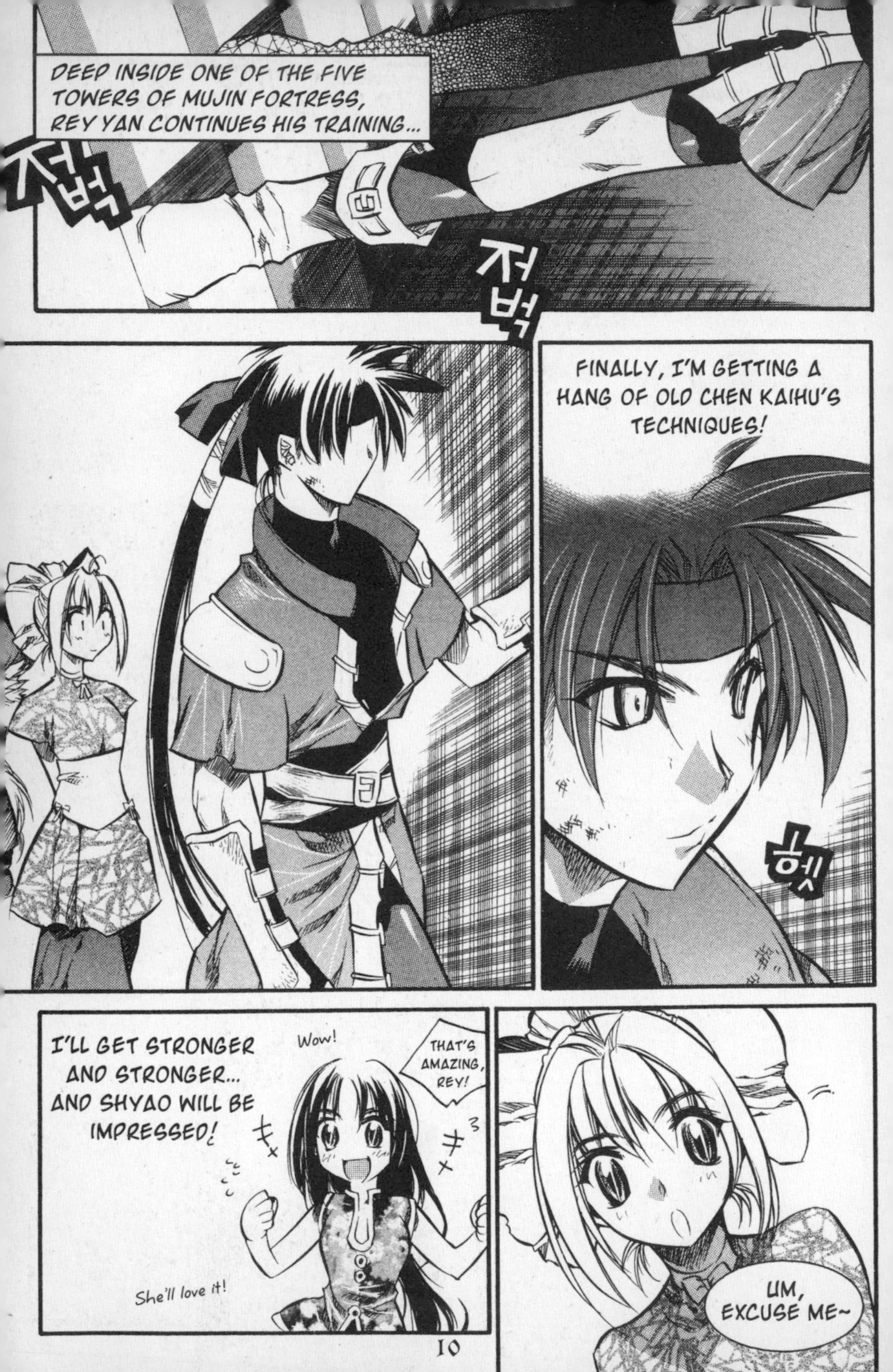
DEEP INSIDE ONE OF THE FIVE TOWERS OF MUJIN FORTRESS, REY YAN CONTINUES HIS TRAINING...
저벅
저벅
FINALLY, I'M GETTING A HANG OF OLD CHEN KAIHU'S TECHNIQUES!
헷
I'LL GET STRONGER AND STRONGER... AND SHYAO WILL BE IMPRESSED¿
Wow!
THAT'S AMAZING, REY!
She'll love it!
UM, EXCUSE ME~

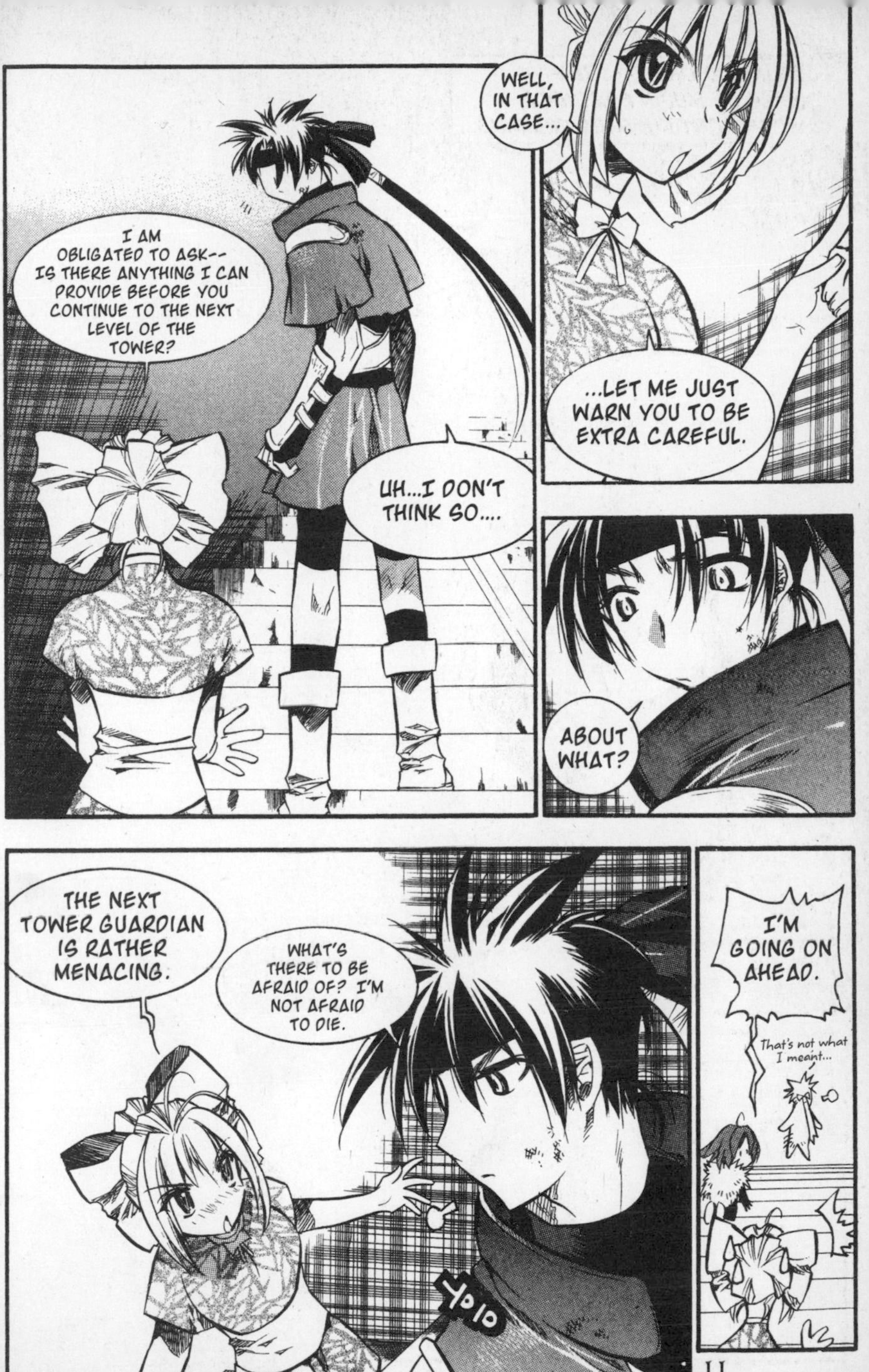
I AM OBLIGATED TO ASK-- IS THERE ANYTHING I CAN PROVIDE BEFORE YOU CONTINUE TO THE NEXT LEVEL OF THE TOWER?
UH...I DON'T THINK SO....
WELL, IN THAT CASE...
...LET ME JUST WARN YOU TO BE EXTRA CAREFUL.
ABOUT WHAT?
THE NEXT TOWER GUARDIAN IS RATHER MENACING.
WHAT'S THERE TO BE AFRAID OF? I'M NOT AFRAID TO DIE.
I'M GOING ON AHEAD.
That's not what I meant...

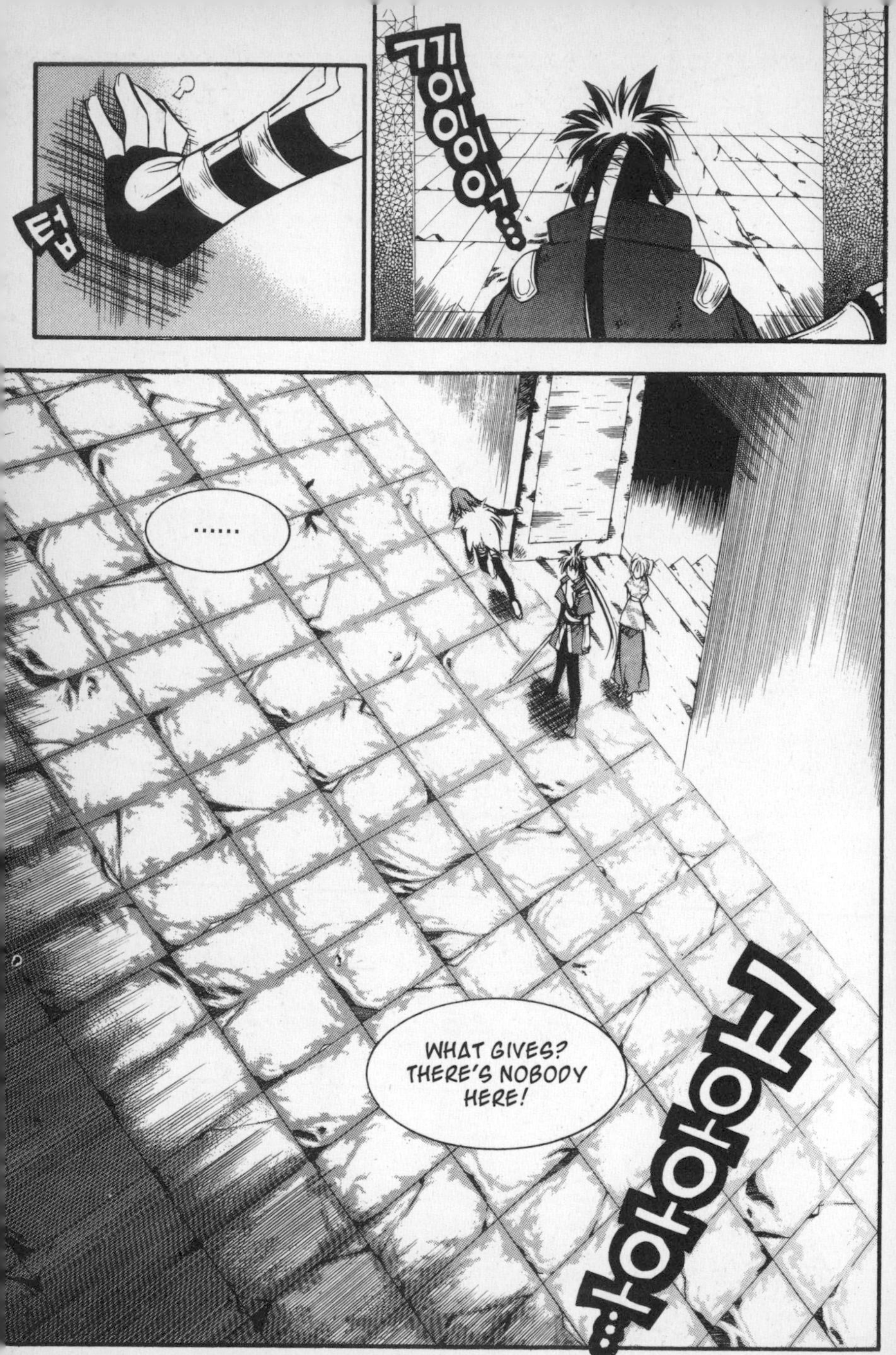
......
WHAT GIVES? THERE'S NOBODY HERE!

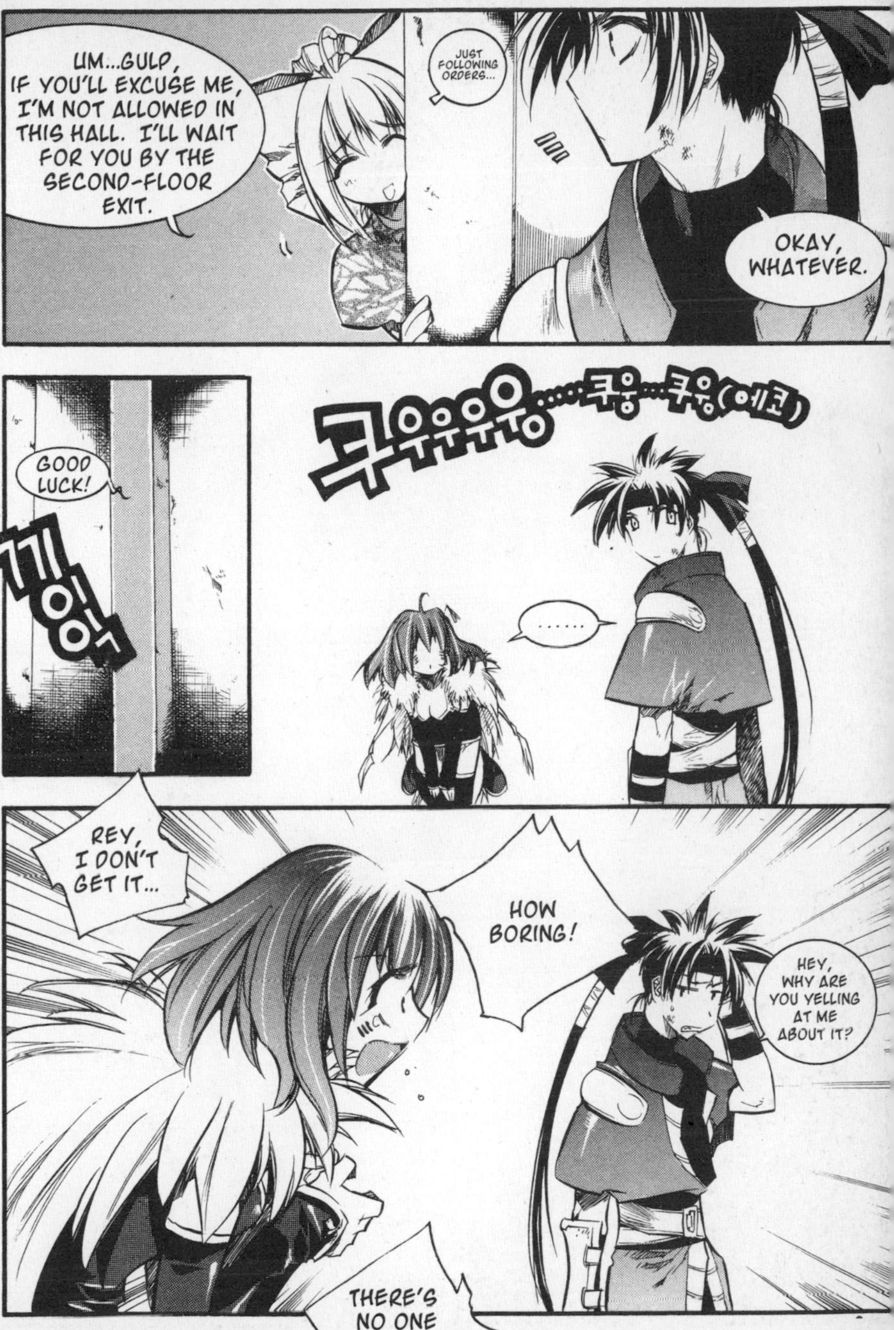
UM...GULP, IF YOU'LL EXCUSE ME, I'M NOT ALLOWED IN THIS HALL. I'LL WAIT FOR YOU BY THE SECOND-FLOOR EXIT.
JUST FOLLOWING ORDERS...
OKAY, WHATEVER.
GOOD LUCK!
끼이익
쿠우우우웅……쿠웅…쿠웅(에코)
......
REY, I DON'T GET IT...
HOW BORING!
HEY, WHY ARE YOU YELLING AT ME ABOUT IT?
THERE'S NO ONE HERE!

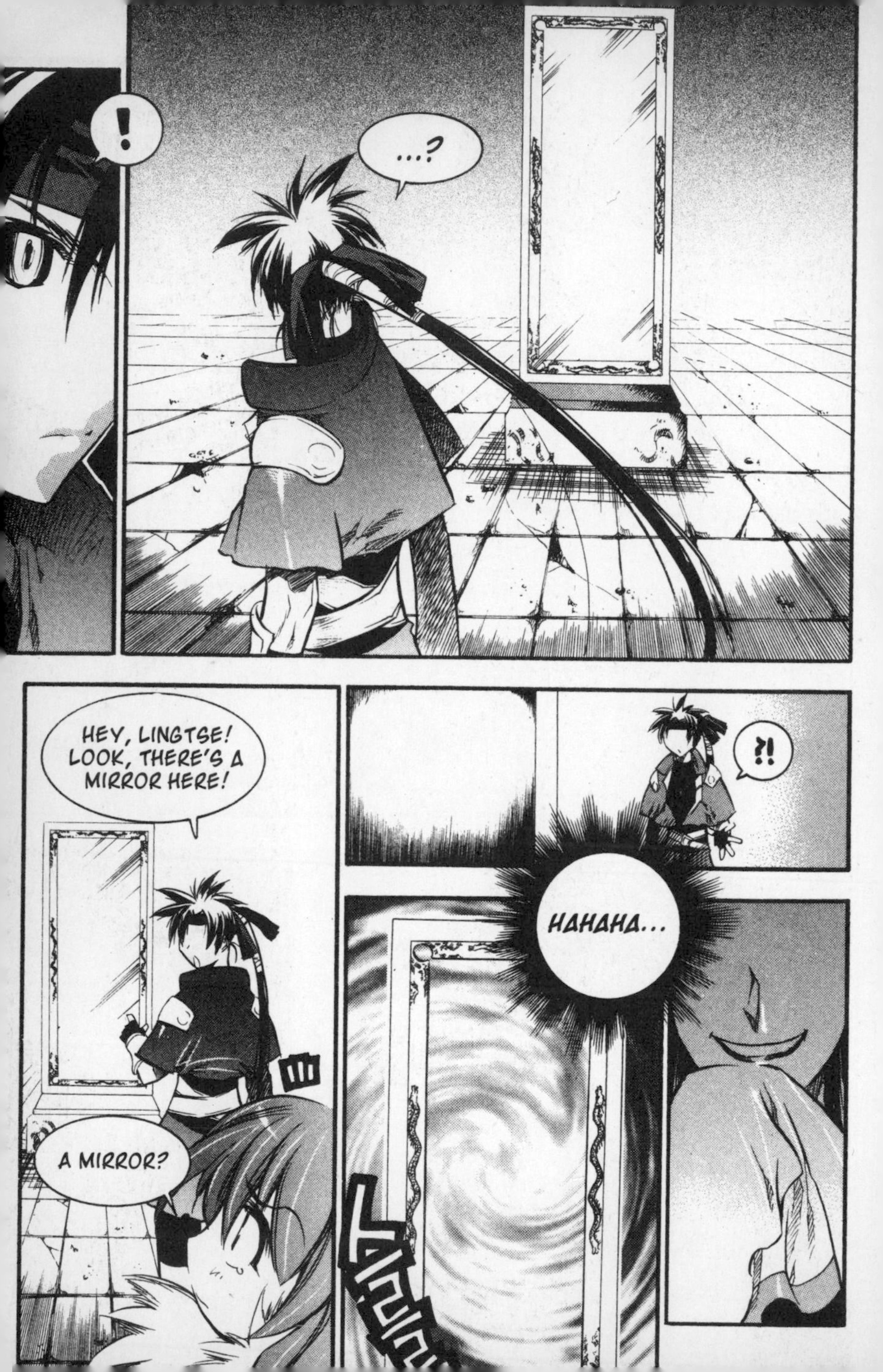
!
...?
HEY, LINGTSE! LOOK, THERE'S A MIRROR HERE!
A MIRROR?
?!
HAHAHA...

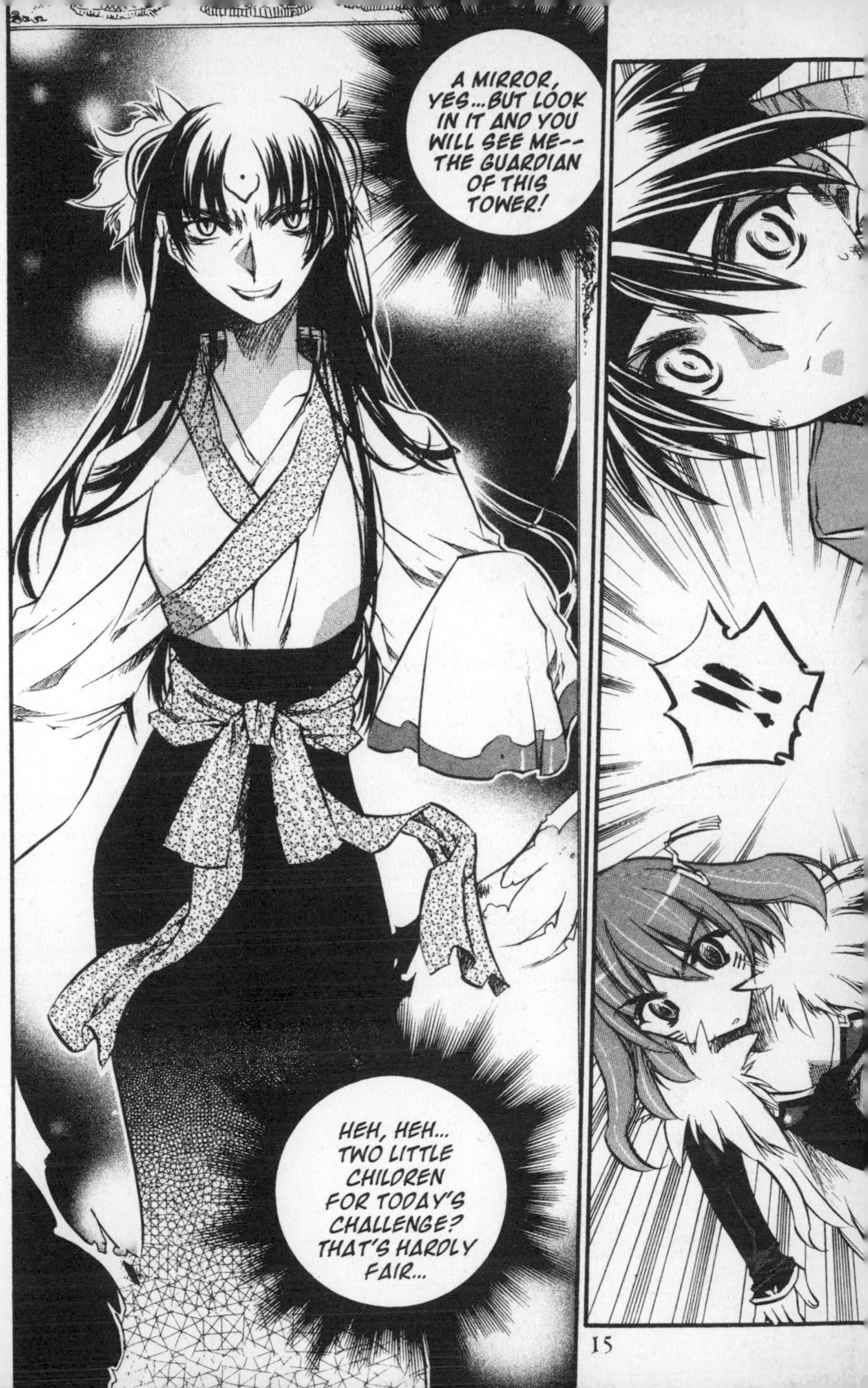
A MIRROR, YES...BUT LOOK IN IT AND YOU WILL SEE ME-- THE GUARDIAN OF THIS TOWER!
HEH, HEH... TWO LITTLE CHILDREN FOR TODAY'S CHALLENGE? THAT'S HARDLY FAIR...
!!

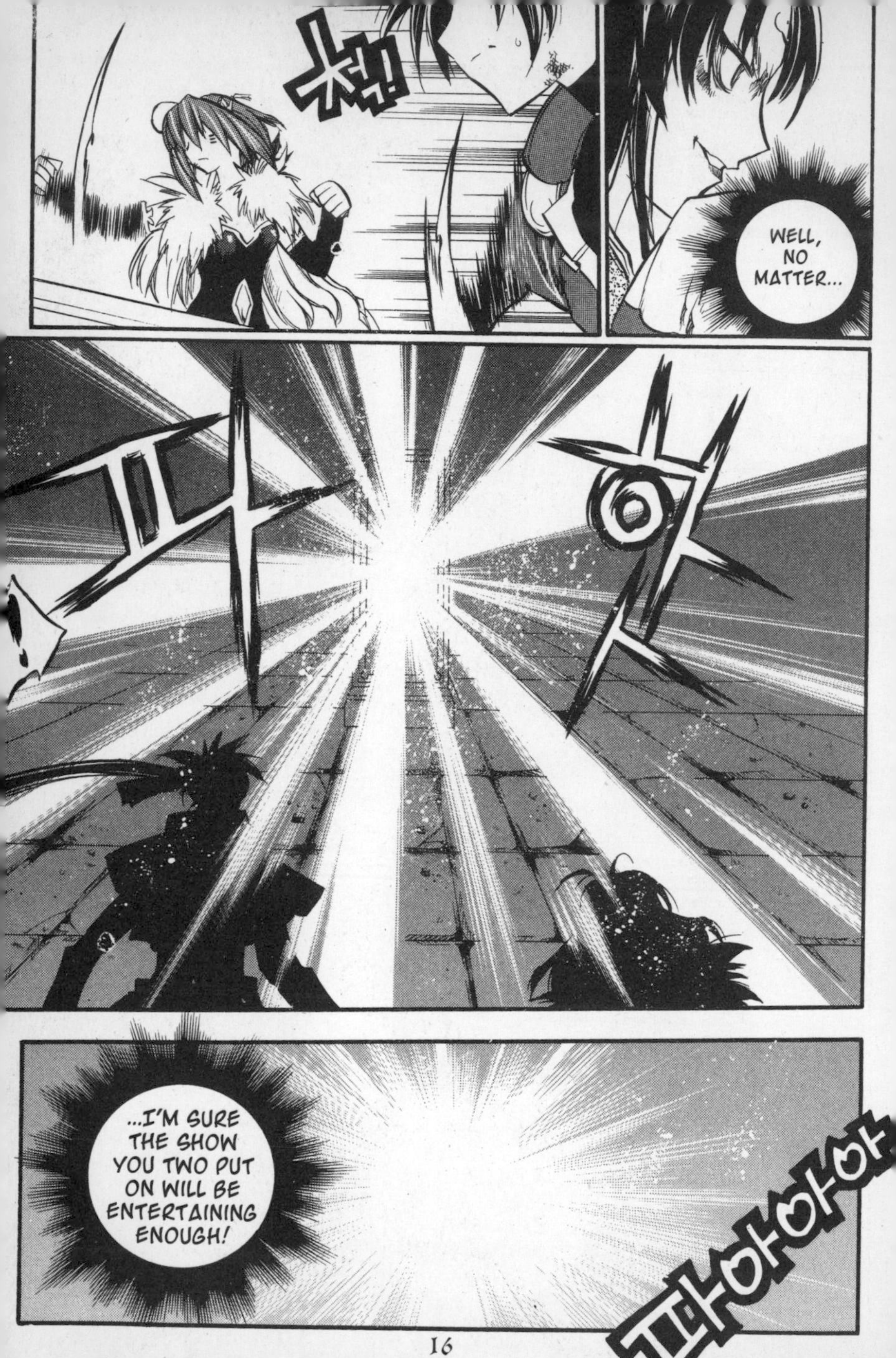
WELL, NO MATTER...
...I'M SURE THE SHOW YOU TWO PUT ON WILL BE ENTERTAINING ENOUGH!

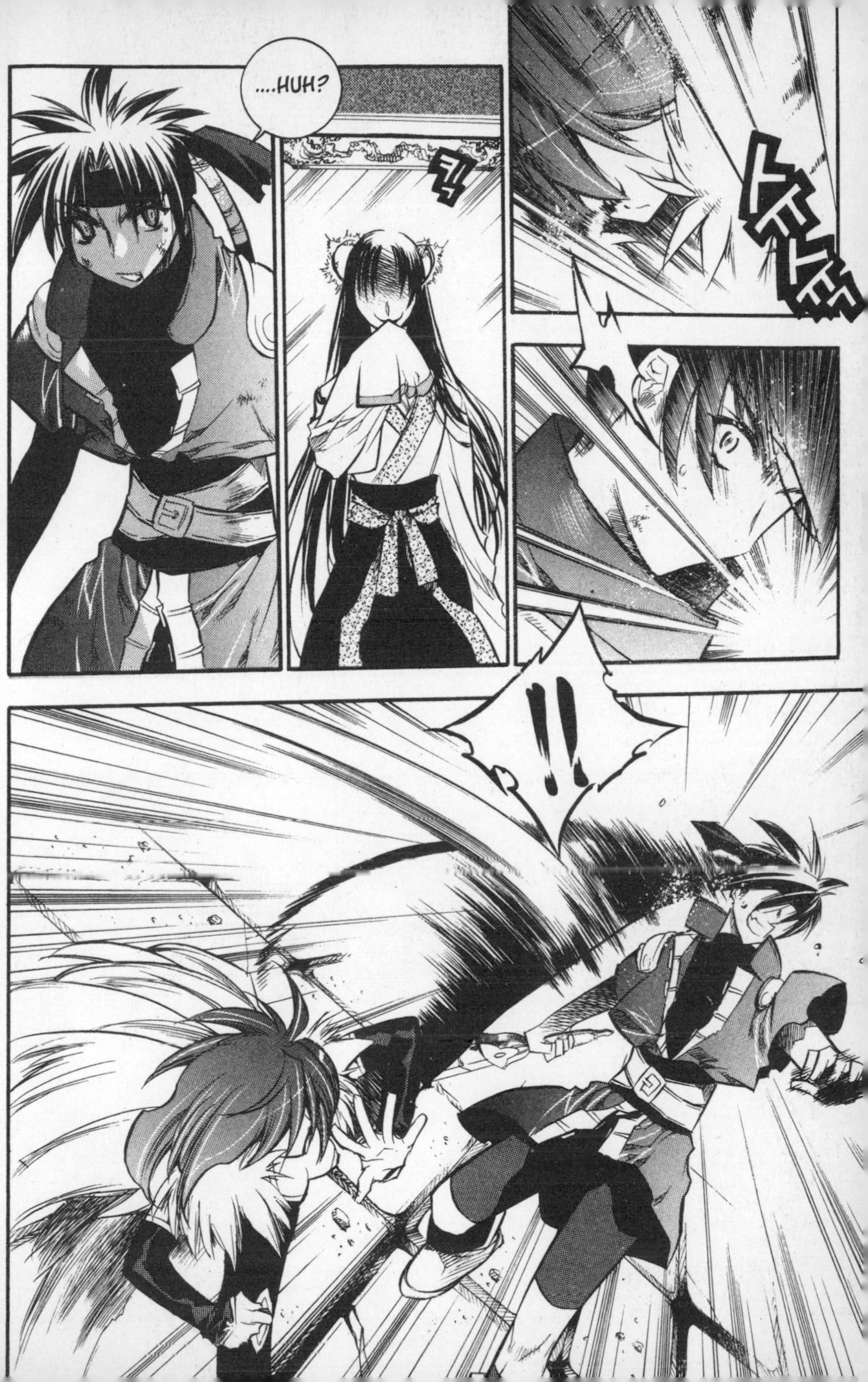
....HUH?
!!

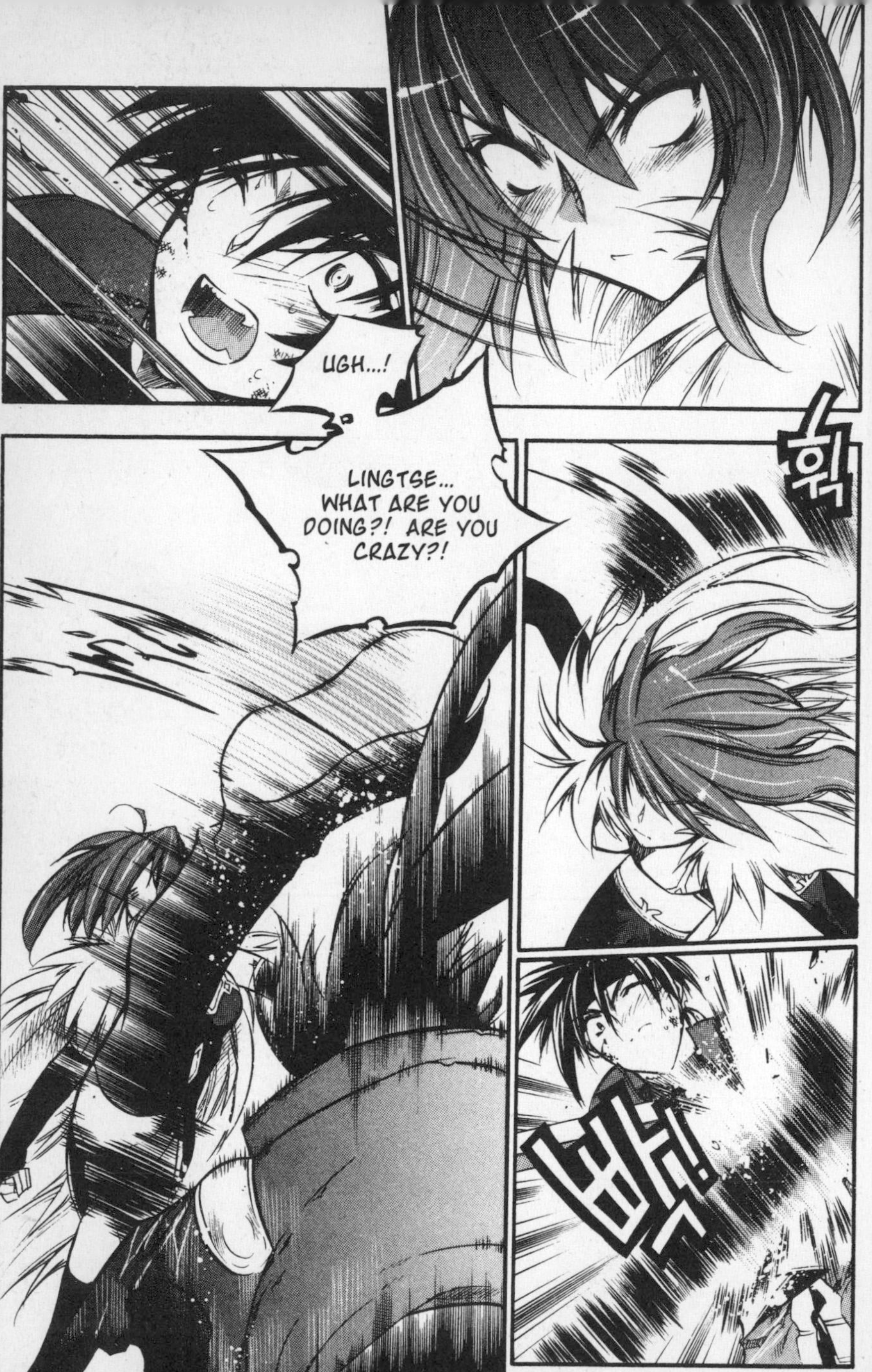
UGH...!
LINGTSE... WHAT ARE YOU DOING?! ARE YOU CRAZY?!

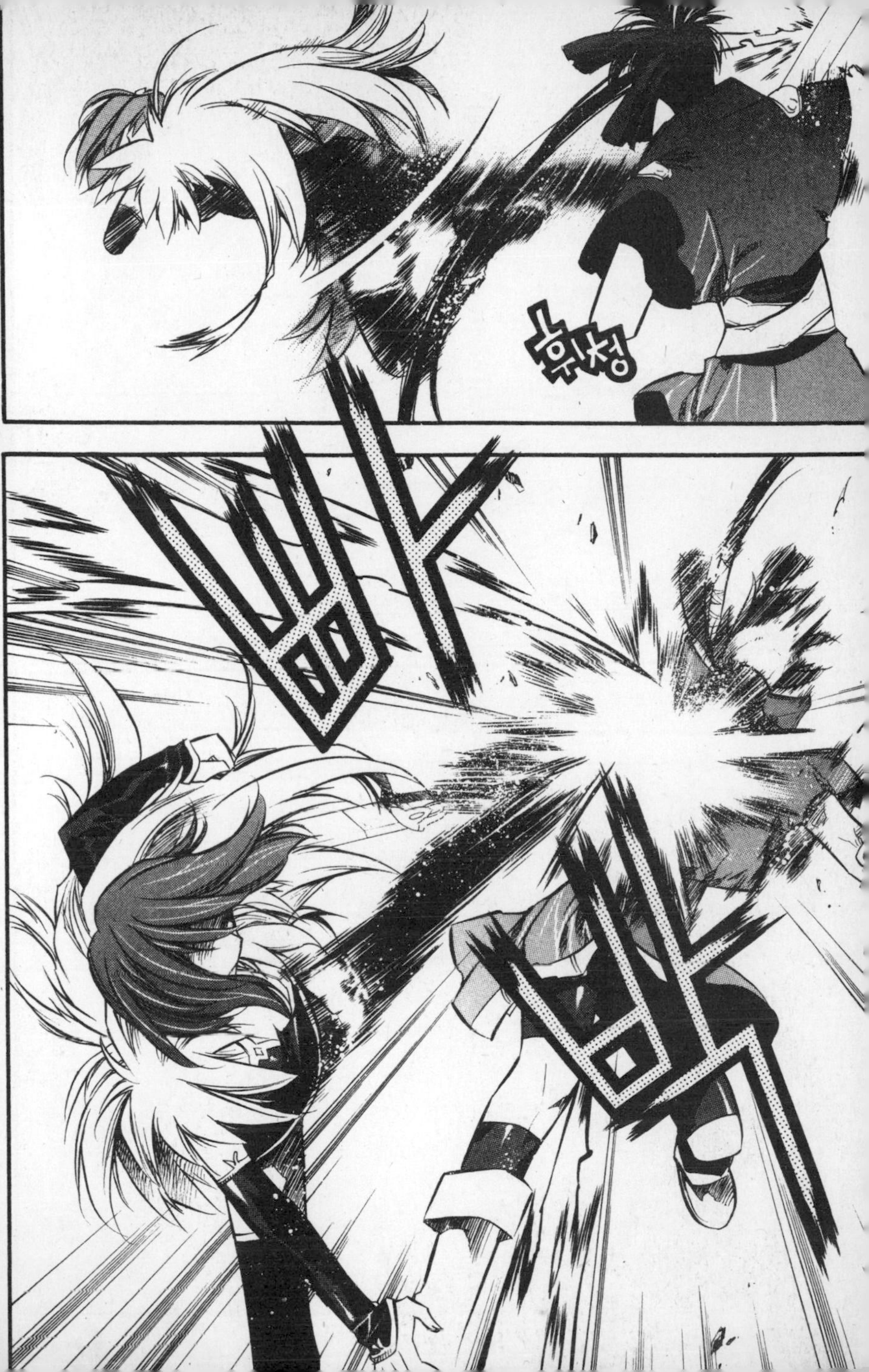
휘청

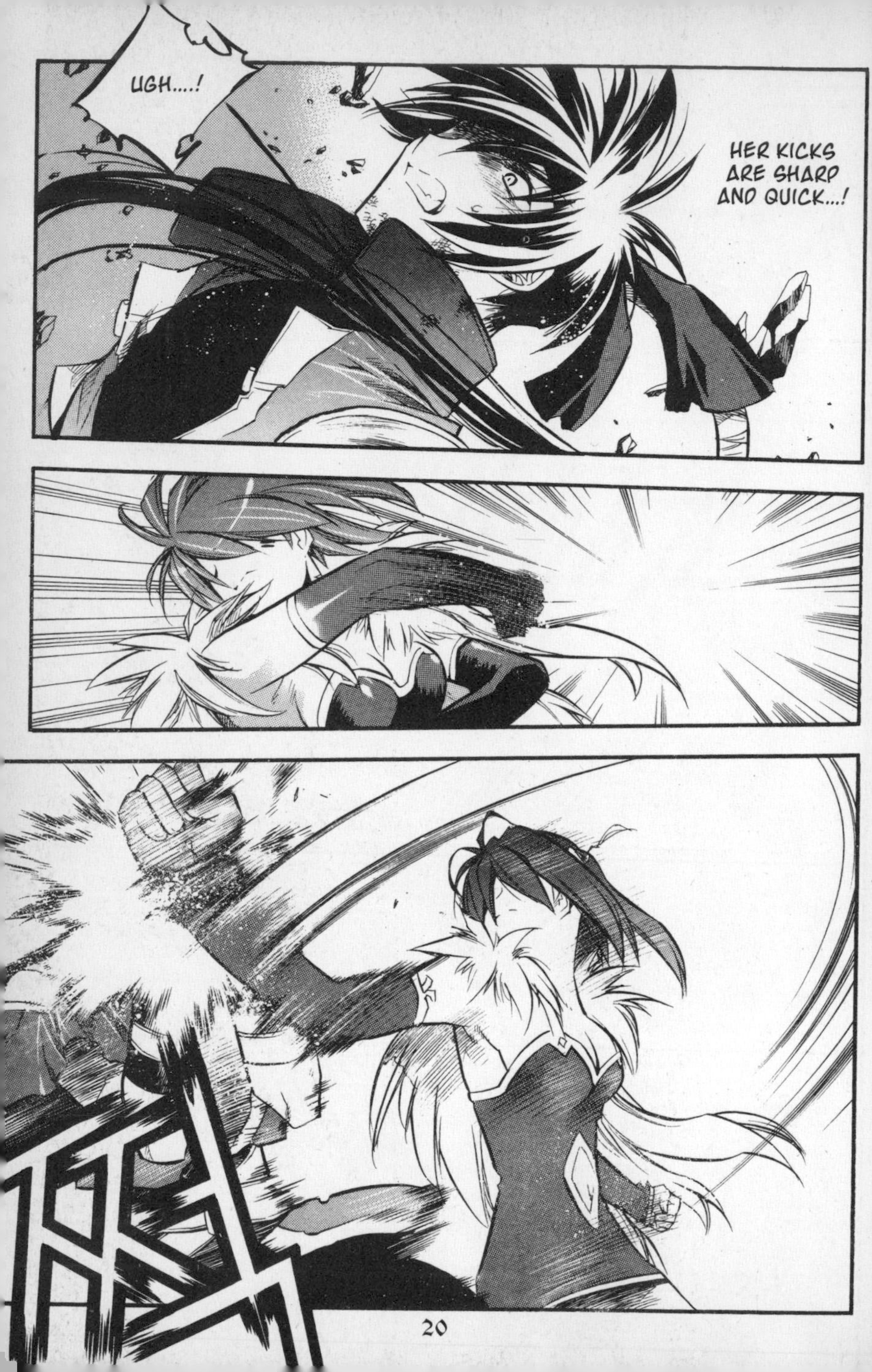
UGH....!
HER KICKS ARE SHARP AND QUICK...!

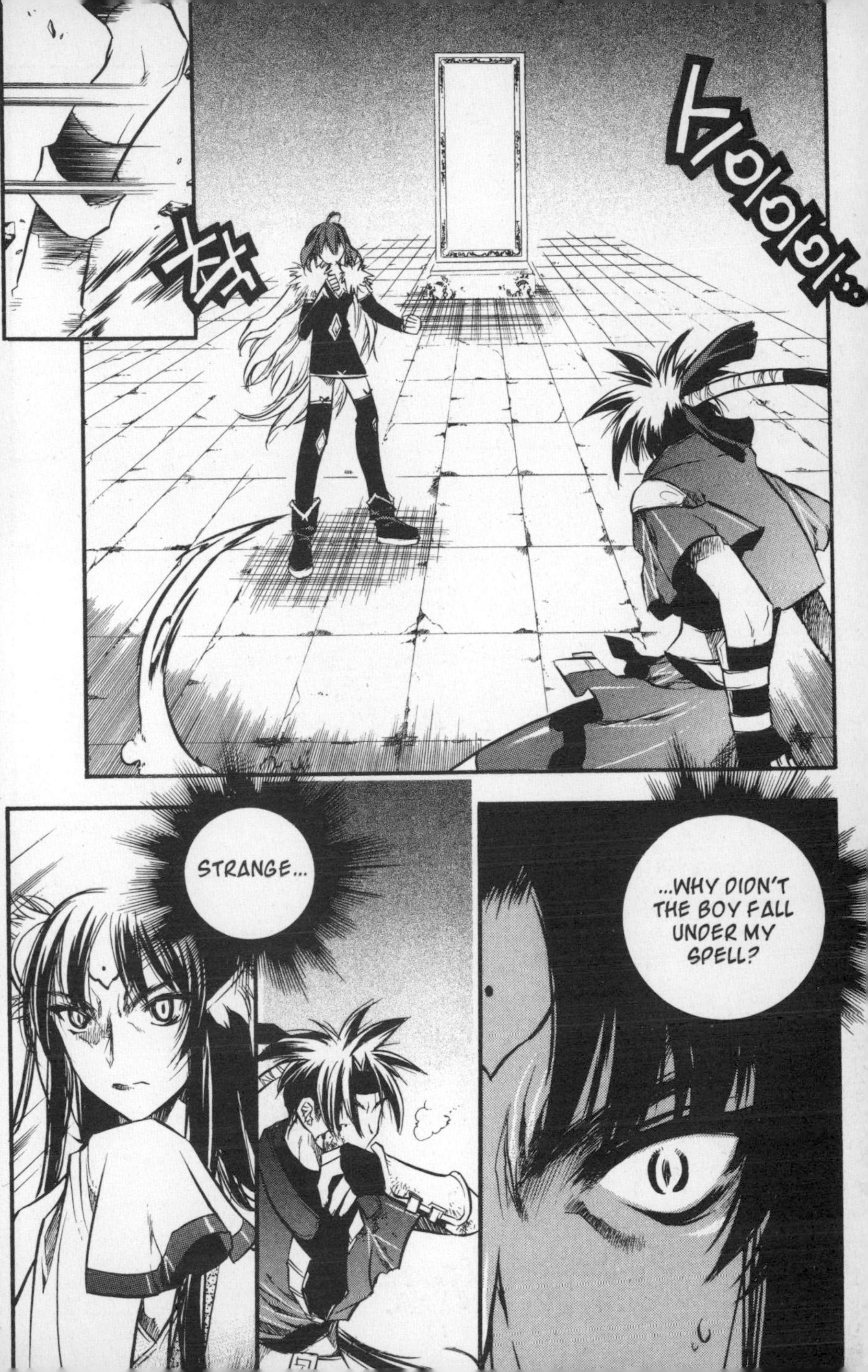
STRANGE...
...WHY DIDN'T THE BOY FALL UNDER MY SPELL?

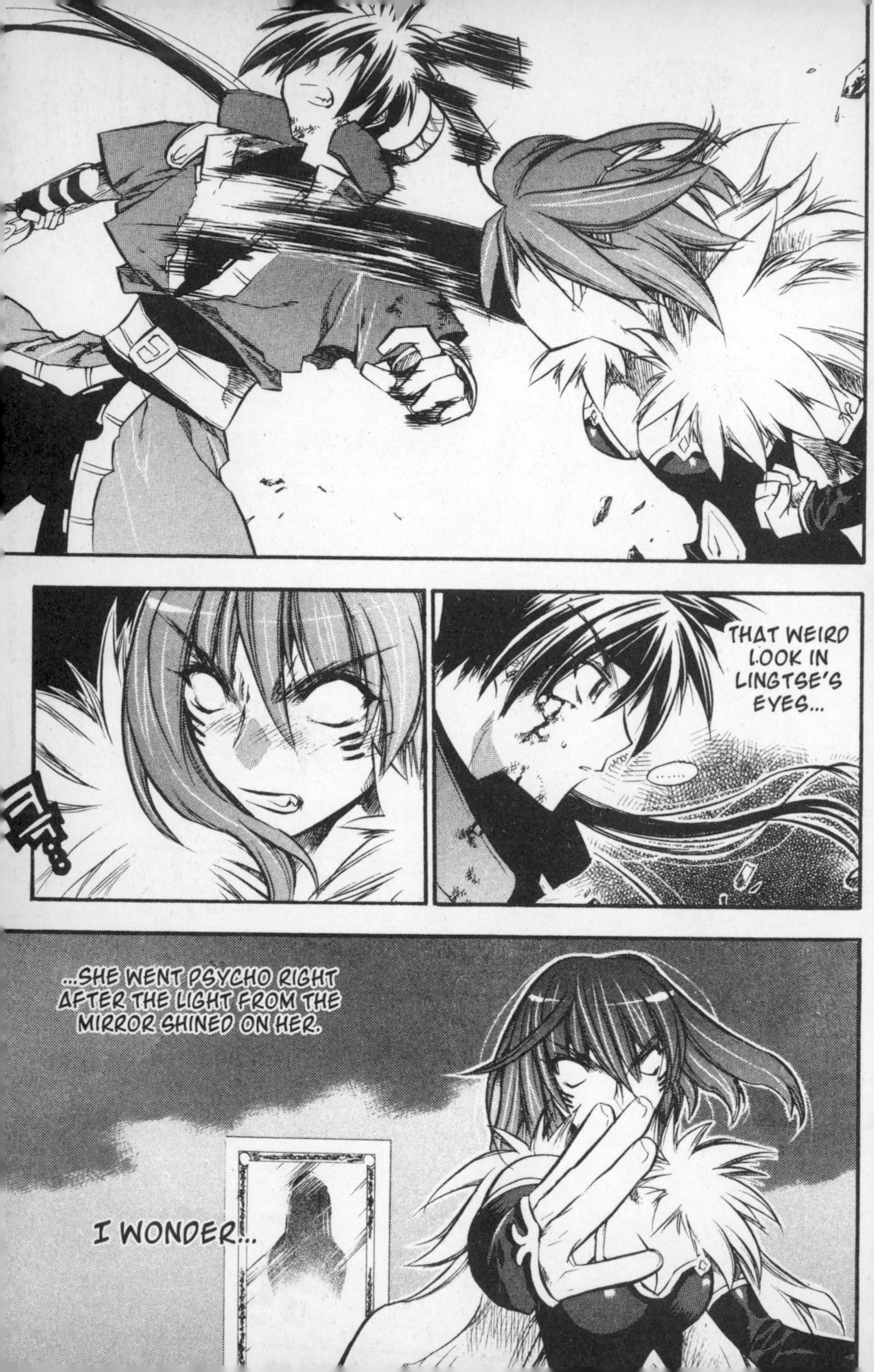
THAT WEIRD LOOK IN LINGTSE'S EYES...
......
...SHE WENT PSYCHO RIGHT AFTER THE LIGHT FROM THE MIRROR SHINED ON HER.
I WONDER...

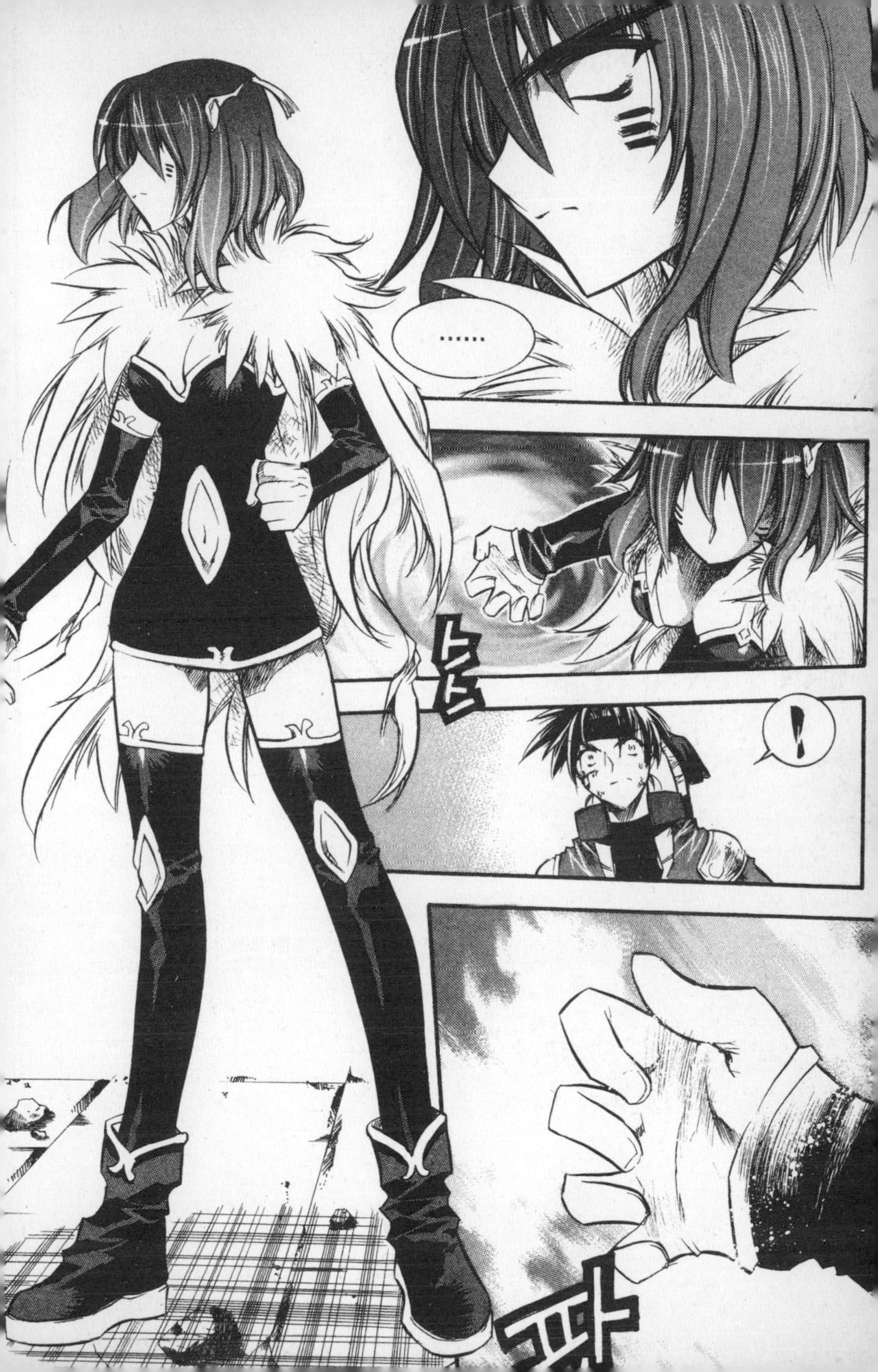
......
トト
!
コット

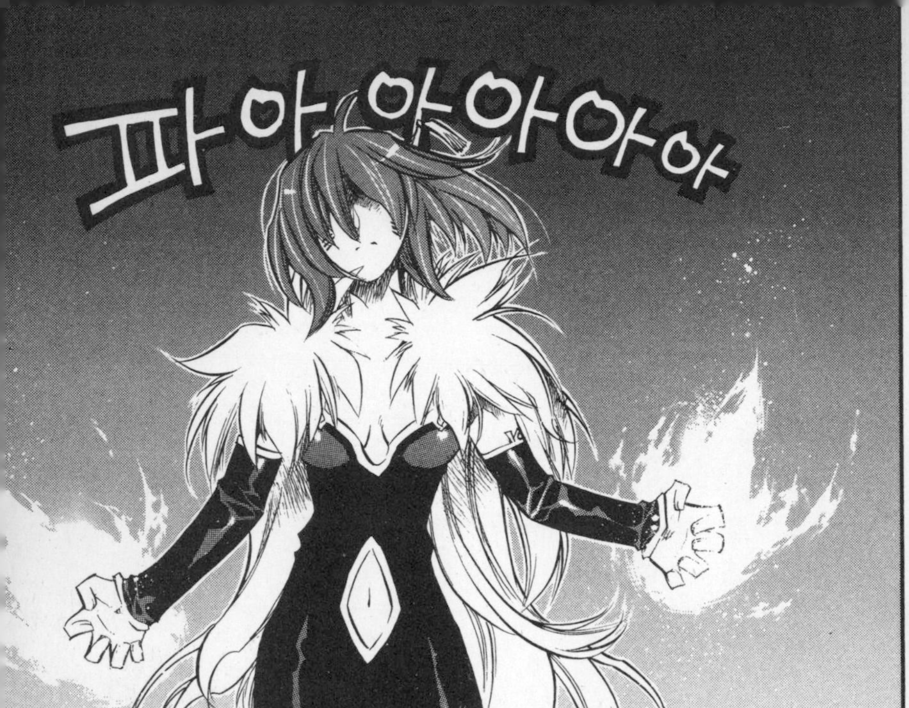
파아아아아아
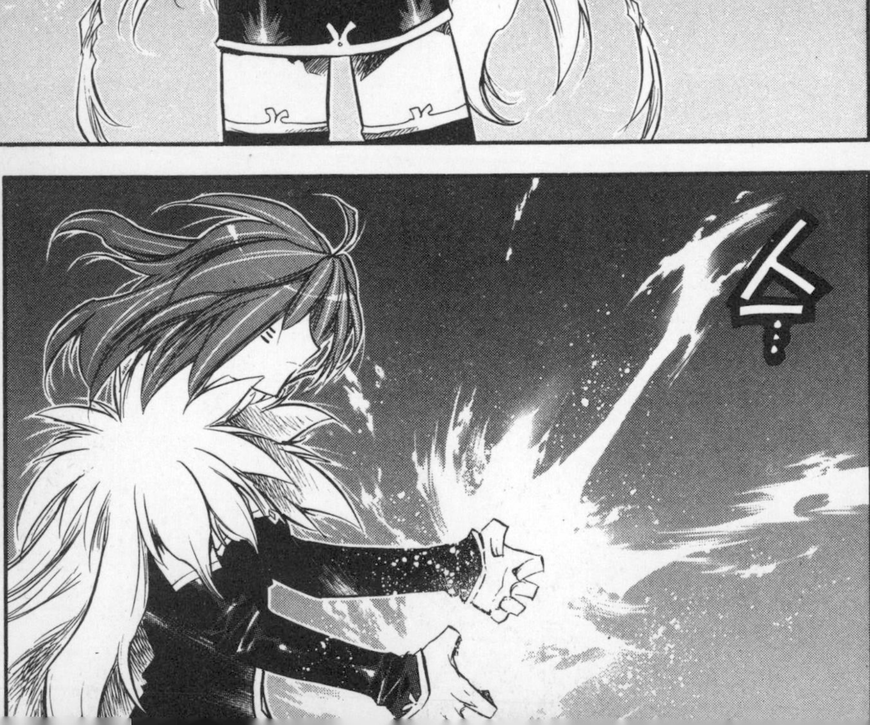
스…

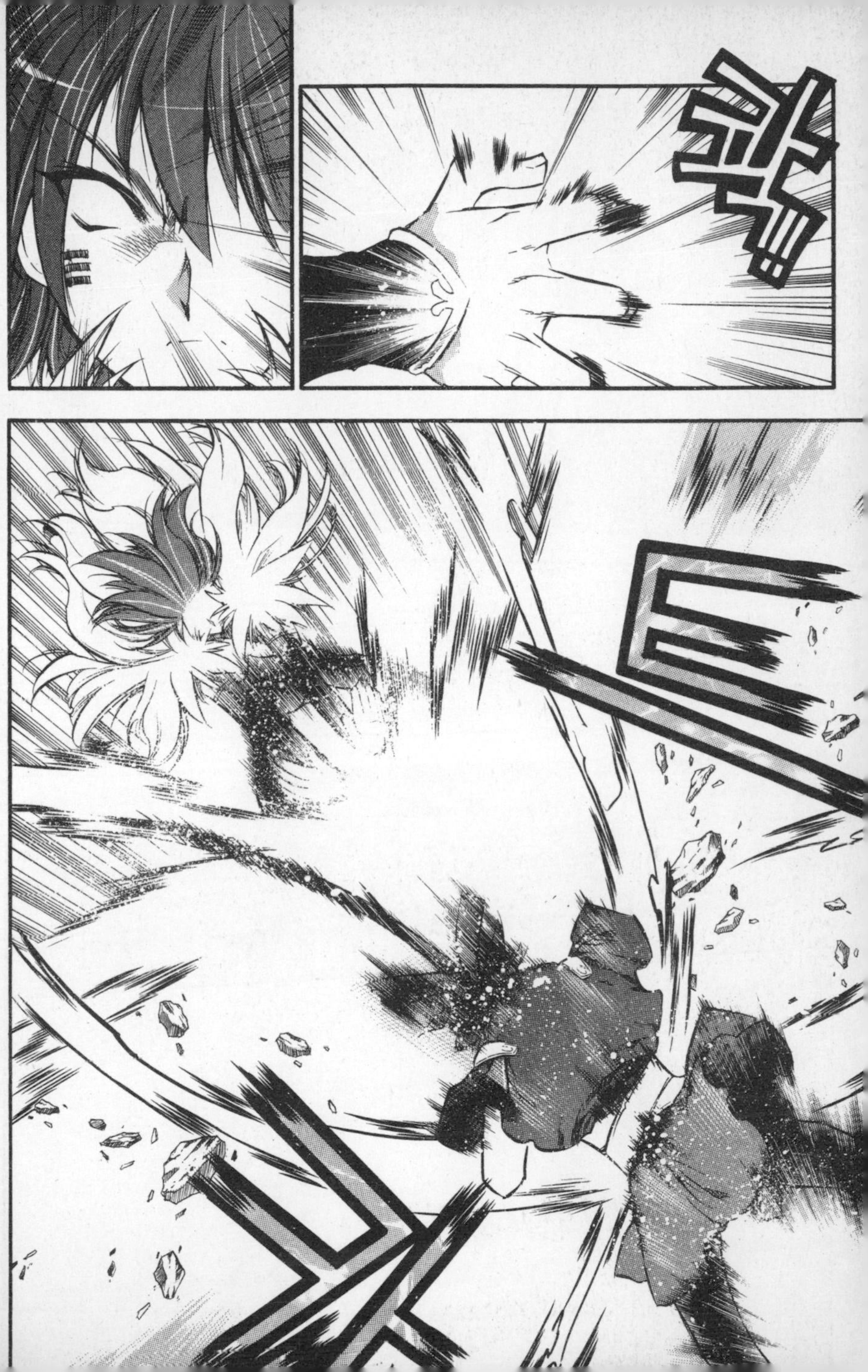

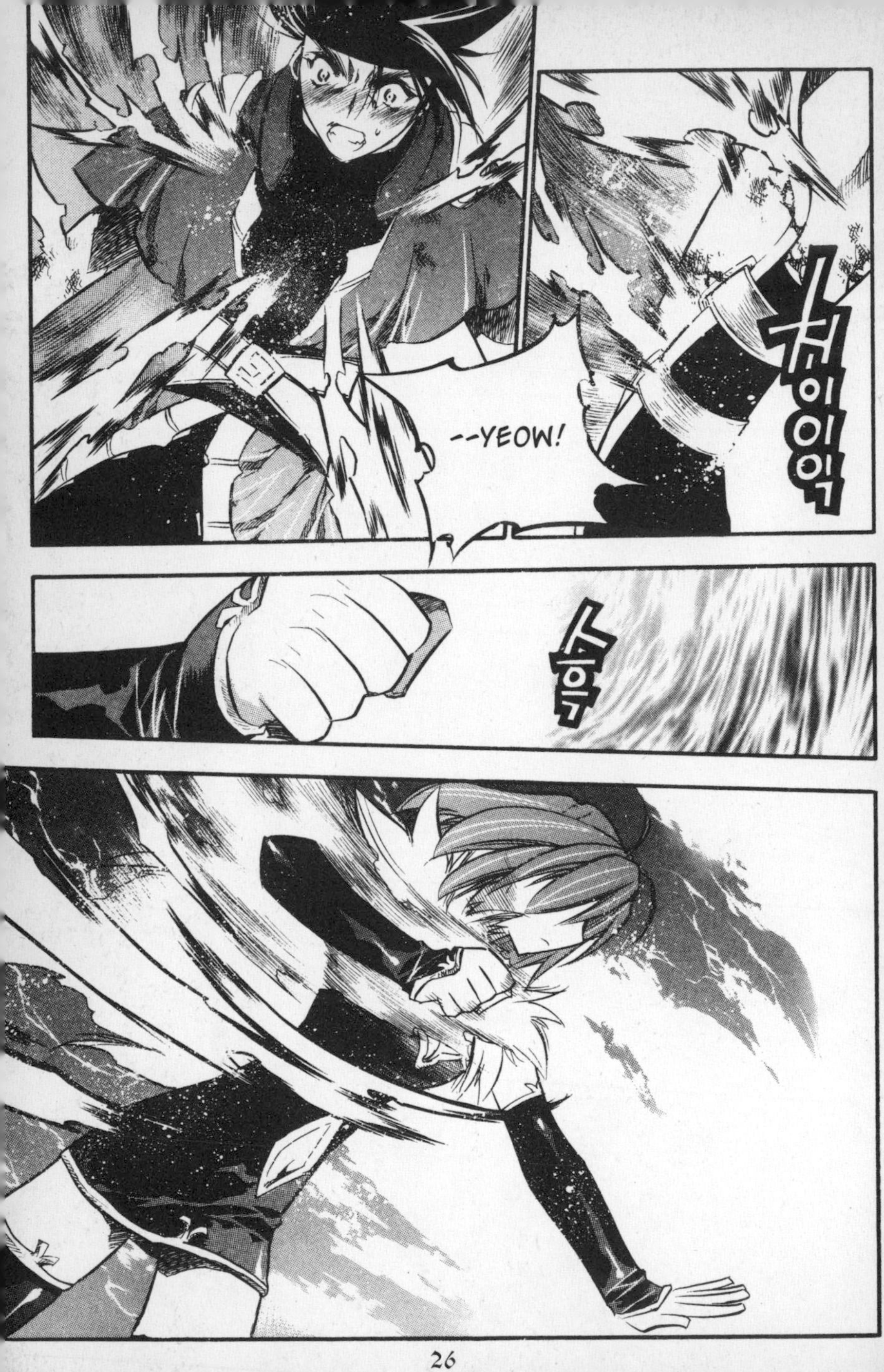

--YEOW!
캐이이익
스윽

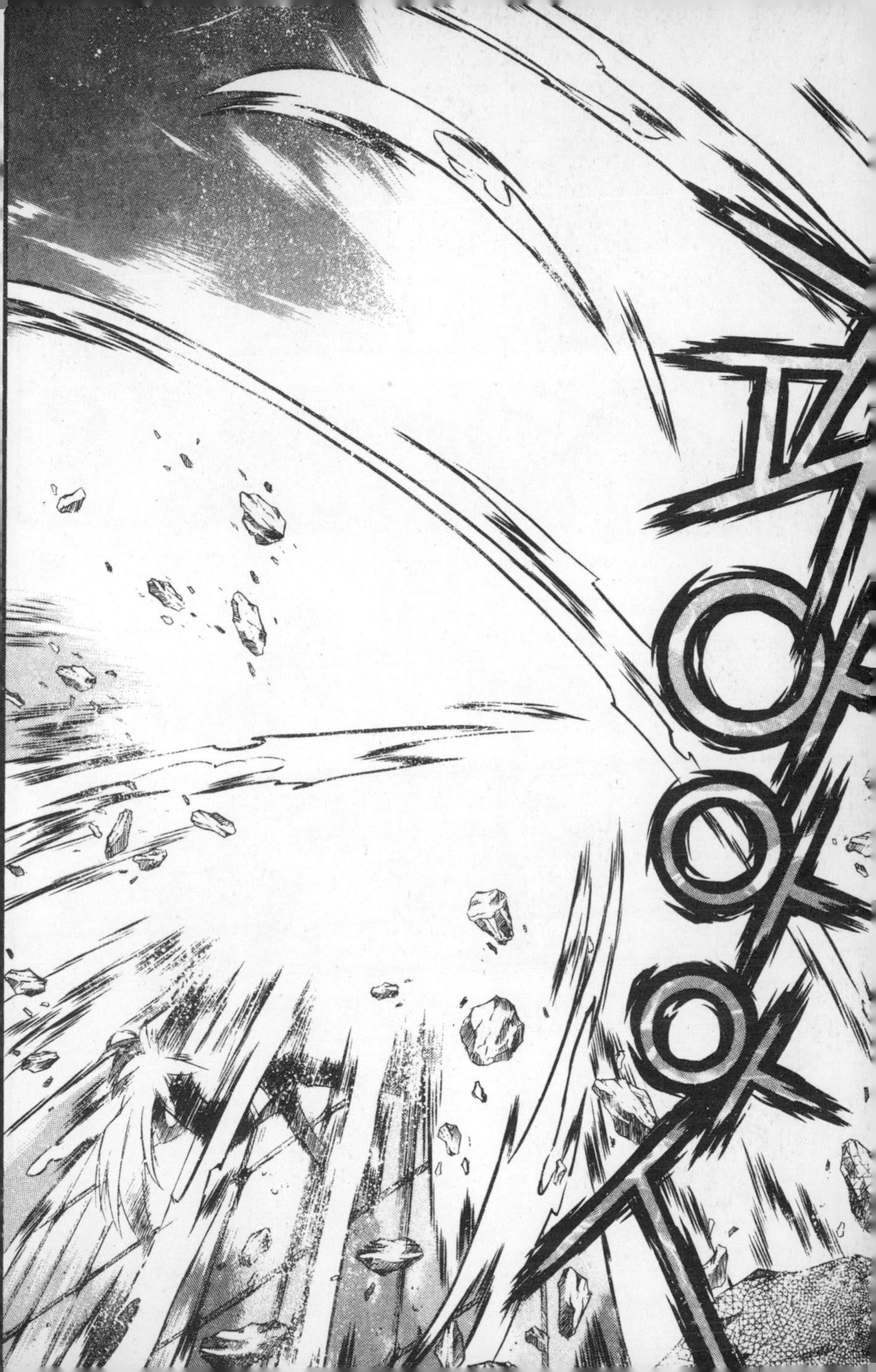

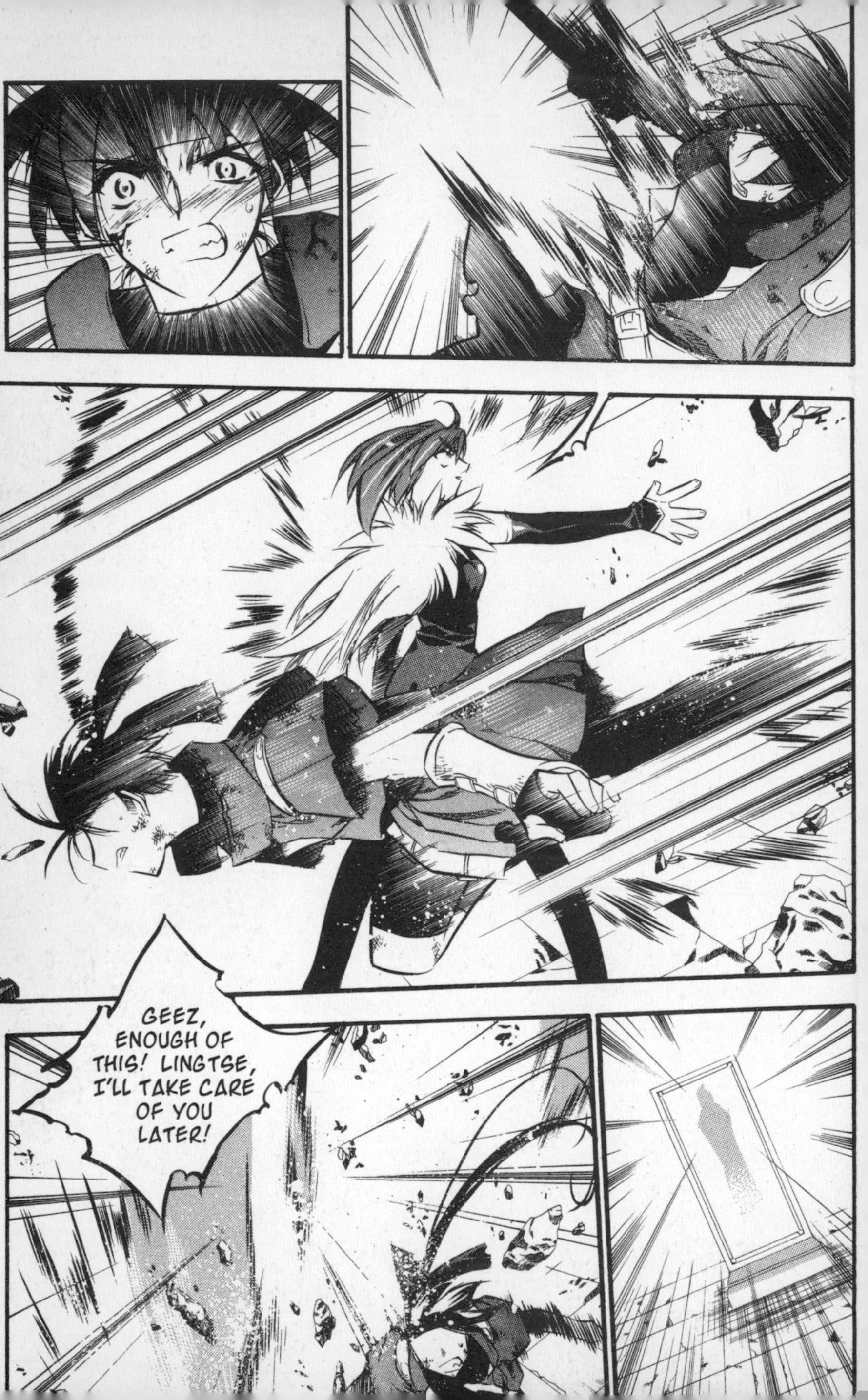
GEEZ, ENOUGH OF THIS! LINGTSE, I'LL TAKE CARE OF YOU LATER!

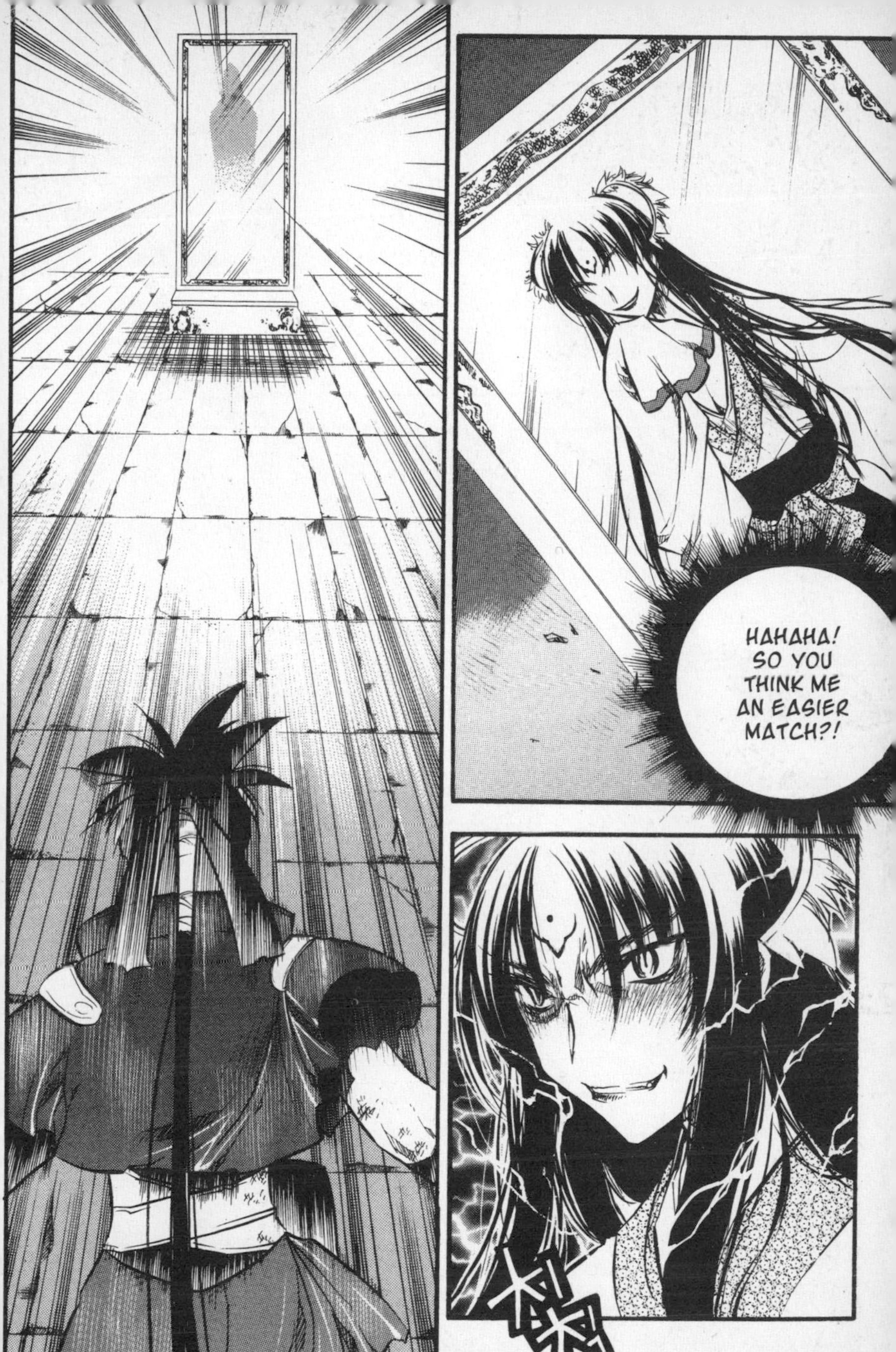
HAHAHA! SO YOU THINK ME AN EASIER MATCH?!

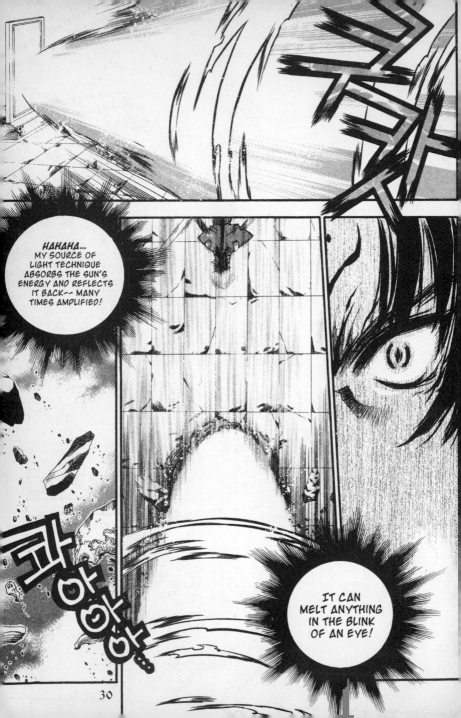

HAHAHA...
MY SOURCE OF
LIGHT TECHNIQUE
ABSORBS THE SUN'S
ENERGY AND REFLECTS
IT BACK-- MANY
TIMES AMPLIFIED!

IT CAN
MELT ANYTHING
IN THE BLINK
OF AN EYE!

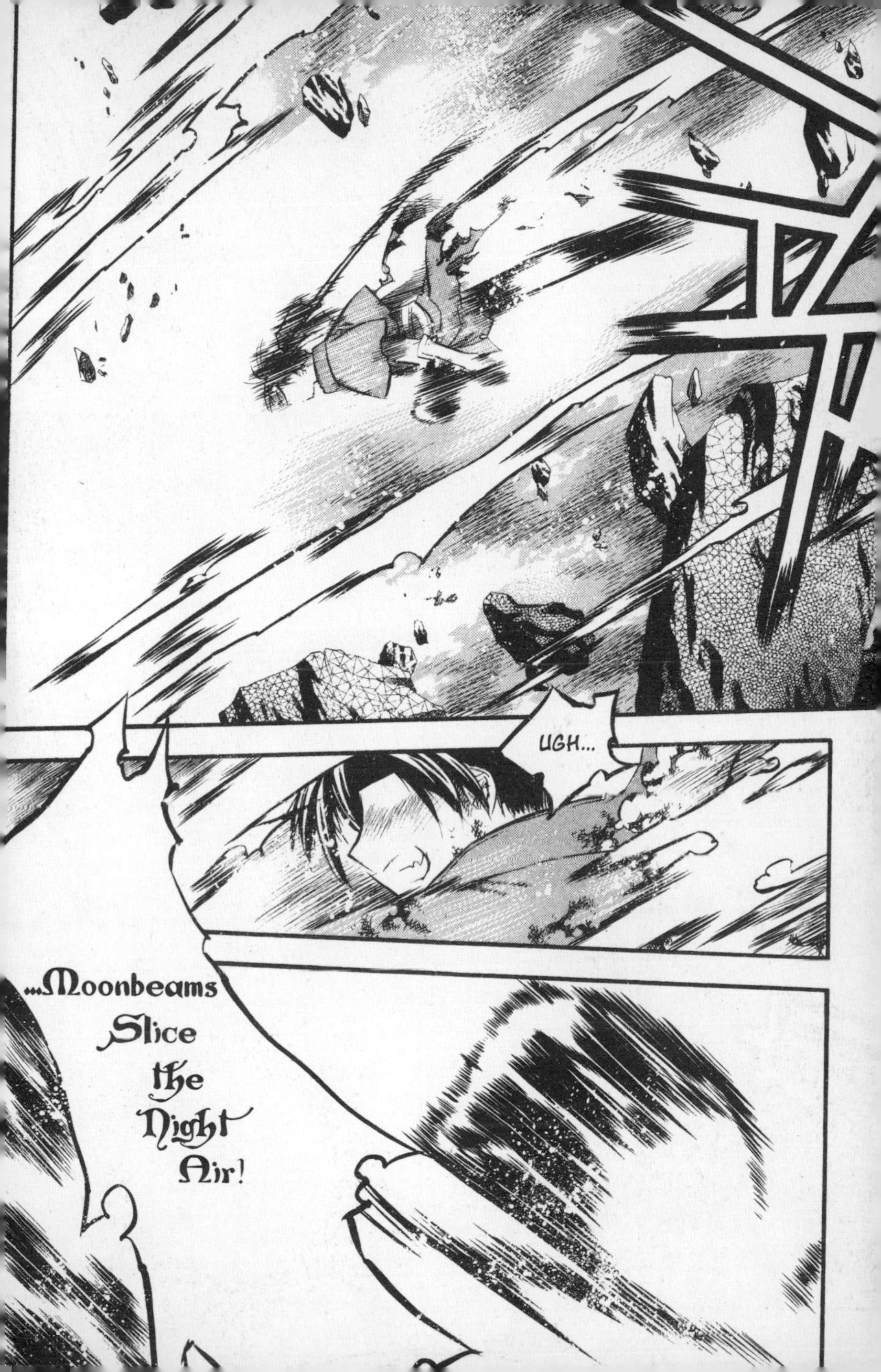
UGH...
...Moonbeams Slice the Night Air!

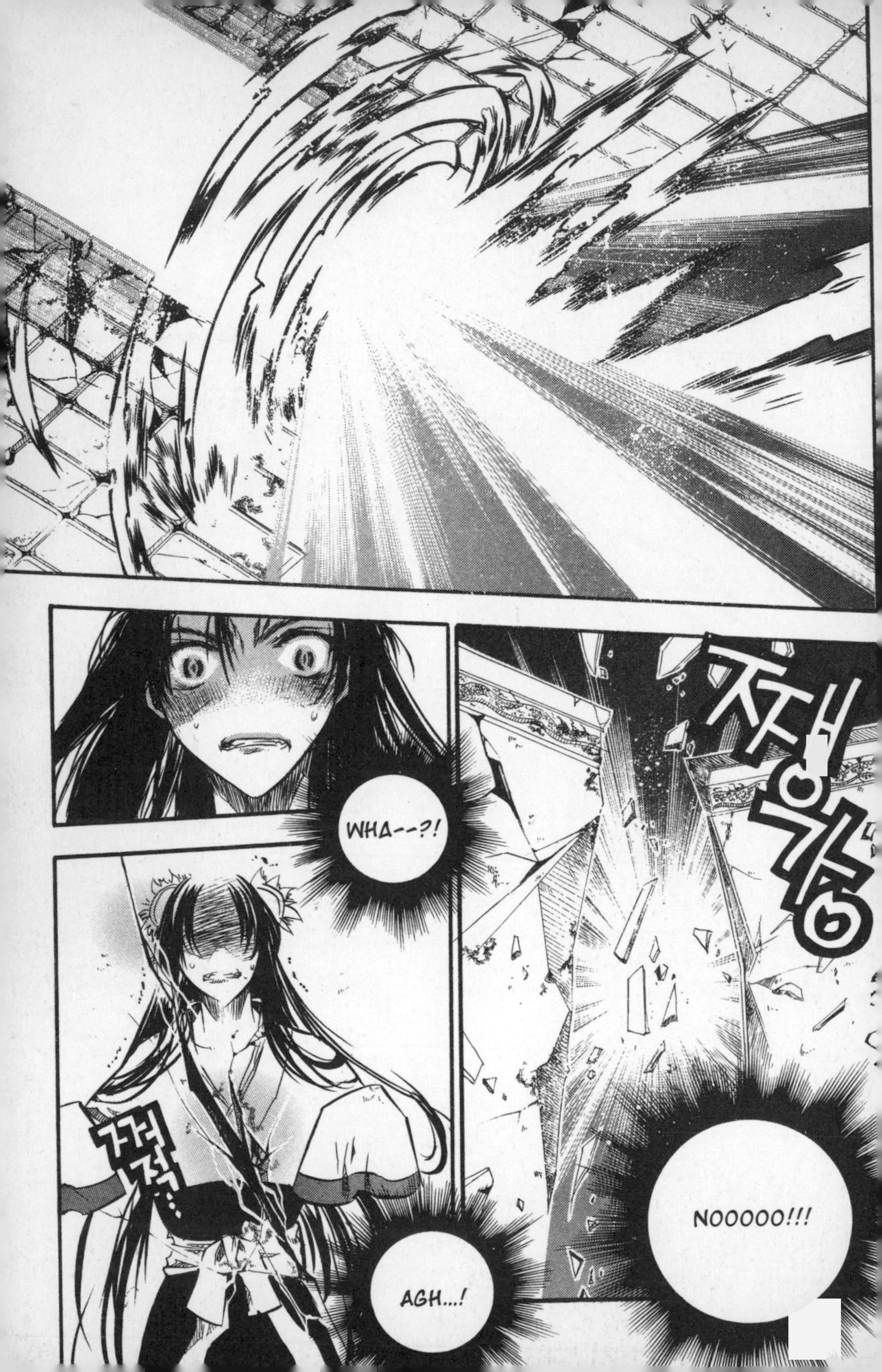
WHA--?!
AGH...!
NOOOOO!!!

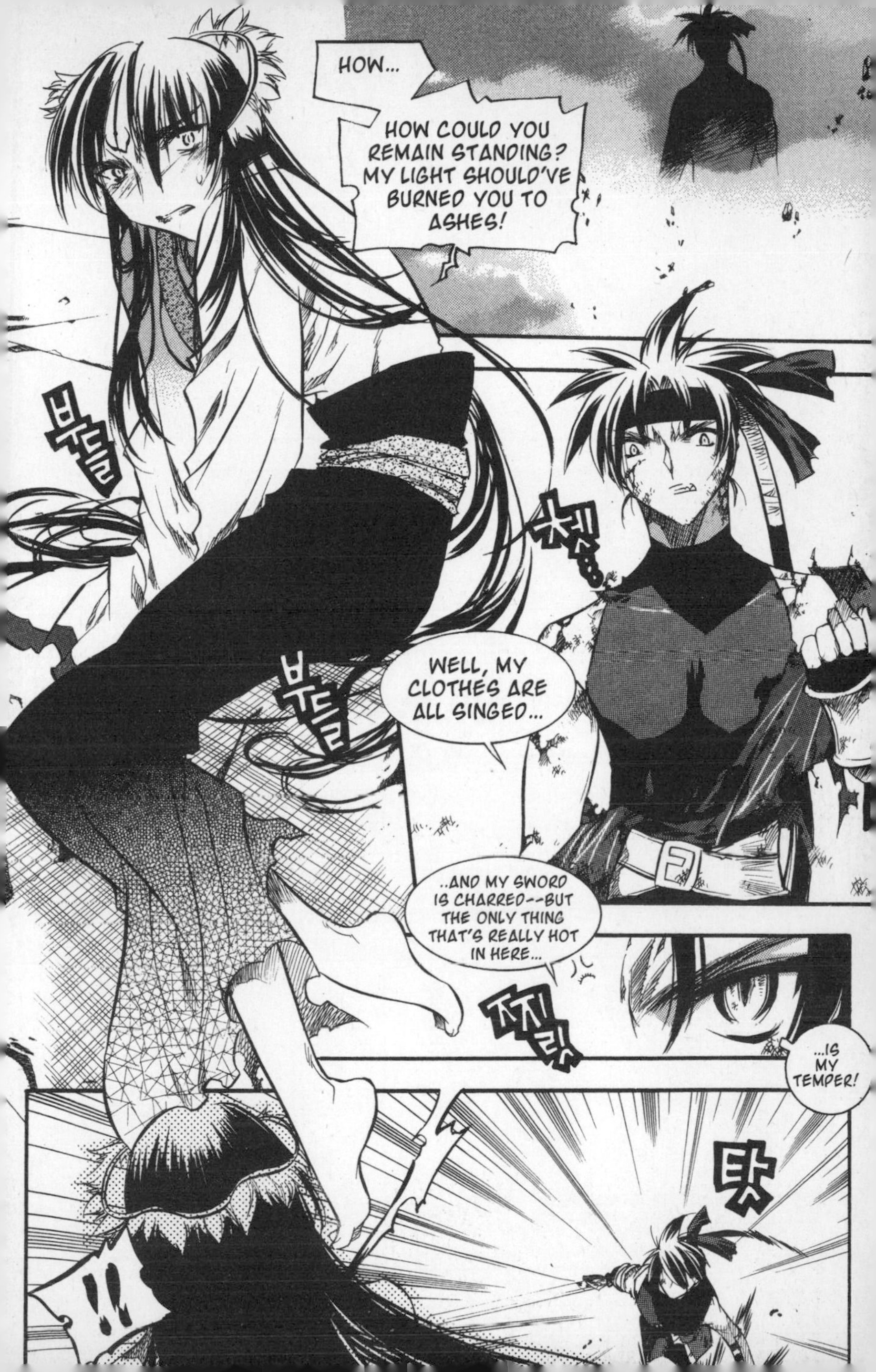
HOW...
HOW COULD YOU REMAIN STANDING? MY LIGHT SHOULD'VE BURNED YOU TO ASHES!
부들
부들
WELL, MY CLOTHES ARE ALL SINGED...
..AND MY SWORD IS CHARRED--BUT THE ONLY THING THAT'S REALLY HOT IN HERE...
...IS MY TEMPER!
탓
!!

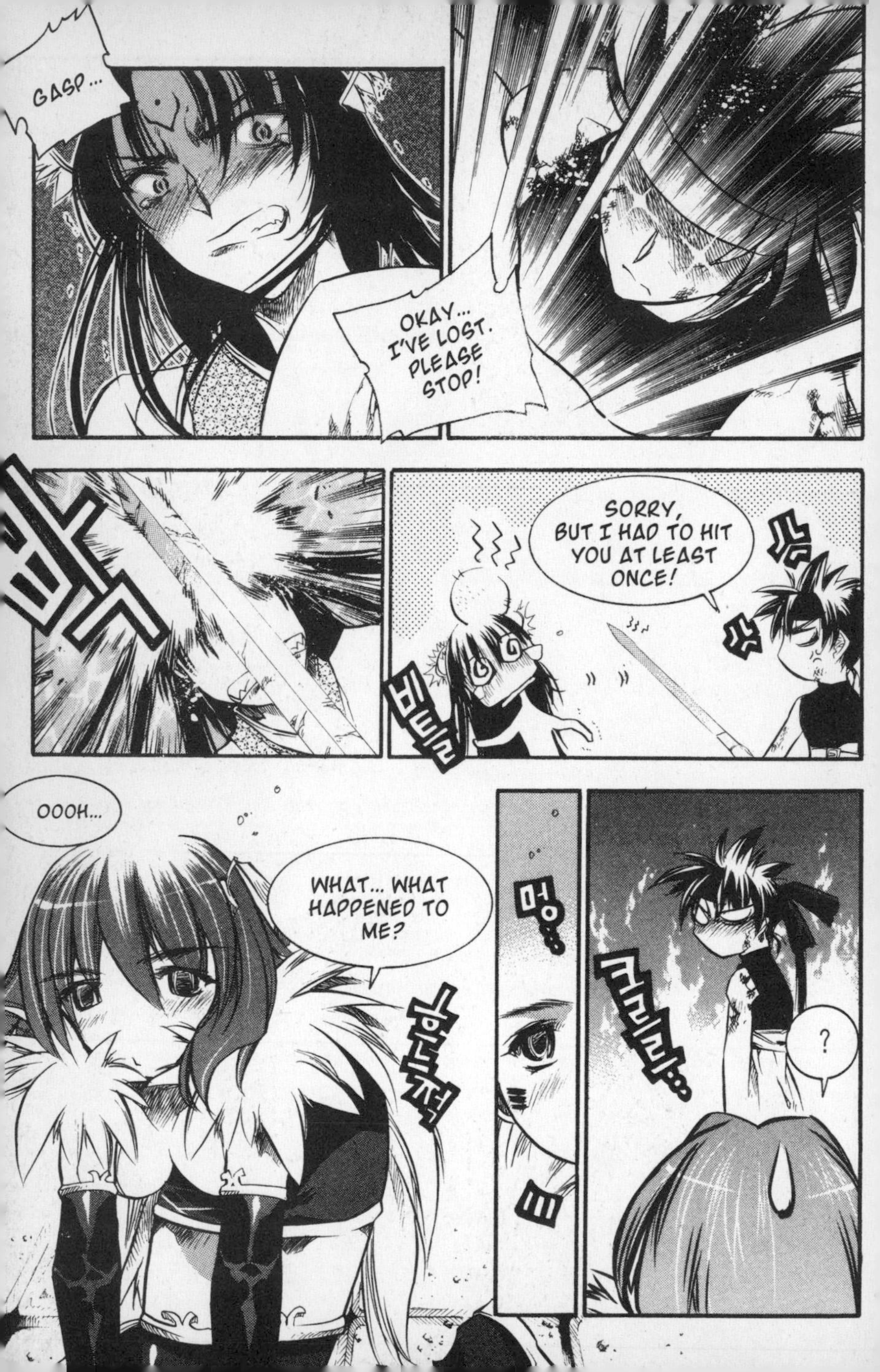
GASP...
OKAY... I'VE LOST. PLEASE STOP!
SORRY, BUT I HAD TO HIT YOU AT LEAST ONCE!
OOOH...
WHAT... WHAT HAPPENED TO ME?
?

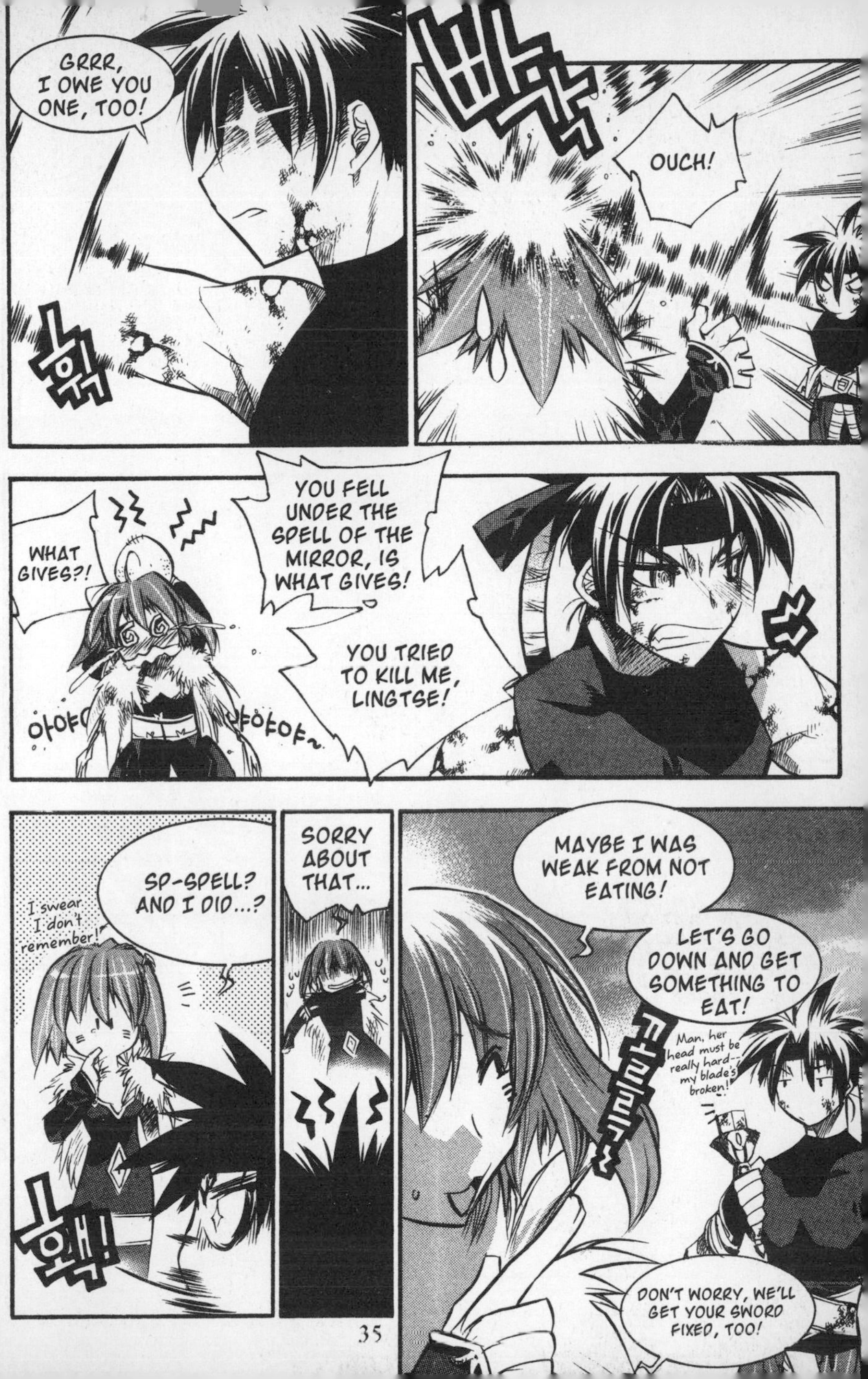
GRRR, I OWE YOU ONE, TOO!
OUCH!
WHAT GIVES?!
YOU FELL UNDER THE SPELL OF THE MIRROR, IS WHAT GIVES!
YOU TRIED TO KILL ME, LINGTSE!
SP-SPELL? AND I DID...?
I swear. I don't remember!
SORRY ABOUT THAT...
MAYBE I WAS WEAK FROM NOT EATING!
LET'S GO DOWN AND GET SOMETHING TO EAT!
Man, her head must be really hard-- my blade's broken!
DON'T WORRY, WE'LL GET YOUR SWORD FIXED, TOO!

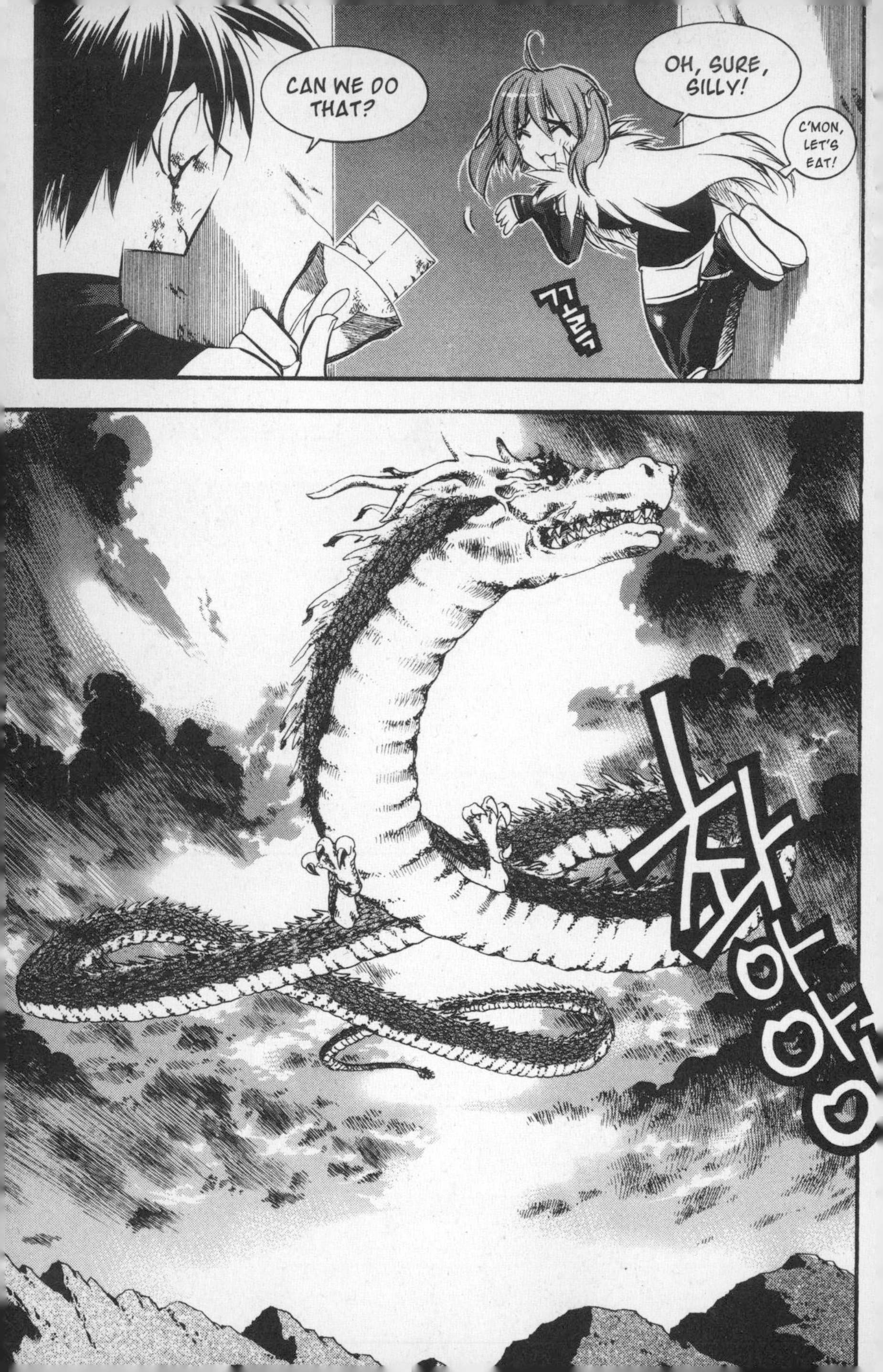
CAN WE DO THAT?
OH, SURE, SILLY!
C'MON, LET'S EAT!

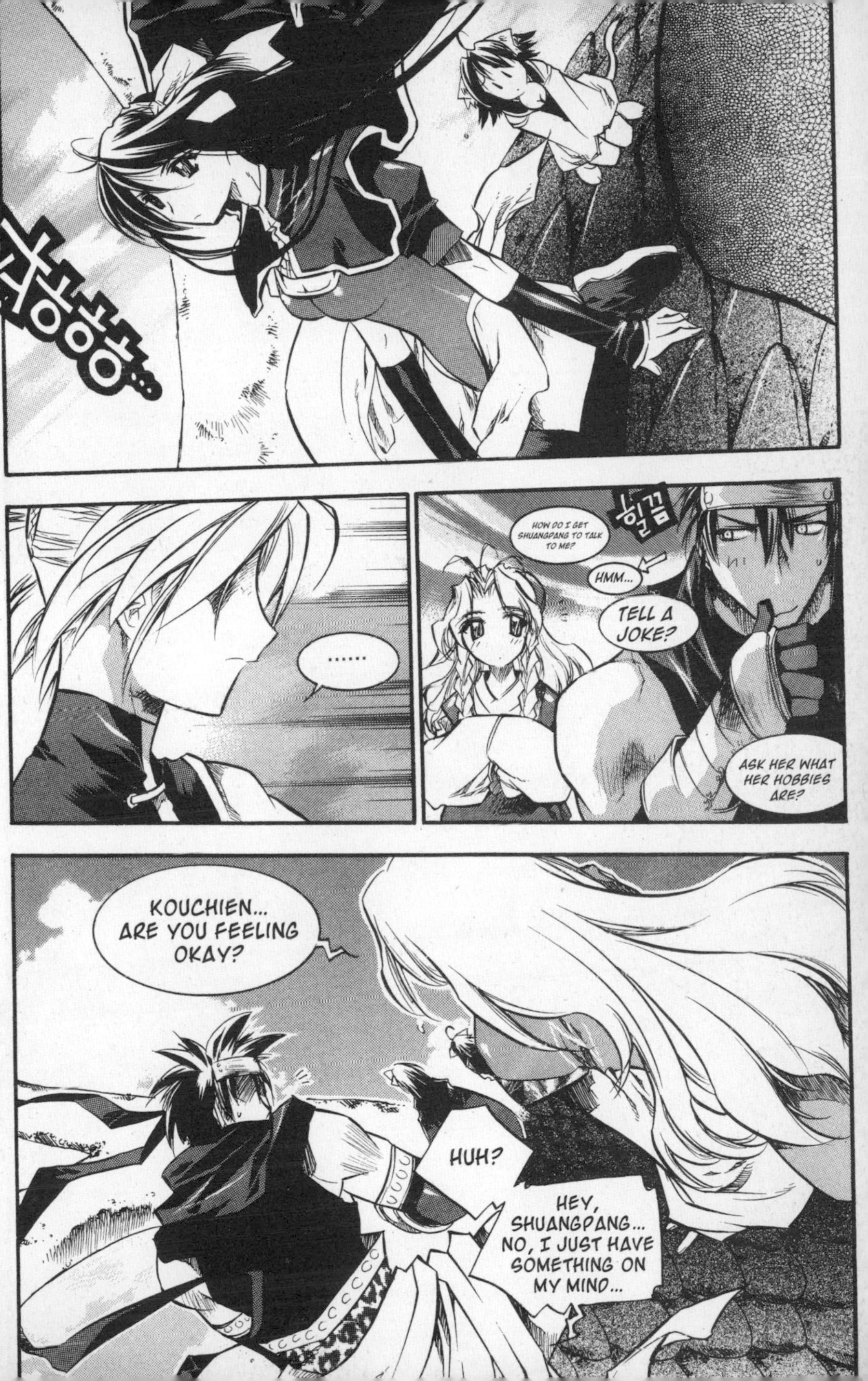
......
힐끔
HOW DO I GET SHUANGPANG TO TALK TO ME?
HMM...
TELL A JOKE?
ASK HER WHAT HER HOBBIES ARE?
KOUCHIEN... ARE YOU FEELING OKAY?
HUH?
HEY, SHUANGPANG... NO, I JUST HAVE SOMETHING ON MY MIND...

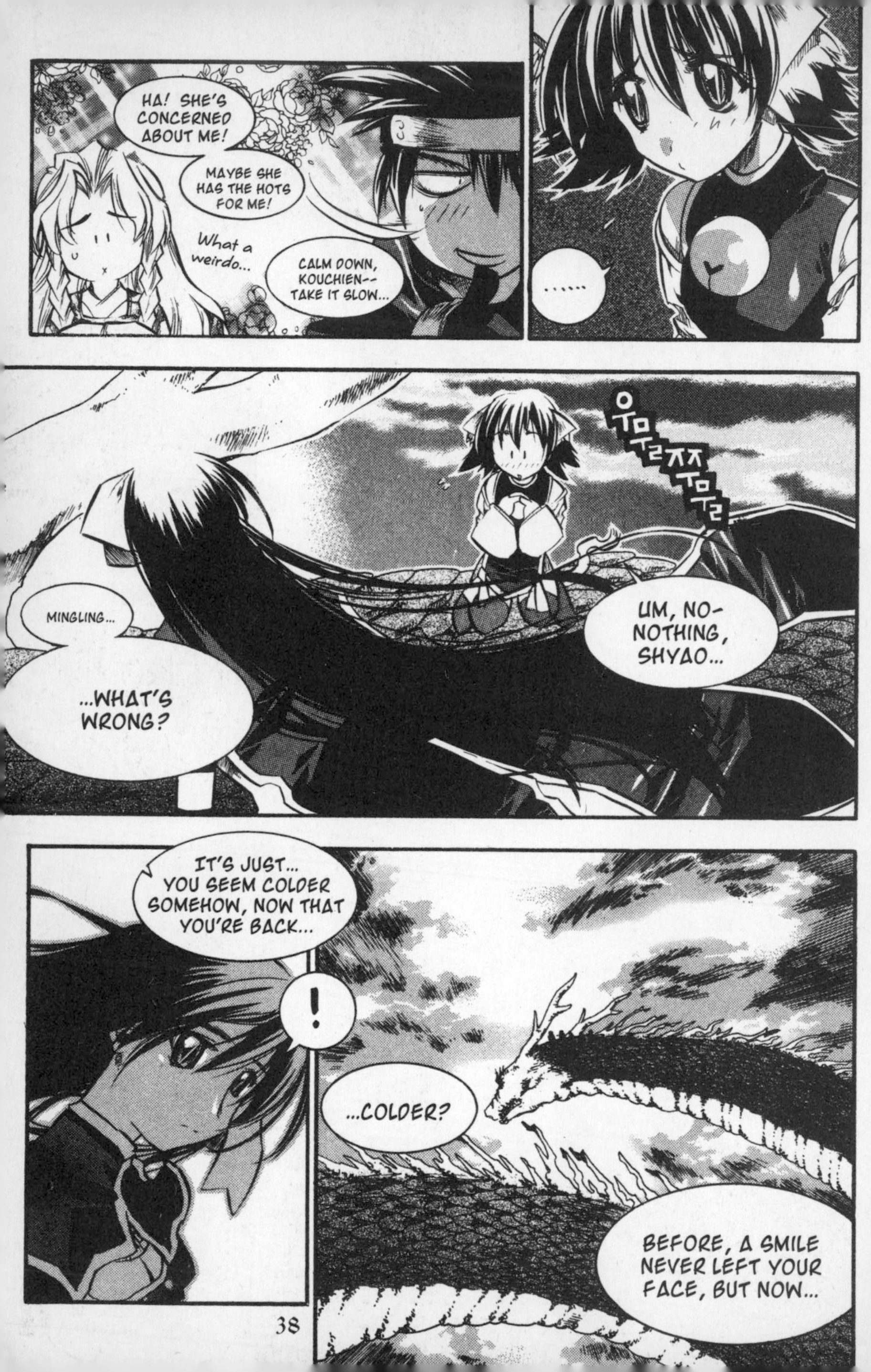
HA! SHE'S CONCERNED ABOUT ME!
MAYBE SHE HAS THE HOTS FOR ME!
What a weirdo...
CALM DOWN, KOUCHIEN--TAKE IT SLOW...
......
우물쭈물
MINGLING...
...WHAT'S WRONG?
UM, NO-NOTHING, SHYAO...
IT'S JUST... YOU SEEM COLDER SOMEHOW, NOW THAT YOU'RE BACK...
!
...COLDER?
BEFORE, A SMILE NEVER LEFT YOUR FACE, BUT NOW...

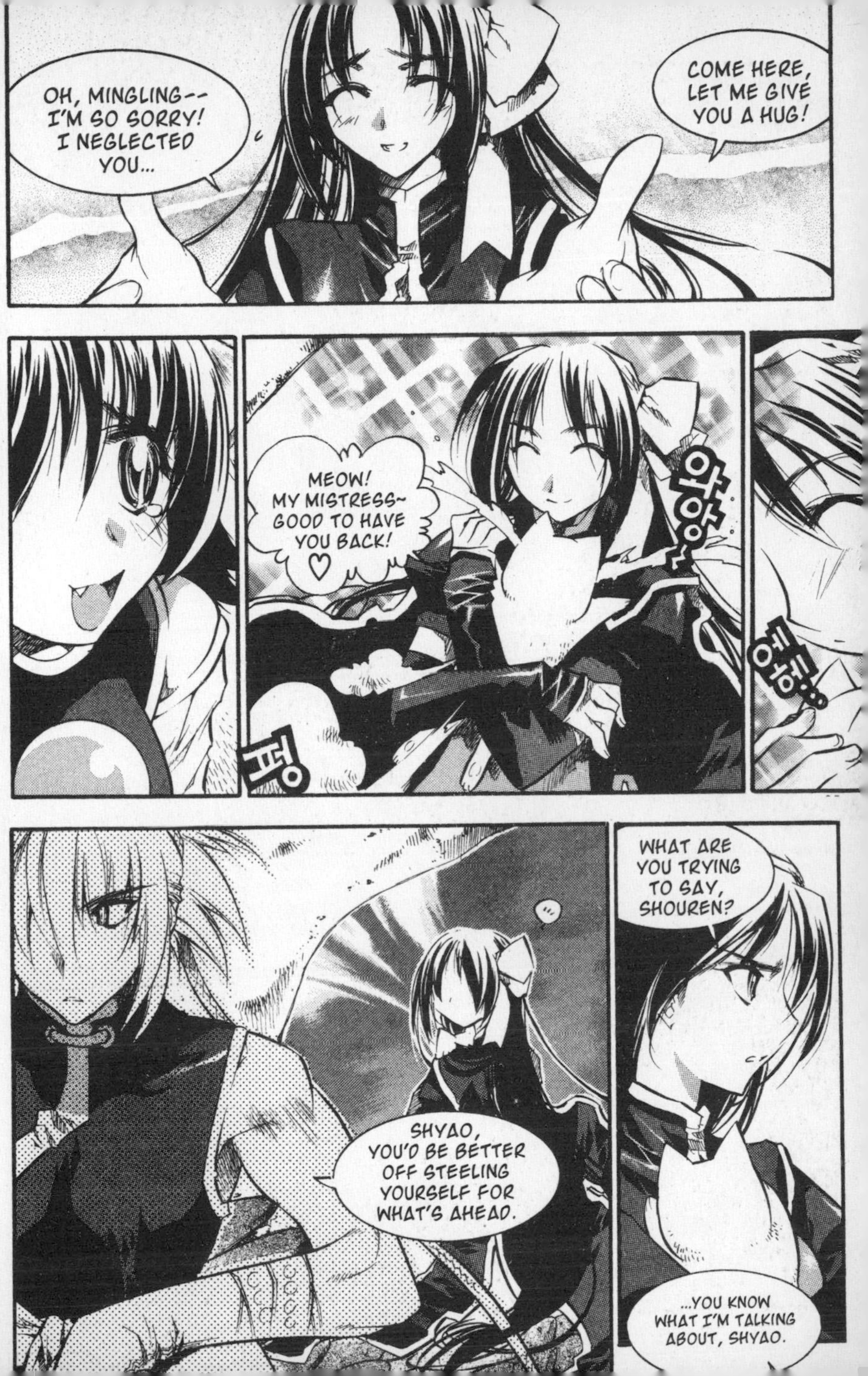
OH, MINGLING-- I'M SO SORRY! I NEGLECTED YOU...
COME HERE, LET ME GIVE YOU A HUG!
MEOW! MY MISTRESS~ GOOD TO HAVE YOU BACK! ♡
야앙~
펑
둥둥..
SHYAO, YOU'D BE BETTER OFF STEELING YOURSELF FOR WHAT'S AHEAD.
WHAT ARE YOU TRYING TO SAY, SHOUREN?
...YOU KNOW WHAT I'M TALKING ABOUT, SHYAO.

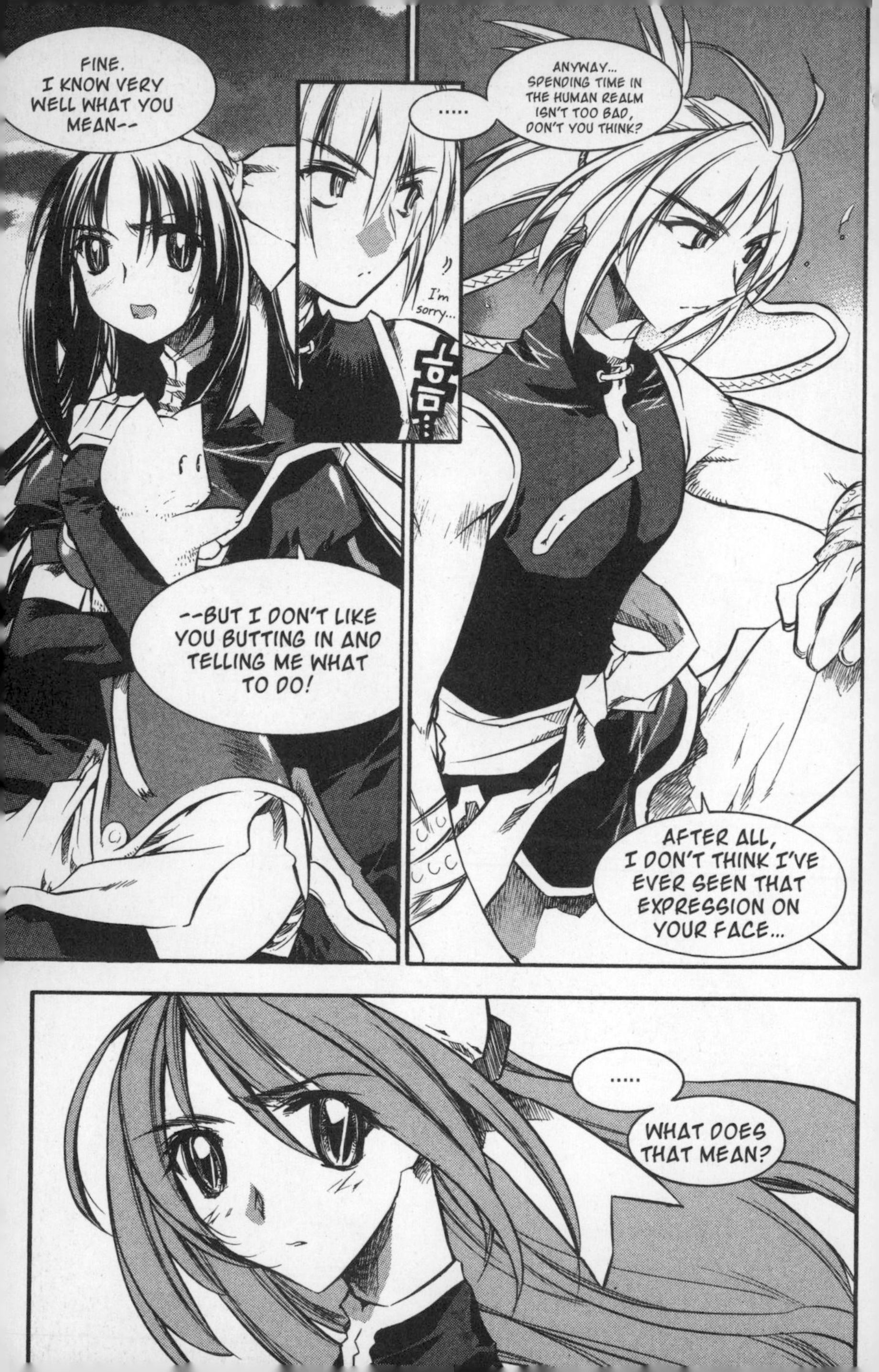
FINE. I KNOW VERY WELL WHAT YOU MEAN--
--BUT I DON'T LIKE YOU BUTTING IN AND TELLING ME WHAT TO DO!
.....
I'm sorry...
흠...
ANYWAY... SPENDING TIME IN THE HUMAN REALM ISN'T TOO BAD, DON'T YOU THINK?
AFTER ALL, I DON'T THINK I'VE EVER SEEN THAT EXPRESSION ON YOUR FACE...
.....
WHAT DOES THAT MEAN?

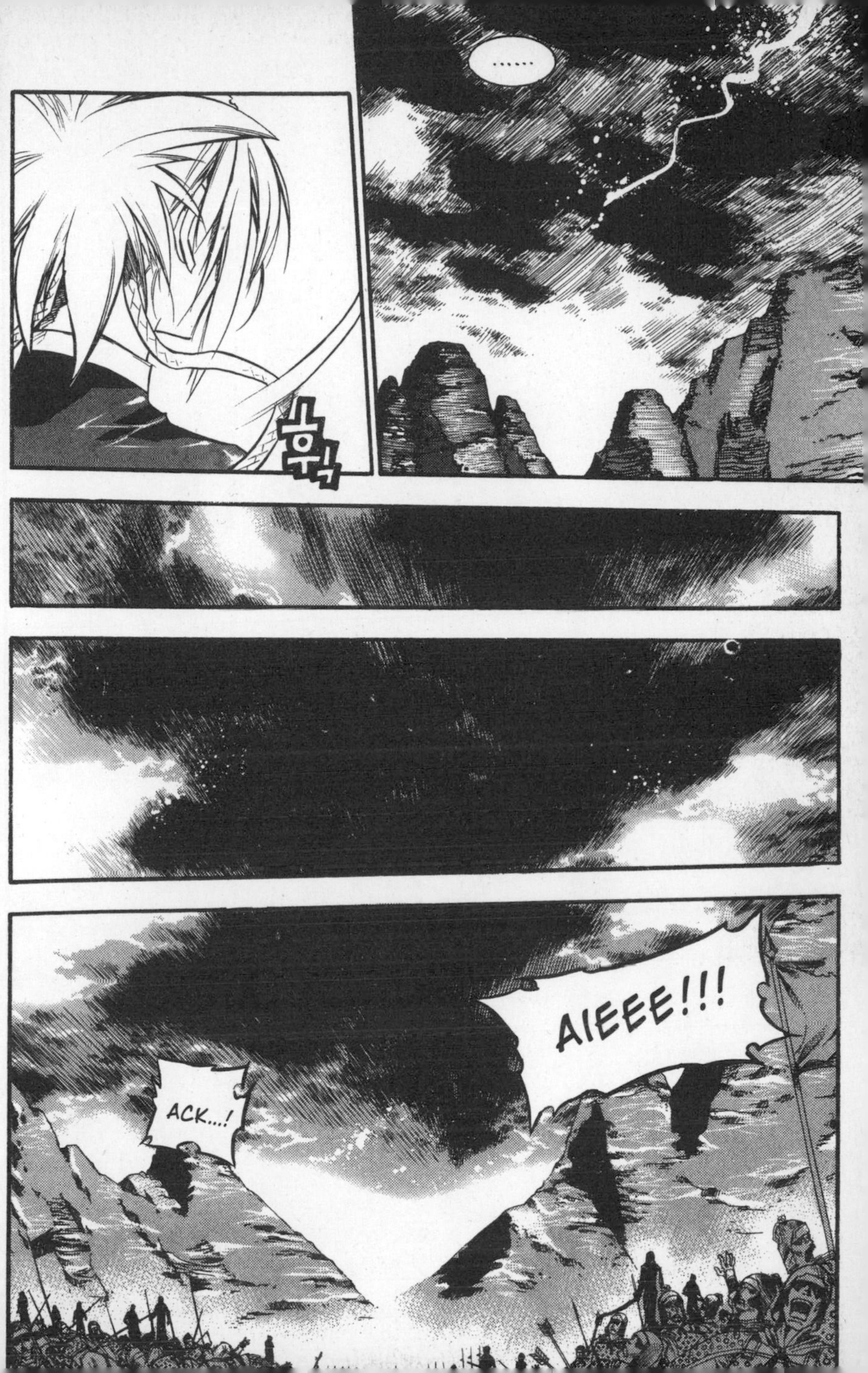
......
휘익
AIEEE!!!
ACK...!

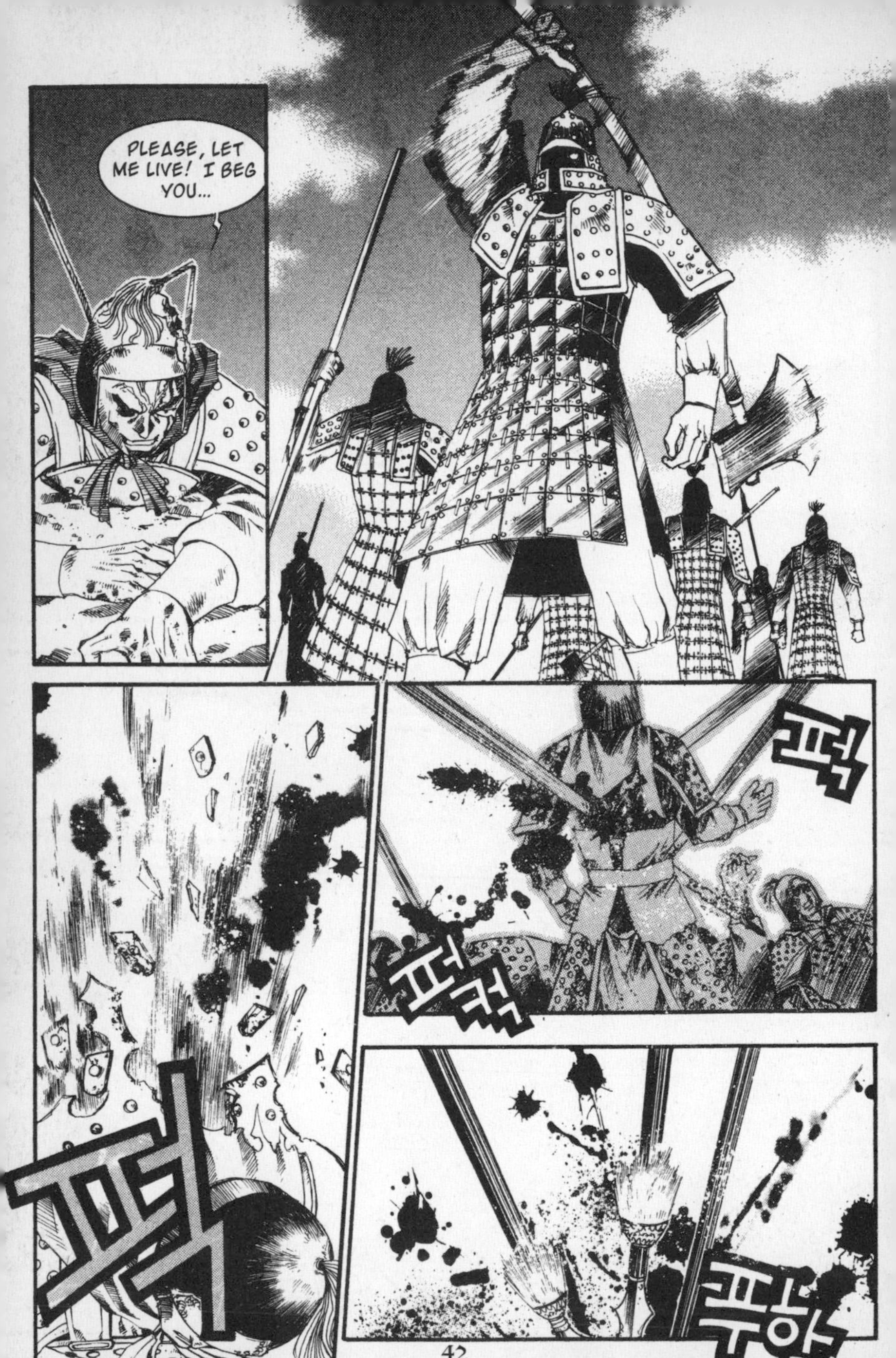
PLEASE, LET ME LIVE! I BEG YOU...
퍽
퍽
퍼걱
푸악

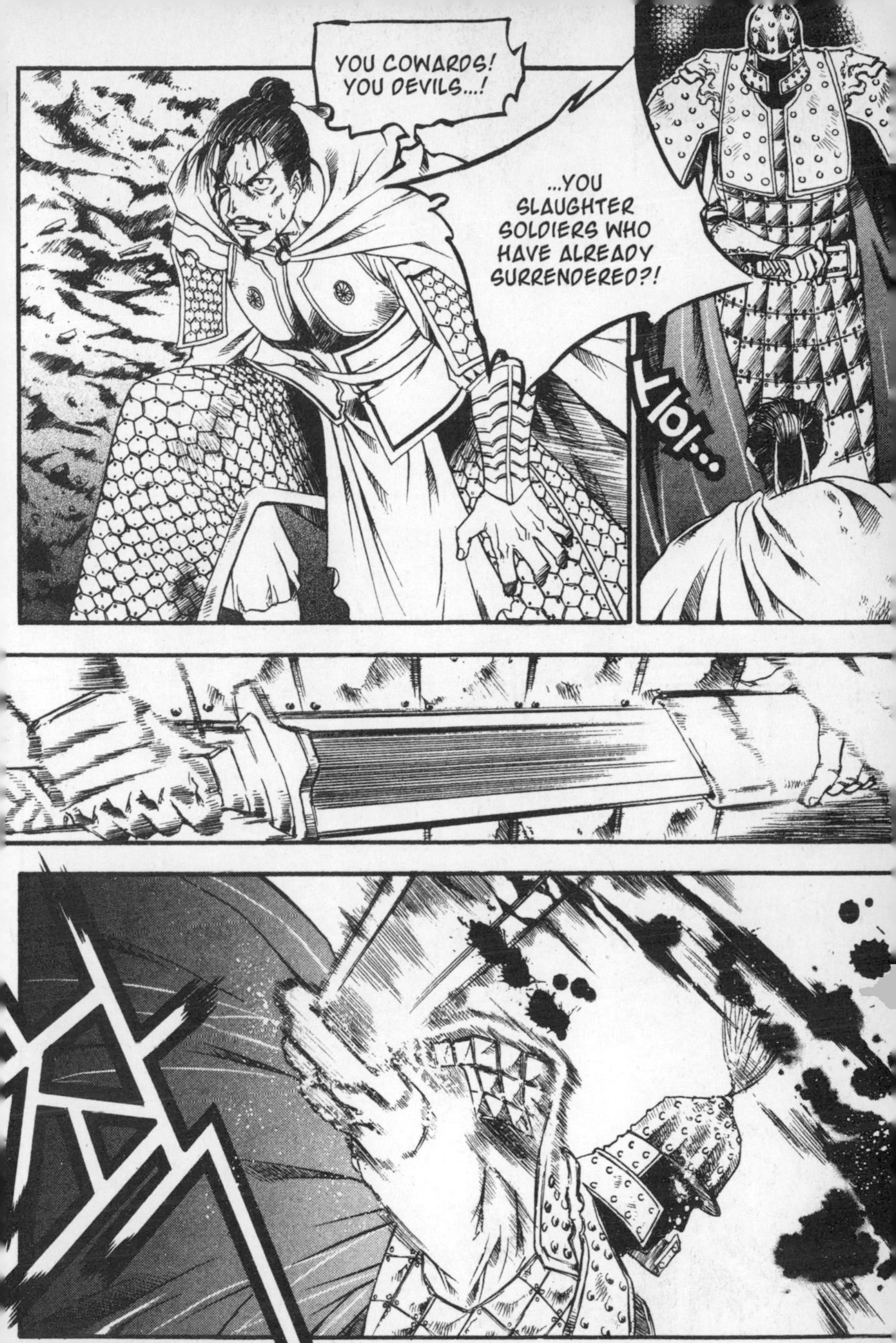
YOU COWARDS! YOU DEVILS...!
...YOU SLAUGHTER SOLDIERS WHO HAVE ALREADY SURRENDERED?!

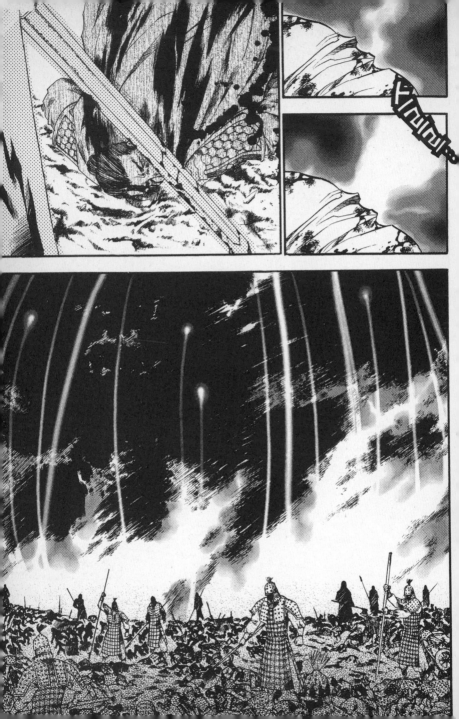

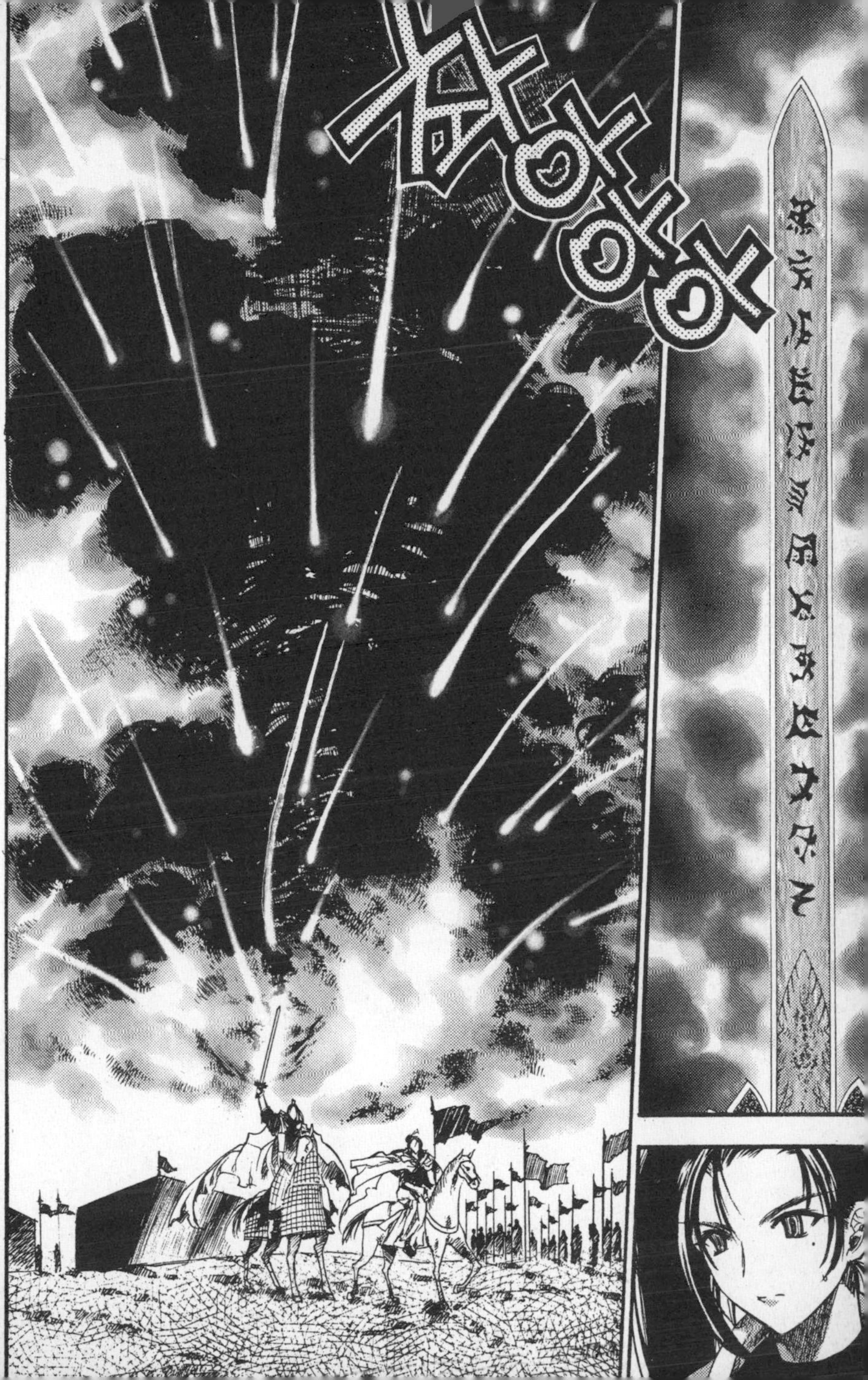
쏴아아아

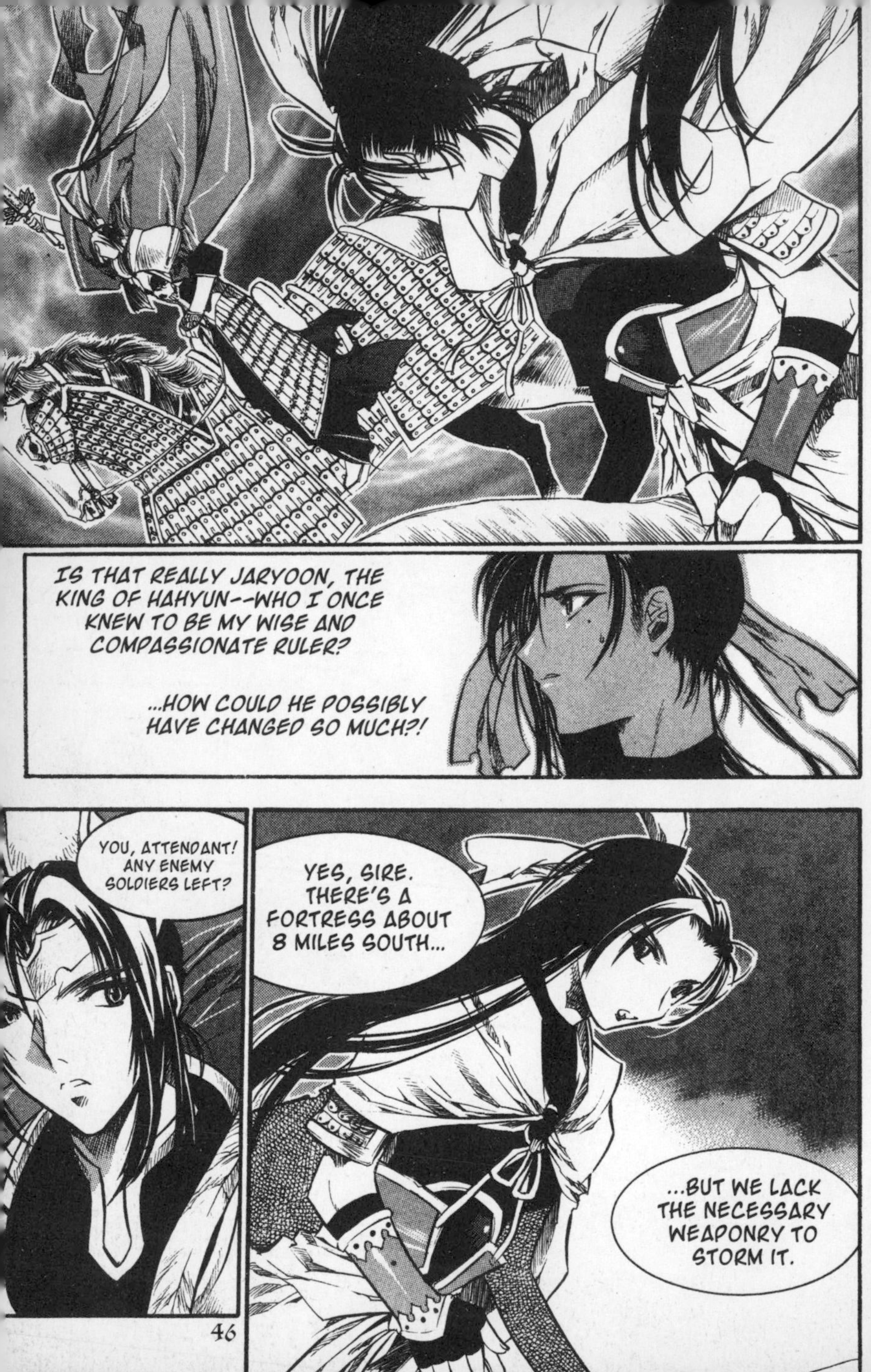
IS THAT REALLY JARYOON, THE KING OF HAHYUN--WHO I ONCE KNEW TO BE MY WISE AND COMPASSIONATE RULER?
...HOW COULD HE POSSIBLY HAVE CHANGED SO MUCH?!
YOU, ATTENDANT! ANY ENEMY SOLDIERS LEFT?
YES, SIRE. THERE'S A FORTRESS ABOUT 8 MILES SOUTH...
...BUT WE LACK THE NECESSARY WEAPONRY TO STORM IT.

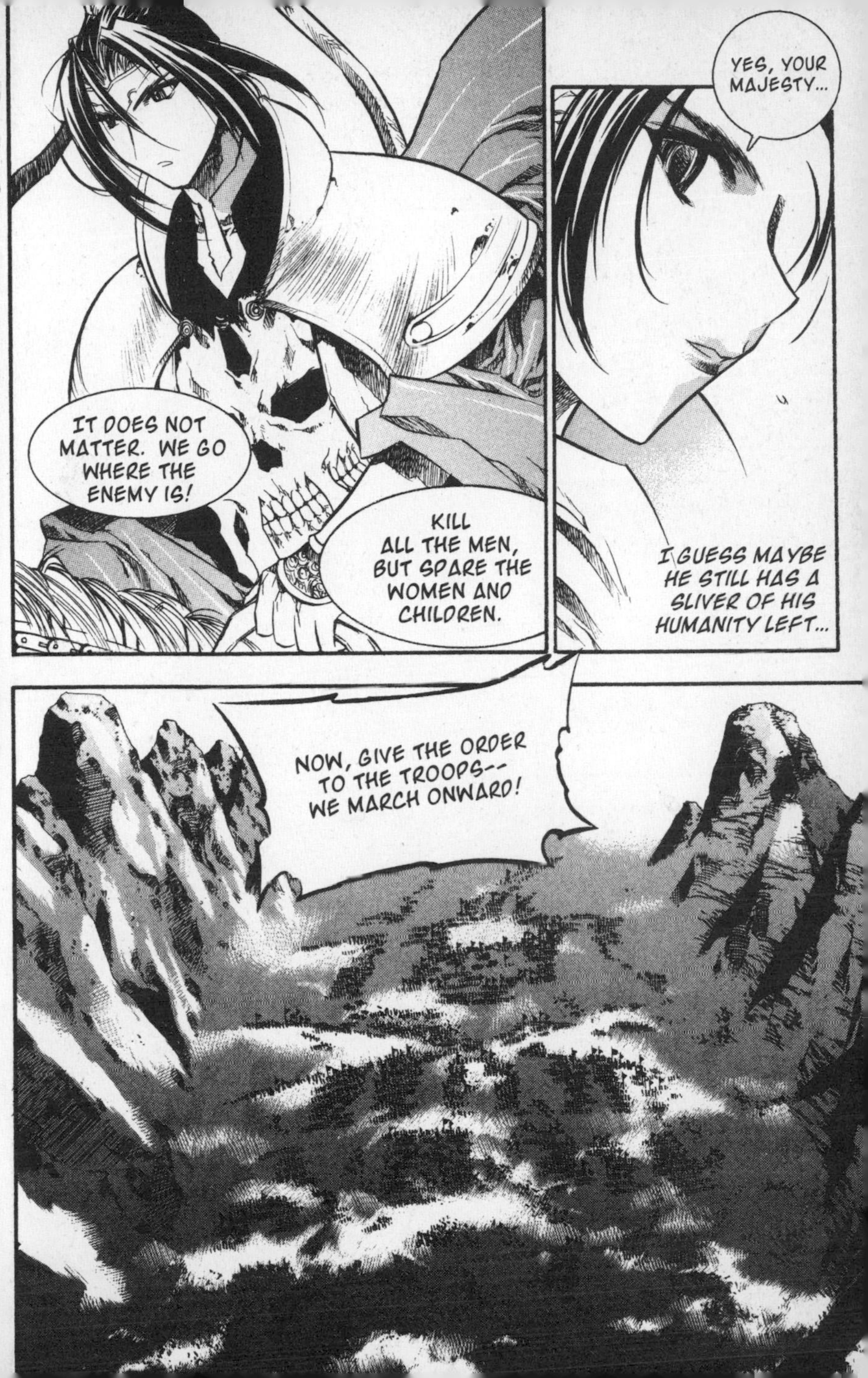
IT DOES NOT MATTER. WE GO WHERE THE ENEMY IS!
KILL ALL THE MEN, BUT SPARE THE WOMEN AND CHILDREN.
YES, YOUR MAJESTY...
I GUESS MAYBE HE STILL HAS A SLIVER OF HIS HUMANITY LEFT...
NOW, GIVE THE ORDER TO THE TROOPS-- WE MARCH ONWARD!

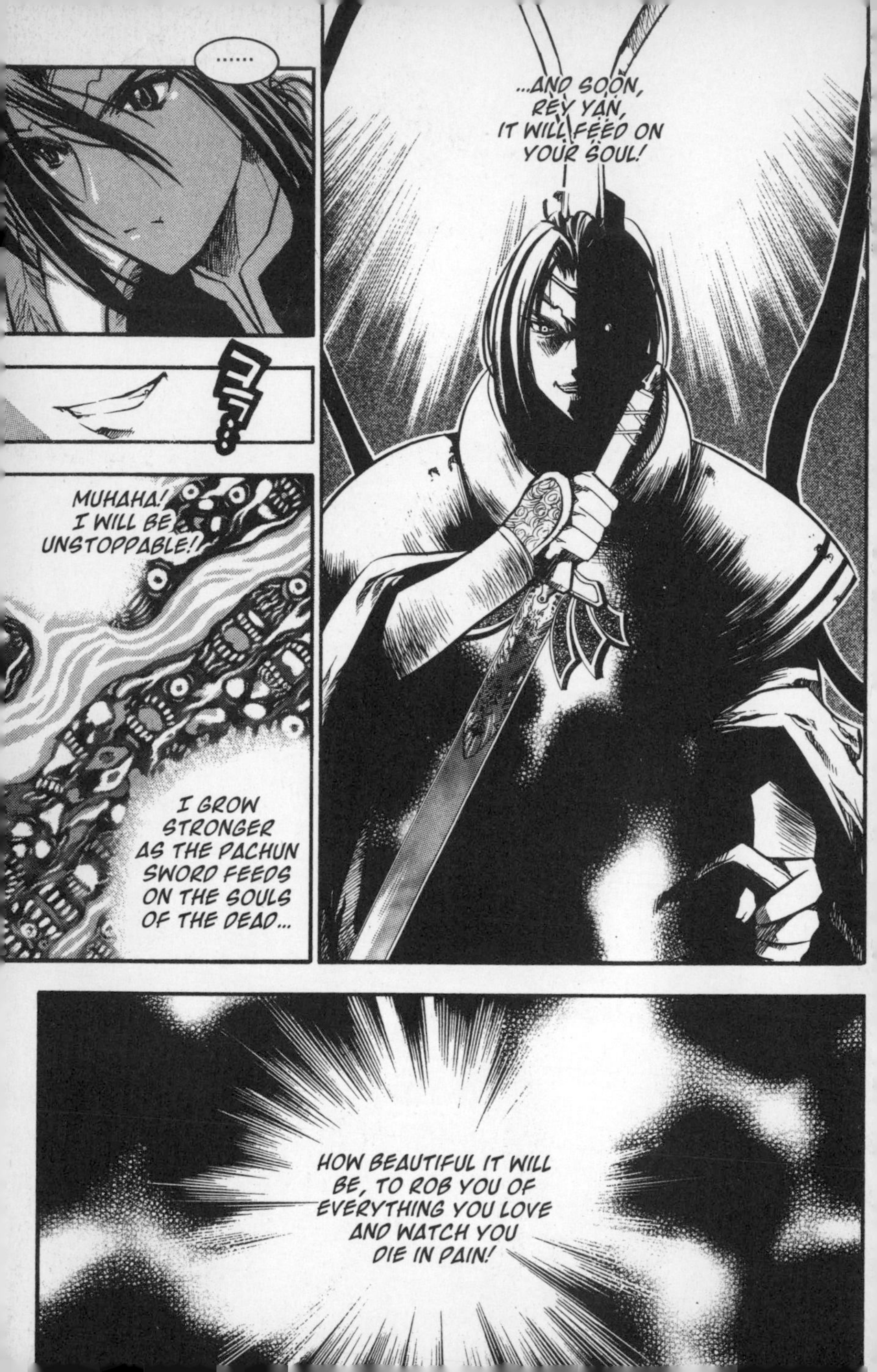
......
MUHAHA! I WILL BE UNSTOPPABLE!
I GROW STRONGER AS THE PACHUN SWORD FEEDS ON THE SOULS OF THE DEAD...
...AND SOON, REY YAN, IT WILL FEED ON YOUR SOUL!
HOW BEAUTIFUL IT WILL BE, TO ROB YOU OF EVERYTHING YOU LOVE AND WATCH YOU DIE IN PAIN!

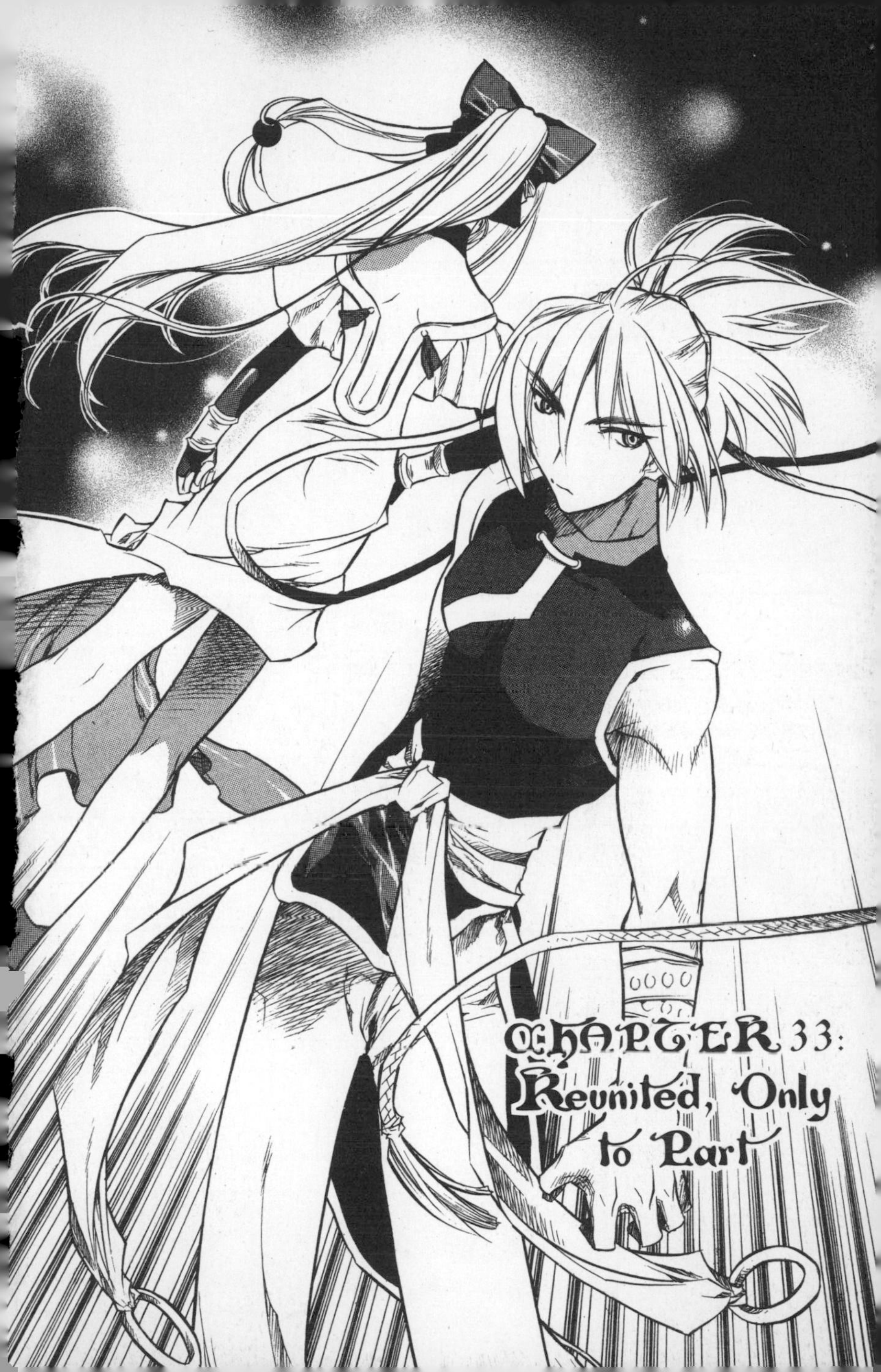
CHAPTER 33:
Reunited, Only to Part

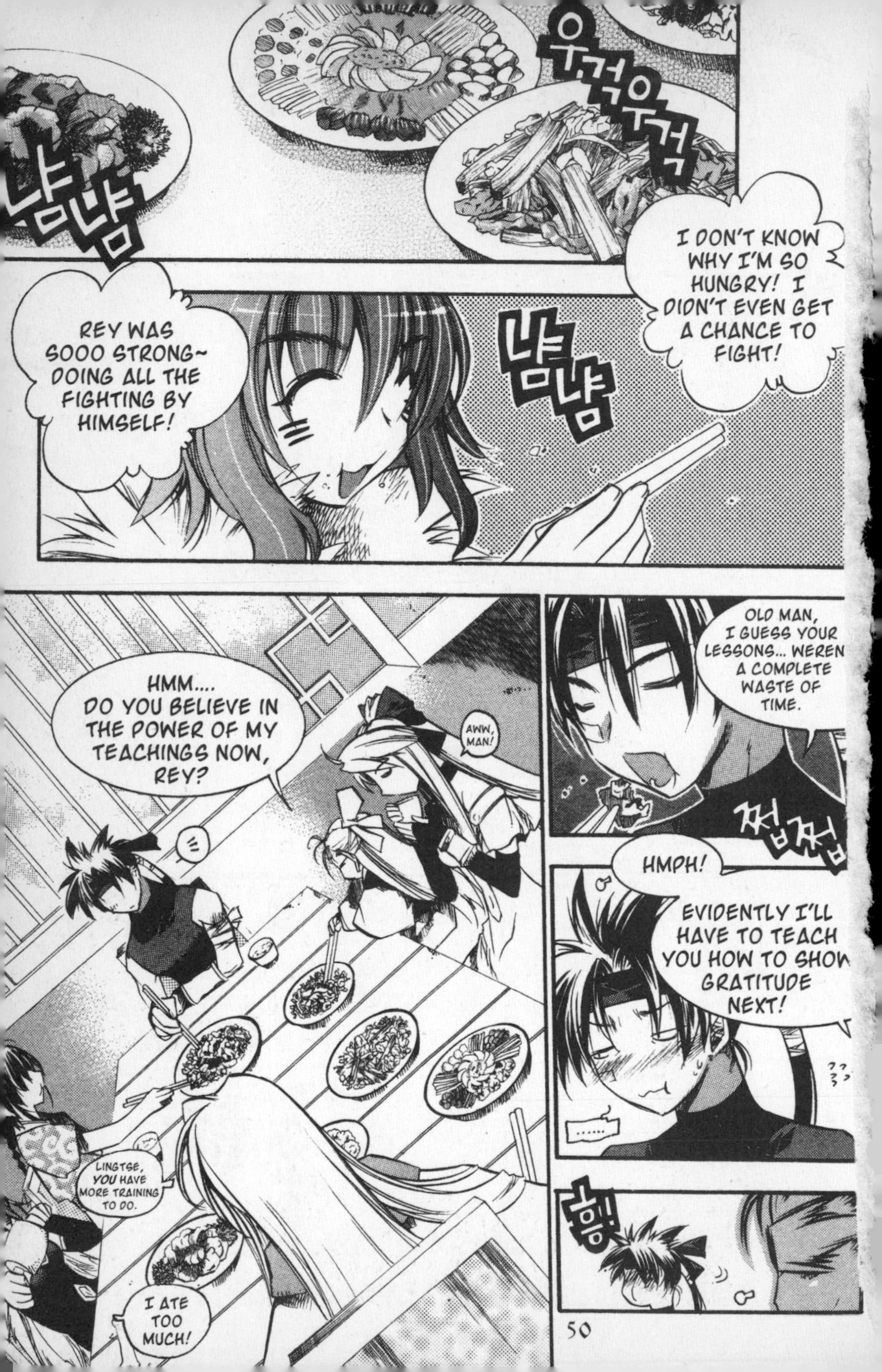

냠냠
우걱우걱
REY WAS SOOO STRONG~ DOING ALL THE FIGHTING BY HIMSELF!
냠냠
I DON'T KNOW WHY I'M SO HUNGRY! I DIDN'T EVEN GET A CHANCE TO FIGHT!
HMM.... DO YOU BELIEVE IN THE POWER OF MY TEACHINGS NOW, REY?
AWW, MAN!
LINGTSE, YOU HAVE MORE TRAINING TO DO.
I ATE TOO MUCH!
OLD MAN, I GUESS YOUR LESSONS... WEREN A COMPLETE WASTE OF TIME.
쩝쩝
HMPH!
EVIDENTLY I'LL HAVE TO TEACH YOU HOW TO SHOW GRATITUDE NEXT!
......
흥

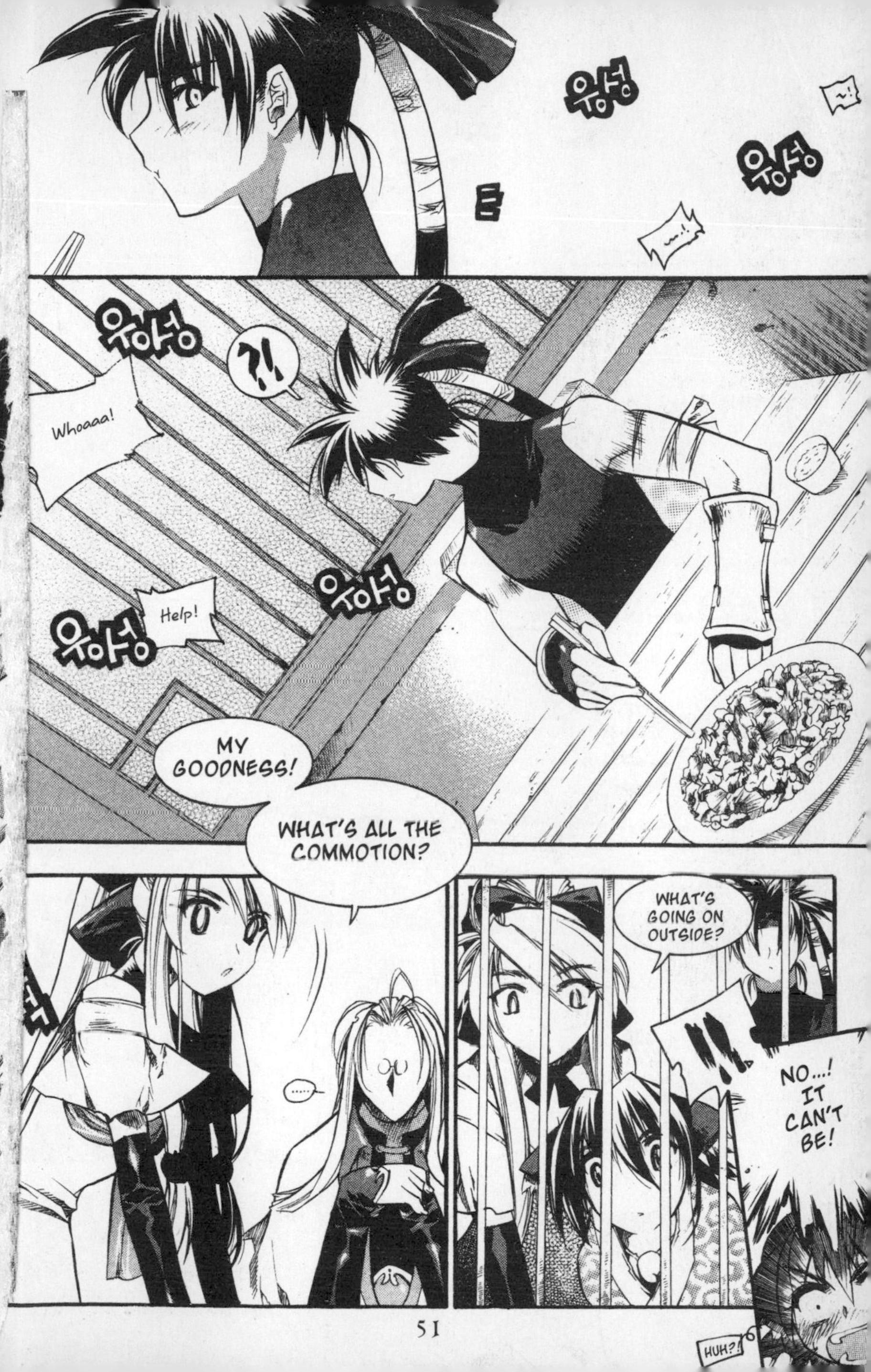

~!
~~!
Whoaaa!
?!
Help!
MY GOODNESS!
WHAT'S ALL THE COMMOTION?
.....
WHAT'S GOING ON OUTSIDE?
!!
NO...! IT CAN'T BE!
HUH?!

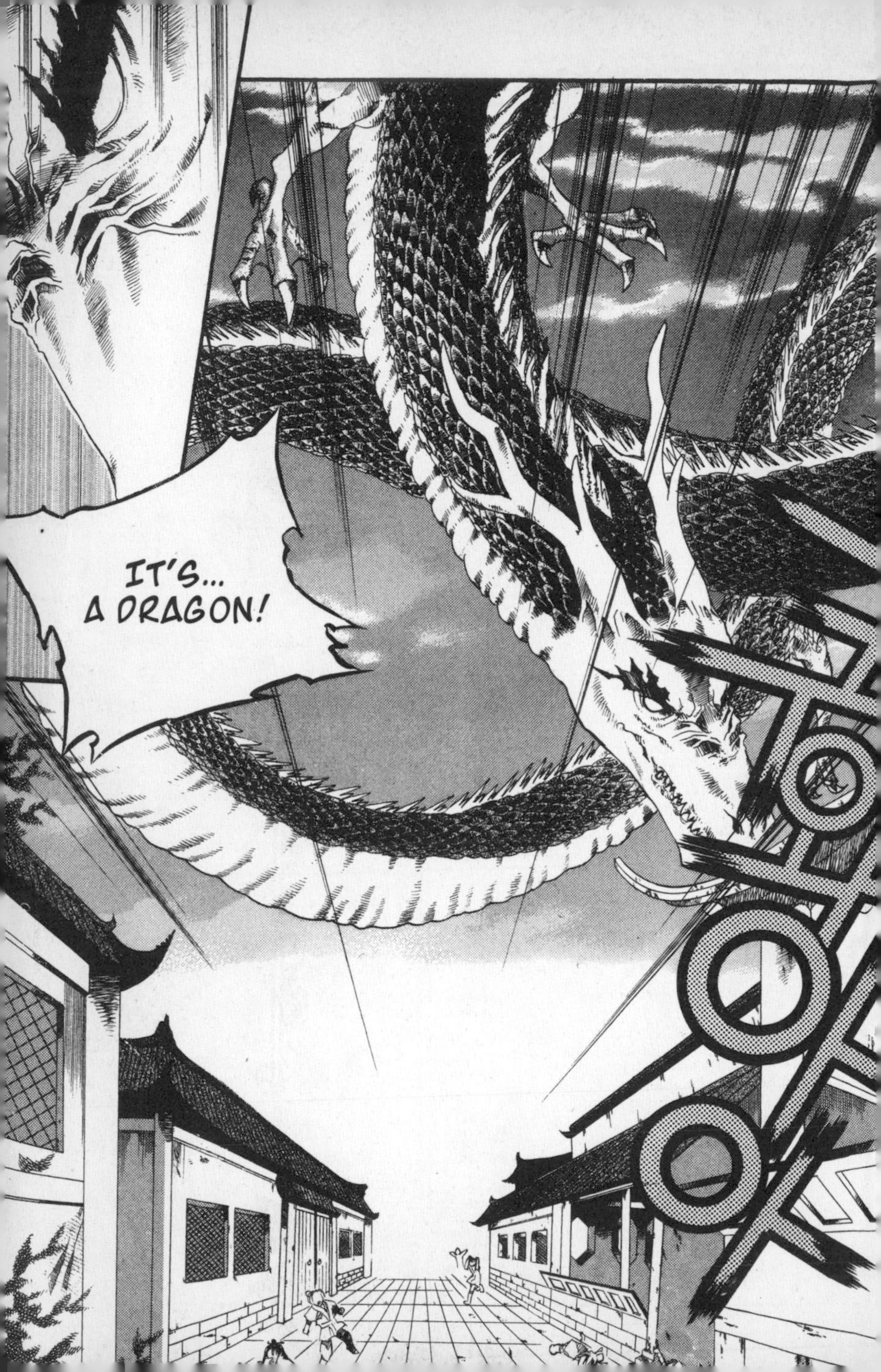
IT'S... A DRAGON!

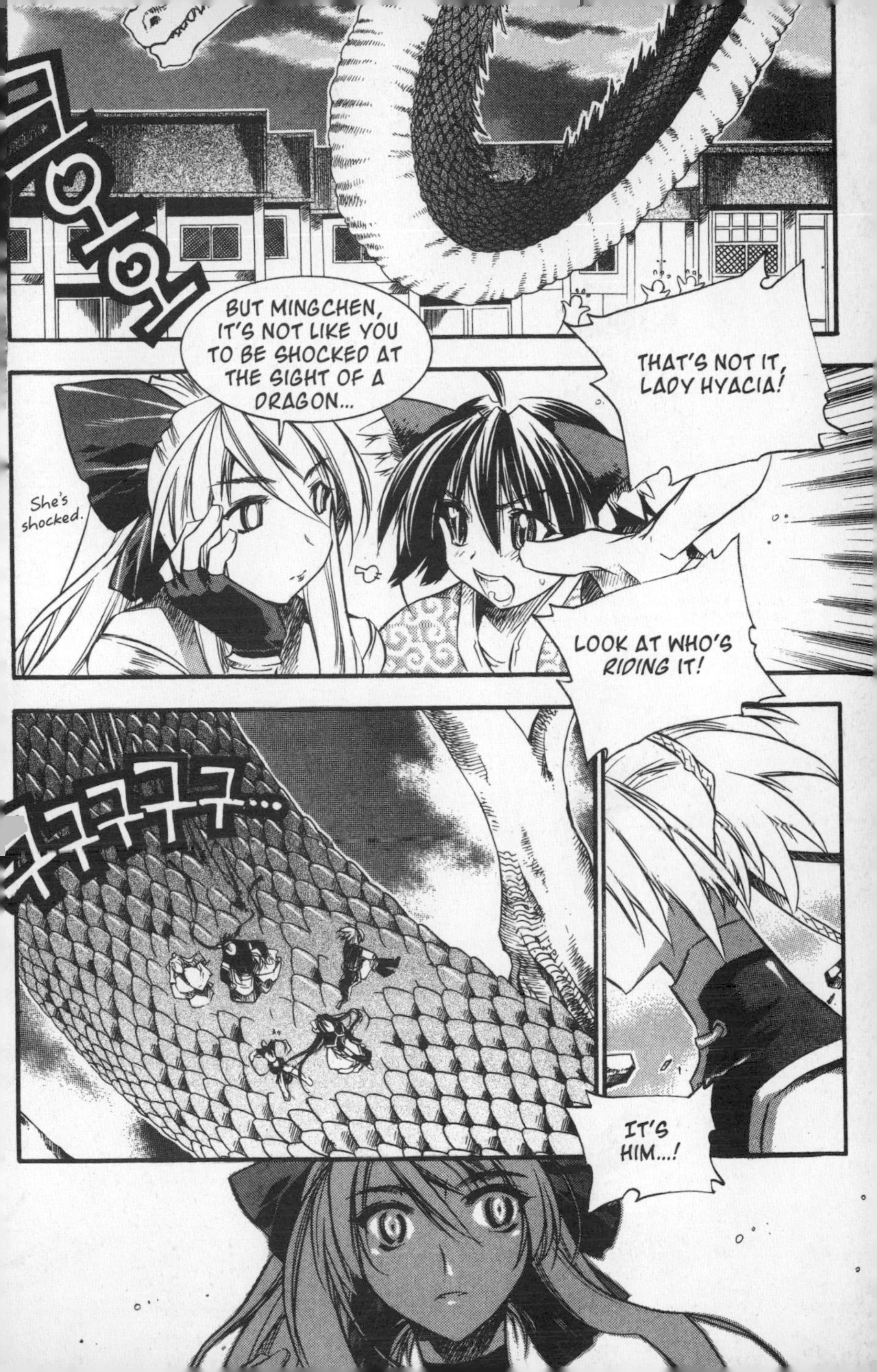
BUT MINGCHEN, IT'S NOT LIKE YOU TO BE SHOCKED AT THE SIGHT OF A DRAGON...
She's shocked.
THAT'S NOT IT, LADY HYACIA!
LOOK AT WHO'S RIDING IT!
IT'S HIM...!

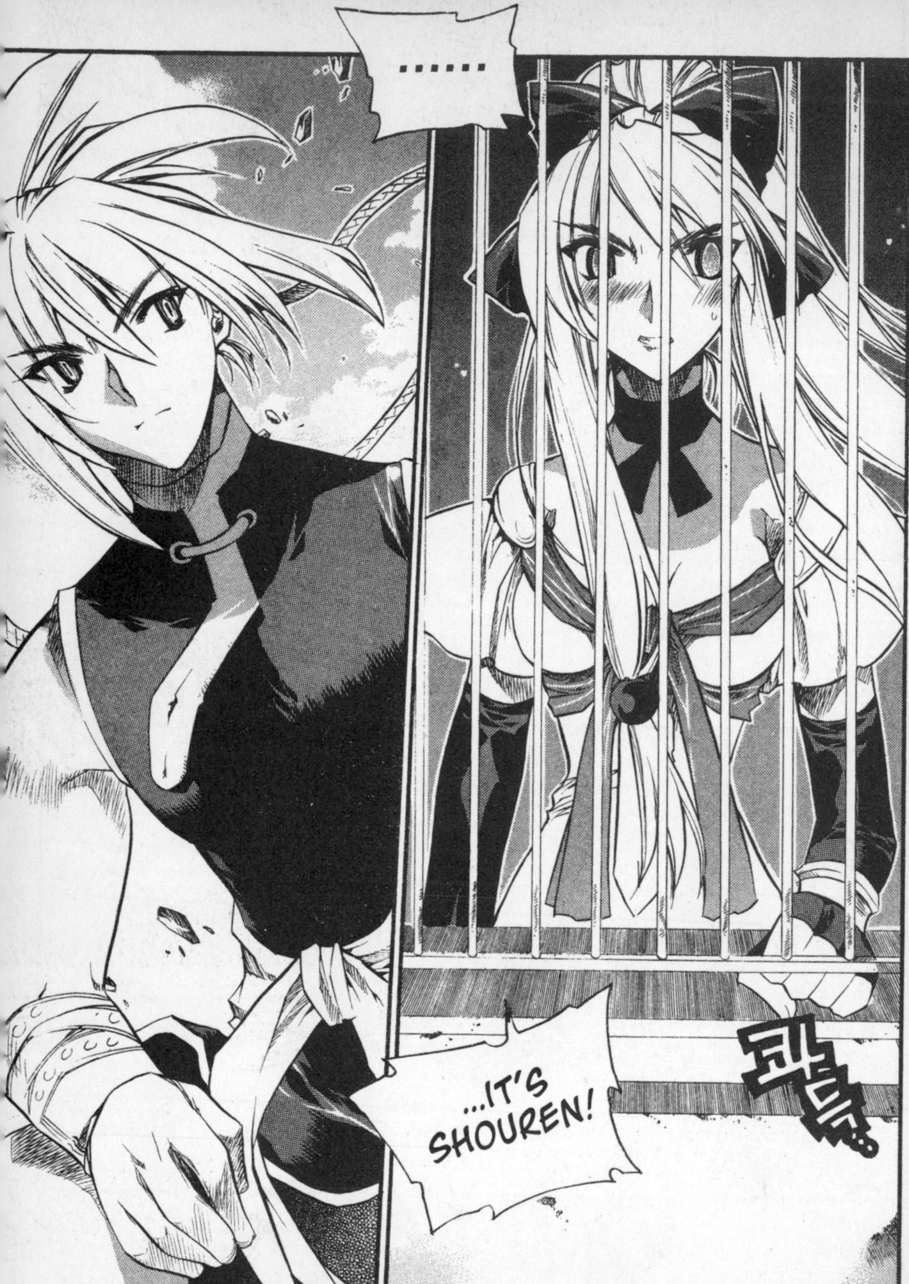
......
...IT'S SHOUREN!

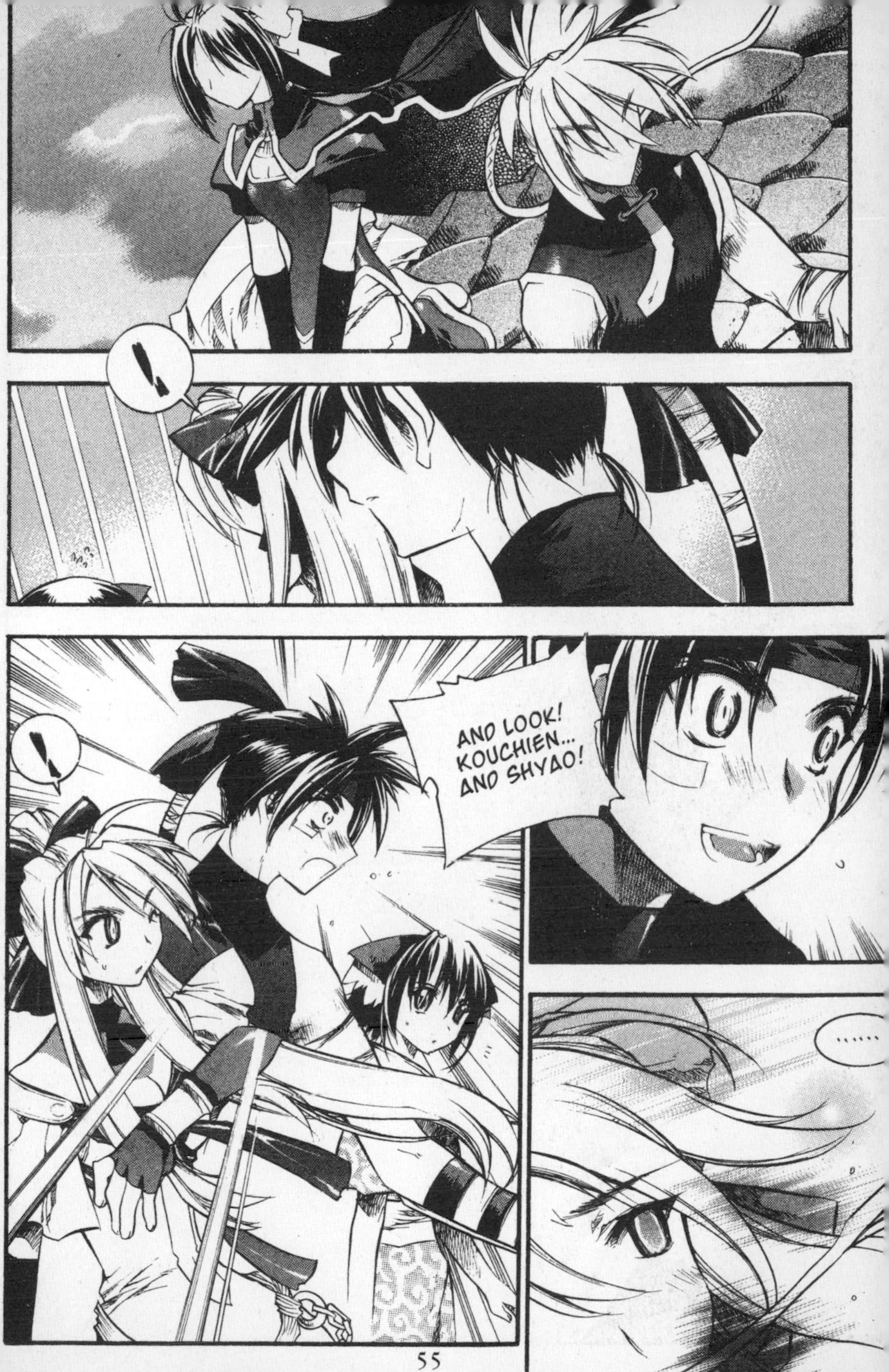
!
!
AND LOOK! KOUCHIEN... AND SHYAO!
......

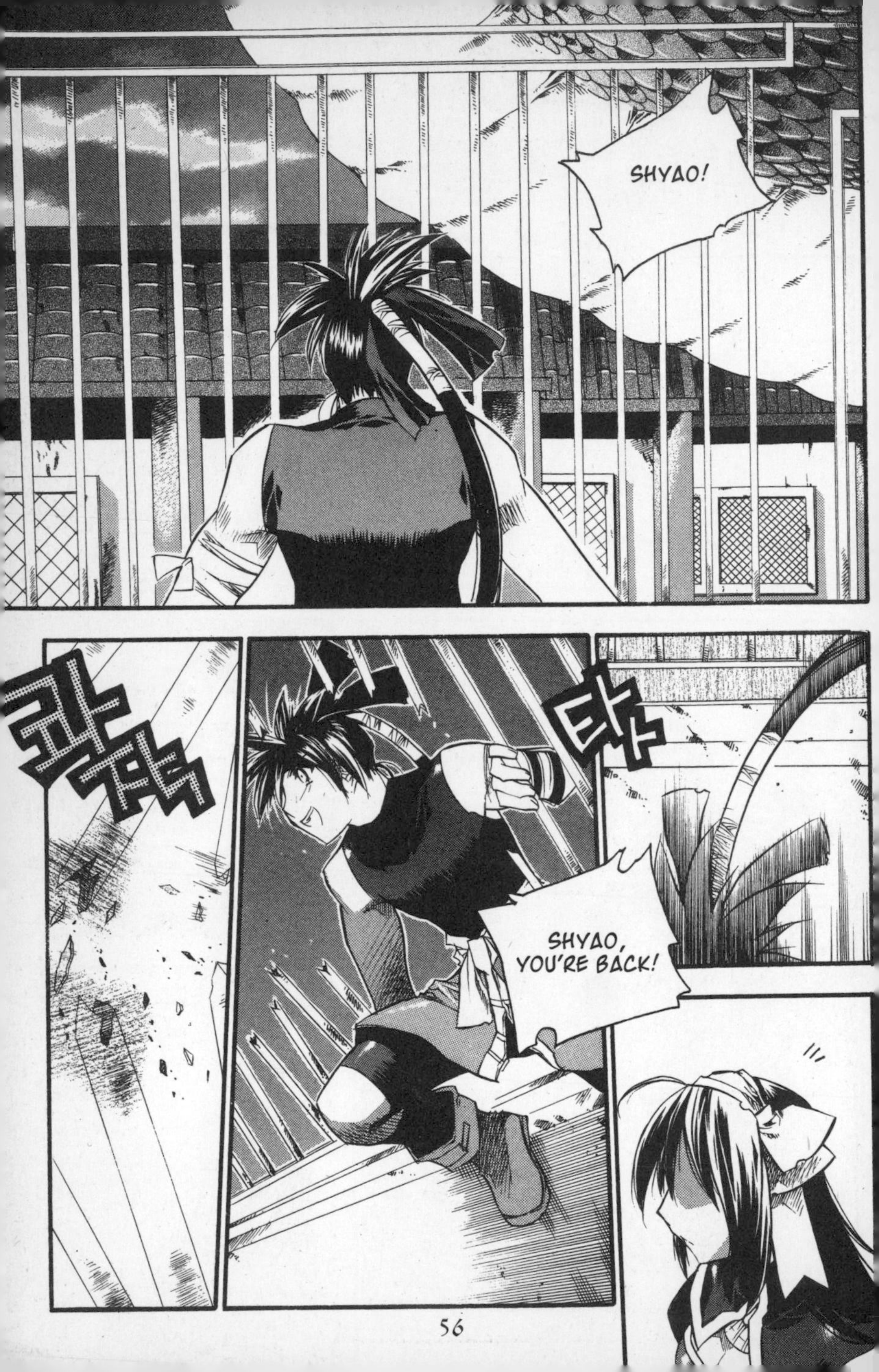
SHYAO!
탁
SHYAO, YOU'RE BACK!

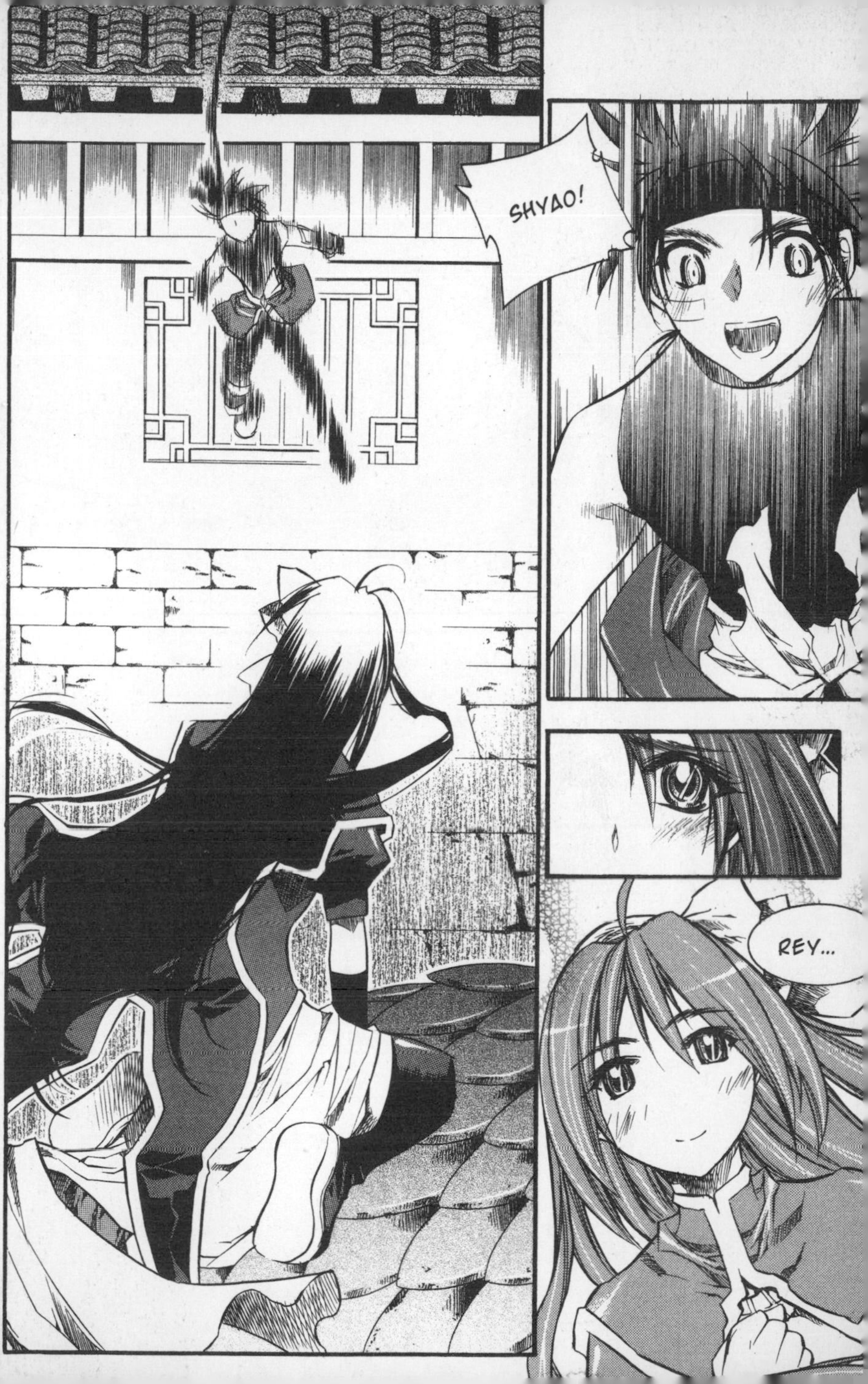
SHYAO!
REY...

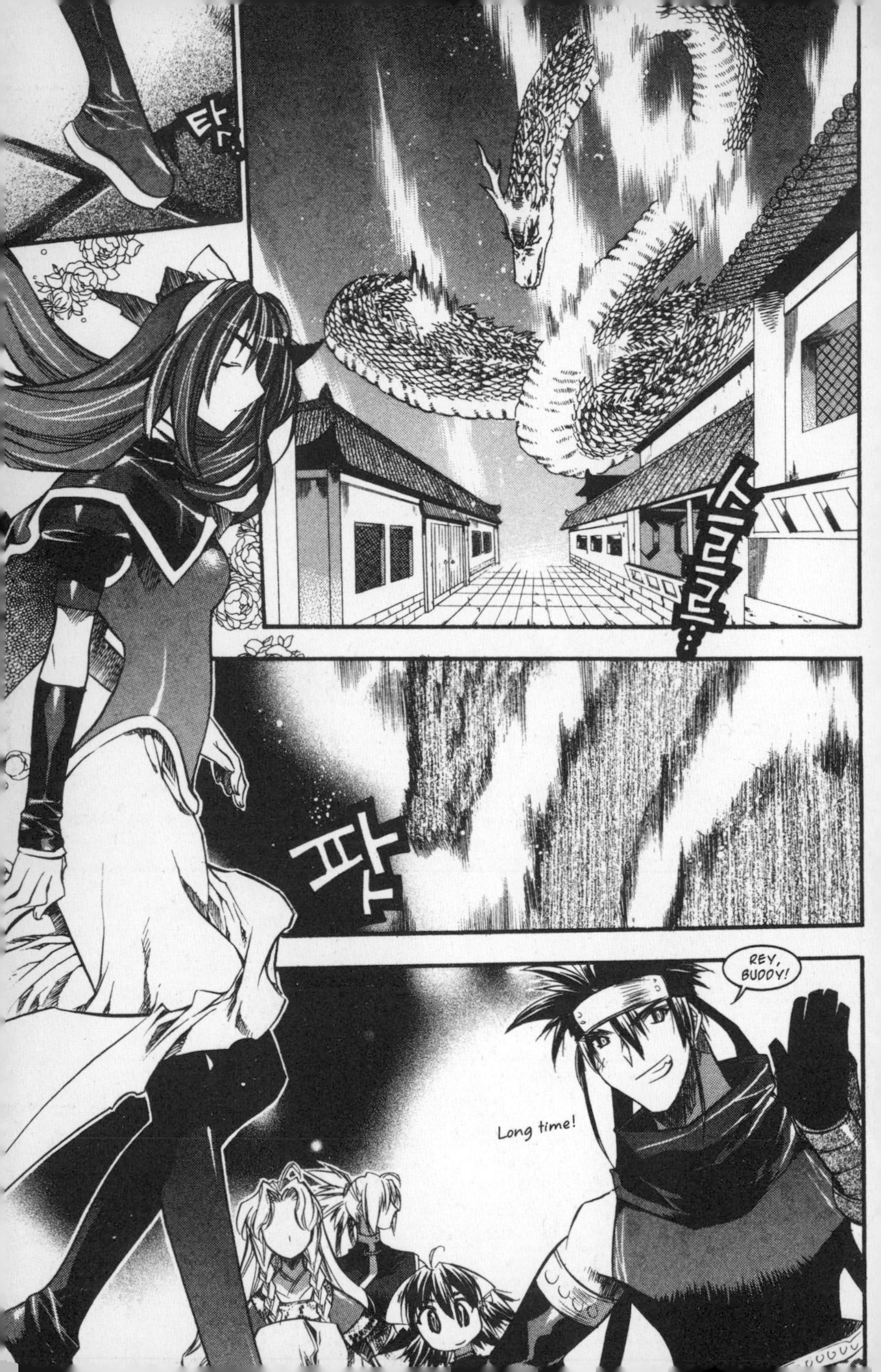
탁..
스르르...
팟
REY, BUDDY!
Long time!

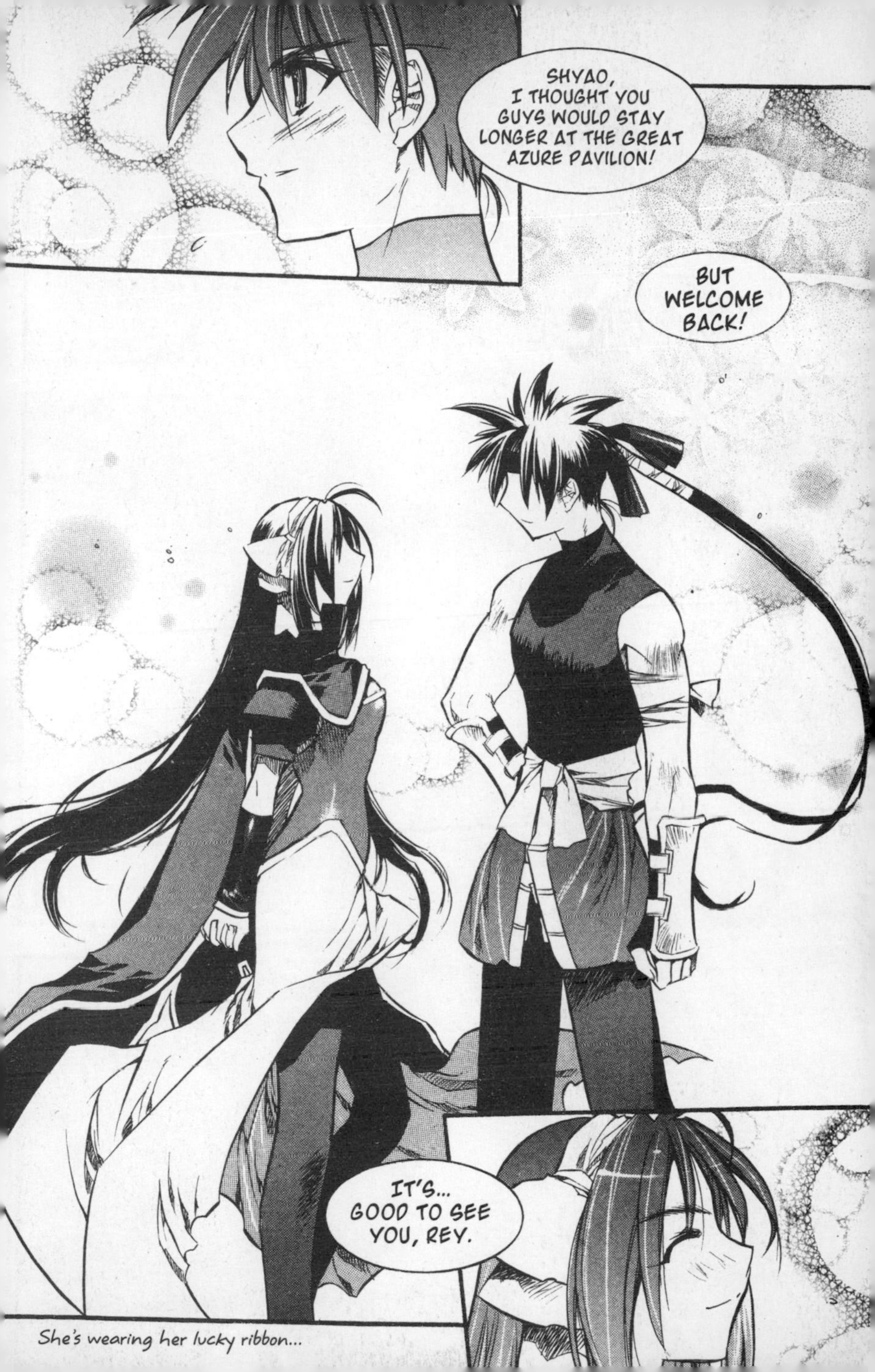
SHYAO, I THOUGHT YOU GUYS WOULD STAY LONGER AT THE GREAT AZURE PAVILION!
BUT WELCOME BACK!
IT'S... GOOD TO SEE YOU, REY.
She's wearing her lucky ribbon...

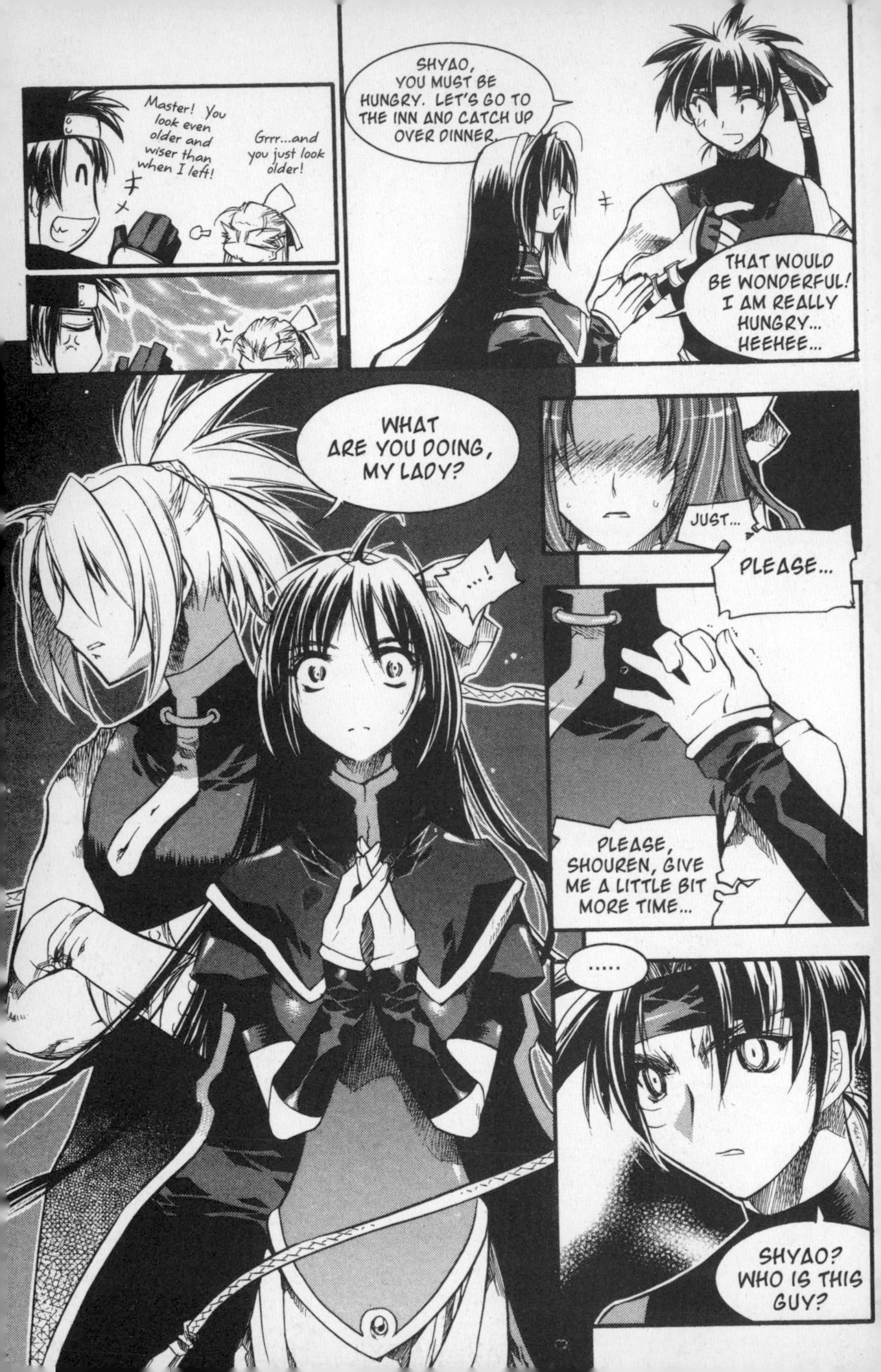
SHYAO, YOU MUST BE HUNGRY. LET'S GO TO THE INN AND CATCH UP OVER DINNER.
THAT WOULD BE WONDERFUL! I AM REALLY HUNGRY... HEEHEE...
Master! You look even older and wiser than when I left!
Grrr...and you just look older!
JUST...
PLEASE...
PLEASE, SHOUREN, GIVE ME A LITTLE BIT MORE TIME...
.....
SHYAO? WHO IS THIS GUY?
WHAT ARE YOU DOING, MY LADY?
...!

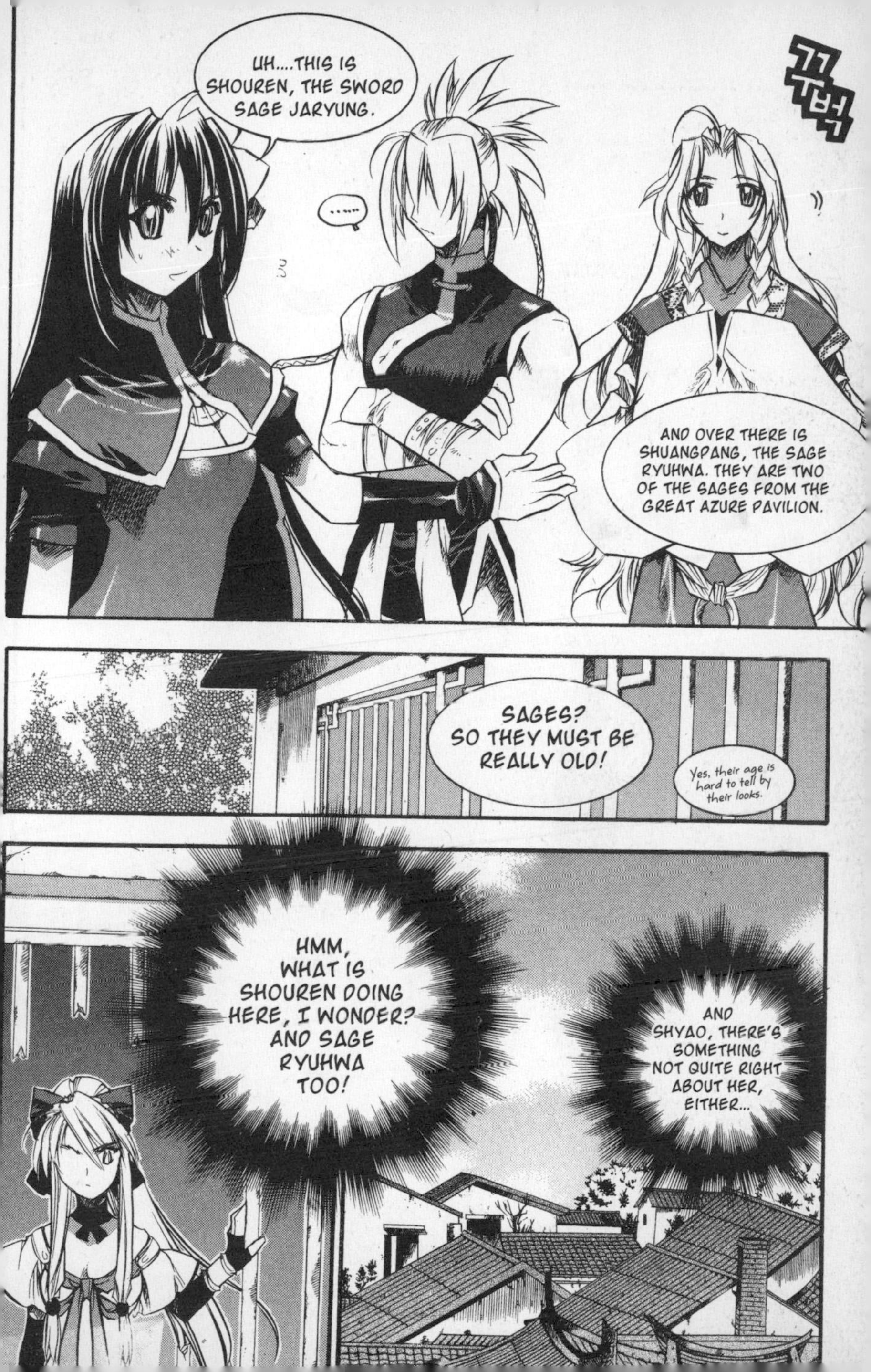
UH....THIS IS SHOUREN, THE SWORD SAGE JARYUNG.
......
AND OVER THERE IS SHUANGPANG, THE SAGE RYUHWA. THEY ARE TWO OF THE SAGES FROM THE GREAT AZURE PAVILION.
SAGES? SO THEY MUST BE REALLY OLD!
Yes, their age is hard to tell by their looks.
HMM, WHAT IS SHOUREN DOING HERE, I WONDER? AND SAGE RYUHWA TOO!
AND SHYAO, THERE'S SOMETHING NOT QUITE RIGHT ABOUT HER, EITHER...

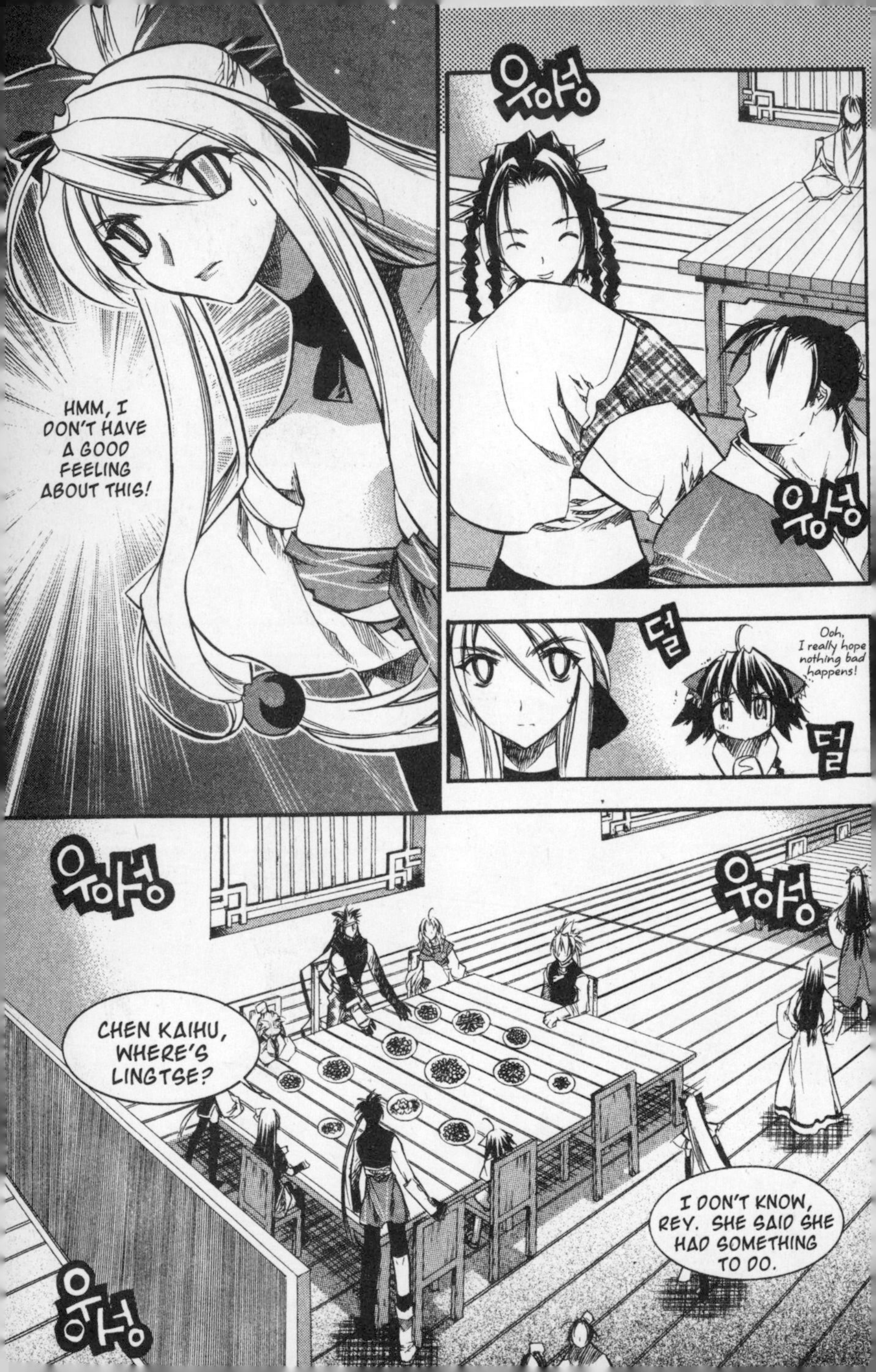
HMM, I DON'T HAVE A GOOD FEELING ABOUT THIS!
우앙
우앙
덜
Ooh, I really hope nothing bad happens!
덜
우앙
우앙
CHEN KAIHU, WHERE'S LINGTSE?
I DON'T KNOW, REY. SHE SAID SHE HAD SOMETHING TO DO.
우앙

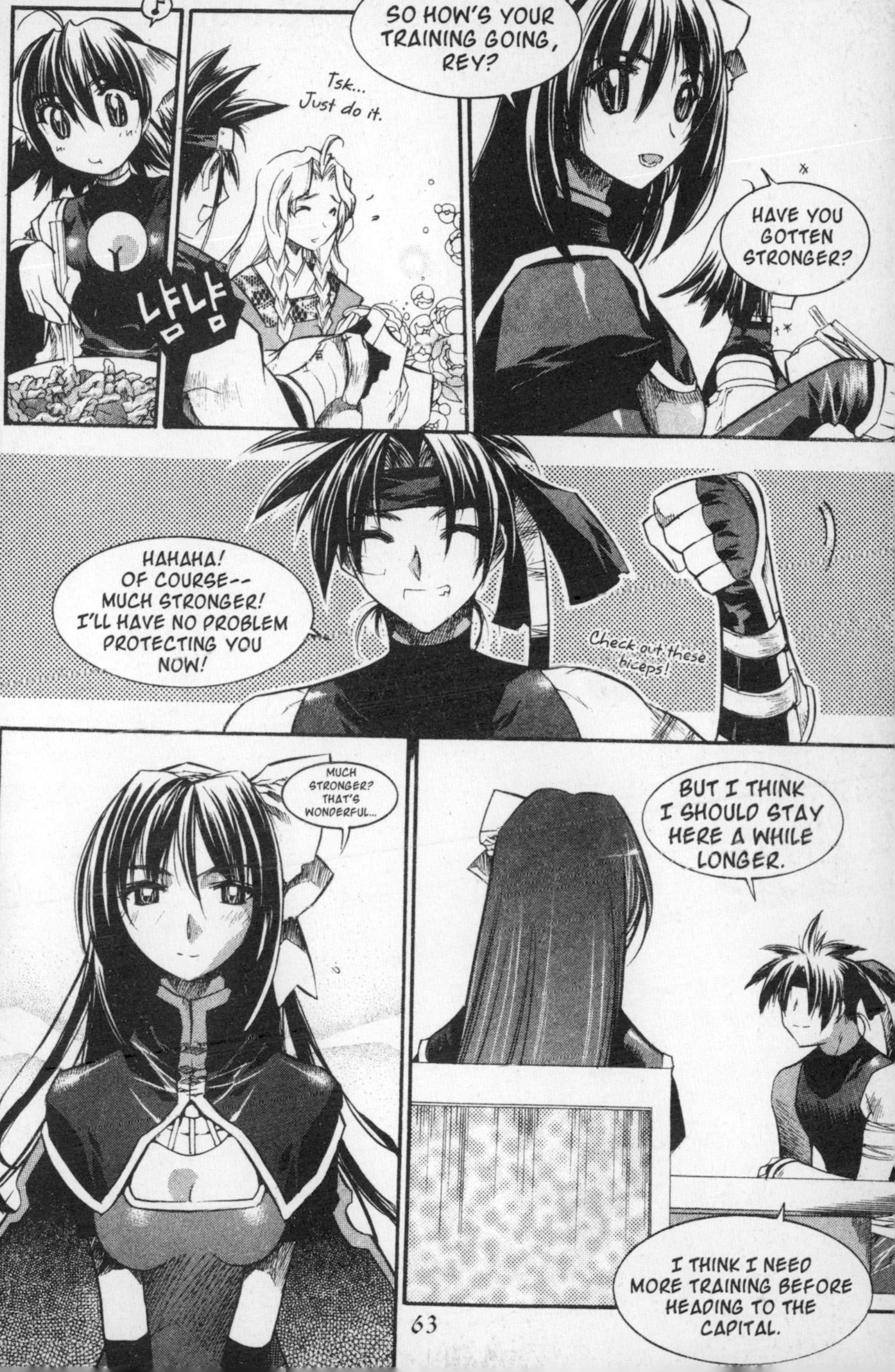
♪
냠냠
Tsk... Just do it.
SO HOW'S YOUR TRAINING GOING, REY?
HAVE YOU GOTTEN STRONGER?
HAHAHA! OF COURSE-- MUCH STRONGER! I'LL HAVE NO PROBLEM PROTECTING YOU NOW!
Check out these biceps!
MUCH STRONGER? THAT'S WONDERFUL...
BUT I THINK I SHOULD STAY HERE A WHILE LONGER.
I THINK I NEED MORE TRAINING BEFORE HEADING TO THE CAPITAL.

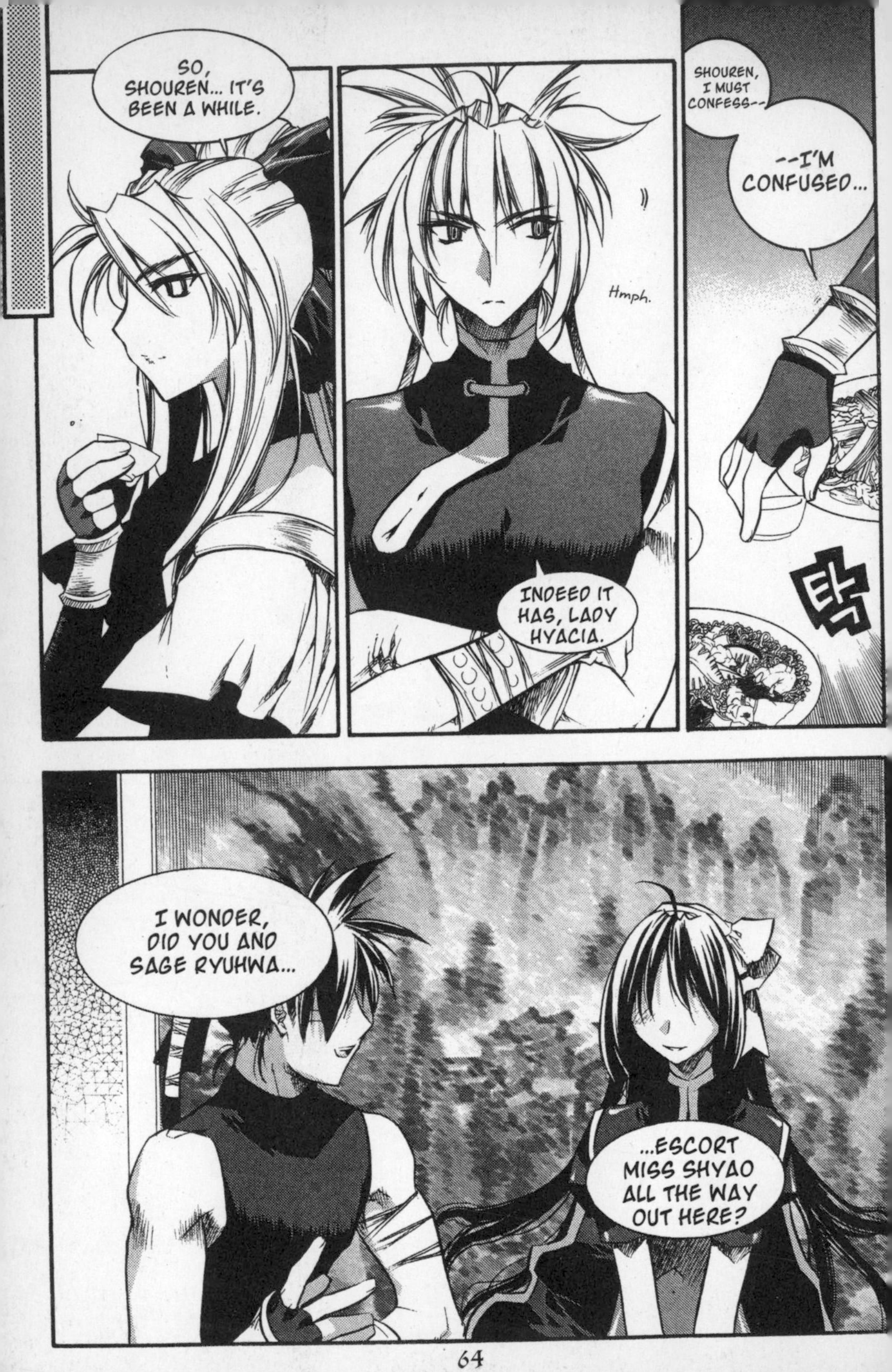
SO, SHOUREN... IT'S BEEN A WHILE.
Hmph.
INDEED IT HAS, LADY HYACIA.
SHOUREN, I MUST CONFESS--
--I'M CONFUSED...
탁
I WONDER, DID YOU AND SAGE RYUHWA...
...ESCORT MISS SHYAO ALL THE WAY OUT HERE?

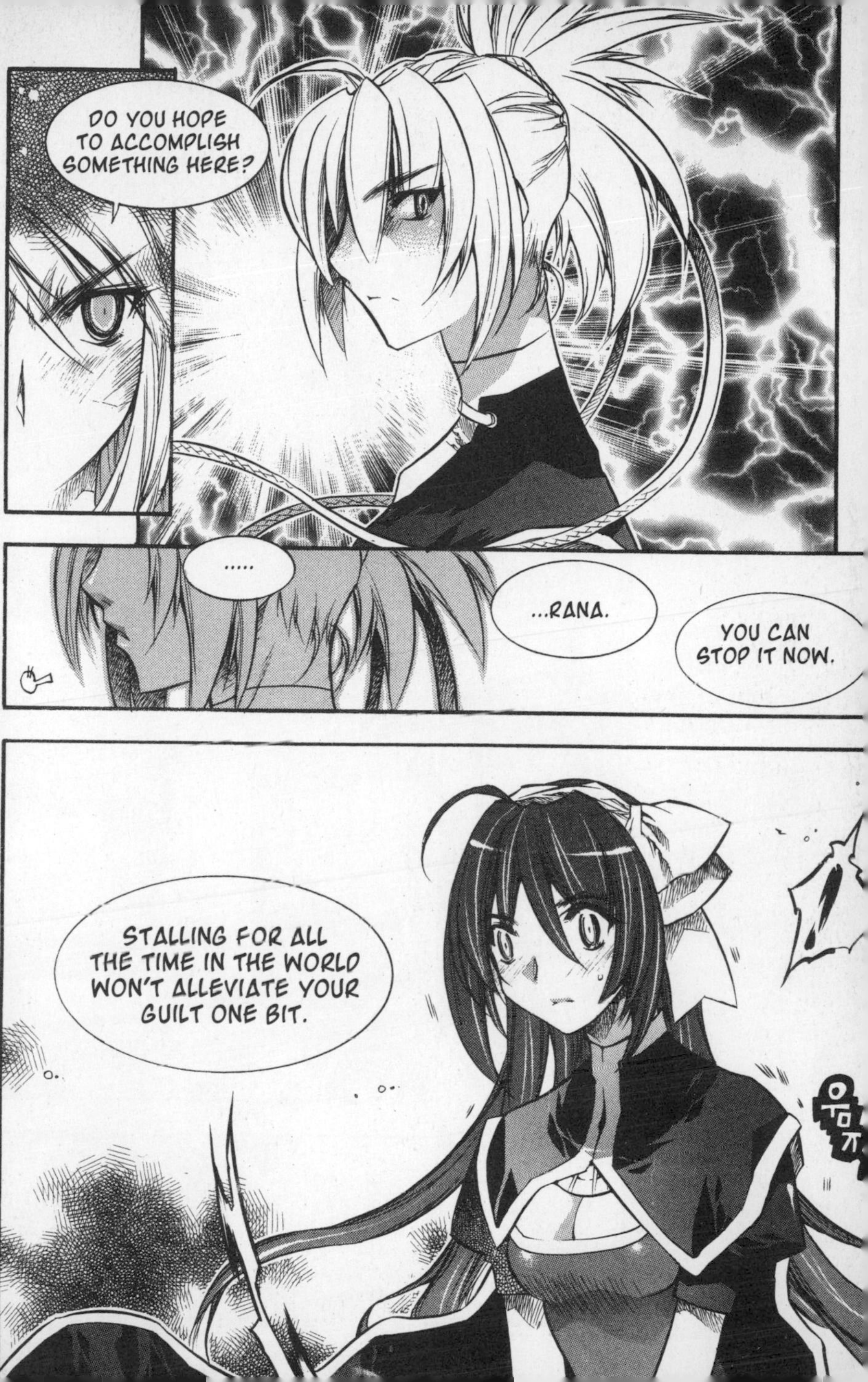
DO YOU HOPE TO ACCOMPLISH SOMETHING HERE?
.....
...RANA.
YOU CAN STOP IT NOW.
STALLING FOR ALL THE TIME IN THE WORLD WON'T ALLEVIATE YOUR GUILT ONE BIT.

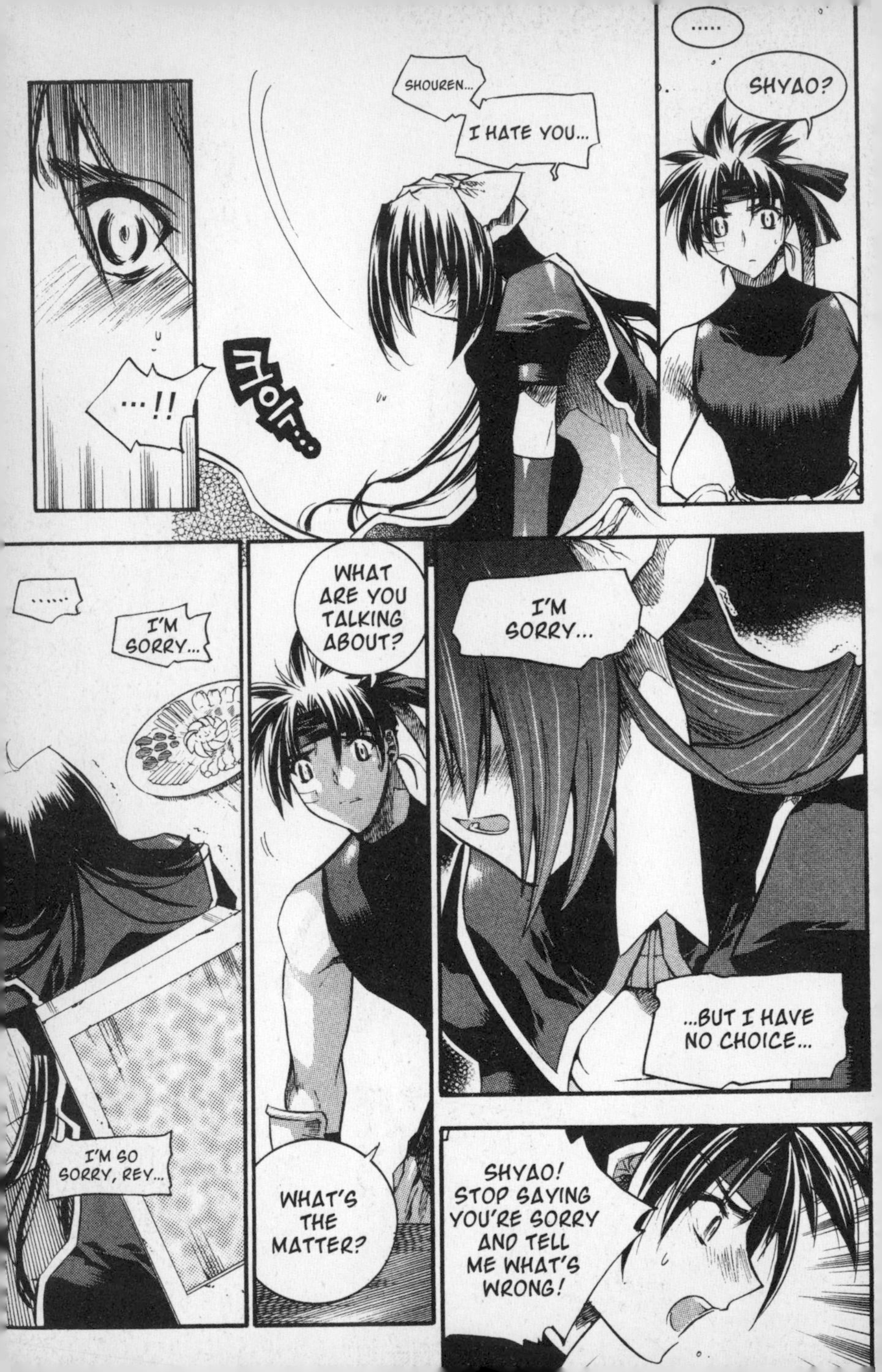

...!!
SHOUREN...
I HATE YOU...
......
SHYAO?
......
I'M SORRY...
I'M SO SORRY, REY...
WHAT ARE YOU TALKING ABOUT?
WHAT'S THE MATTER?
I'M SORRY...
...BUT I HAVE NO CHOICE...
SHYAO! STOP SAYING YOU'RE SORRY AND TELL ME WHAT'S WRONG!

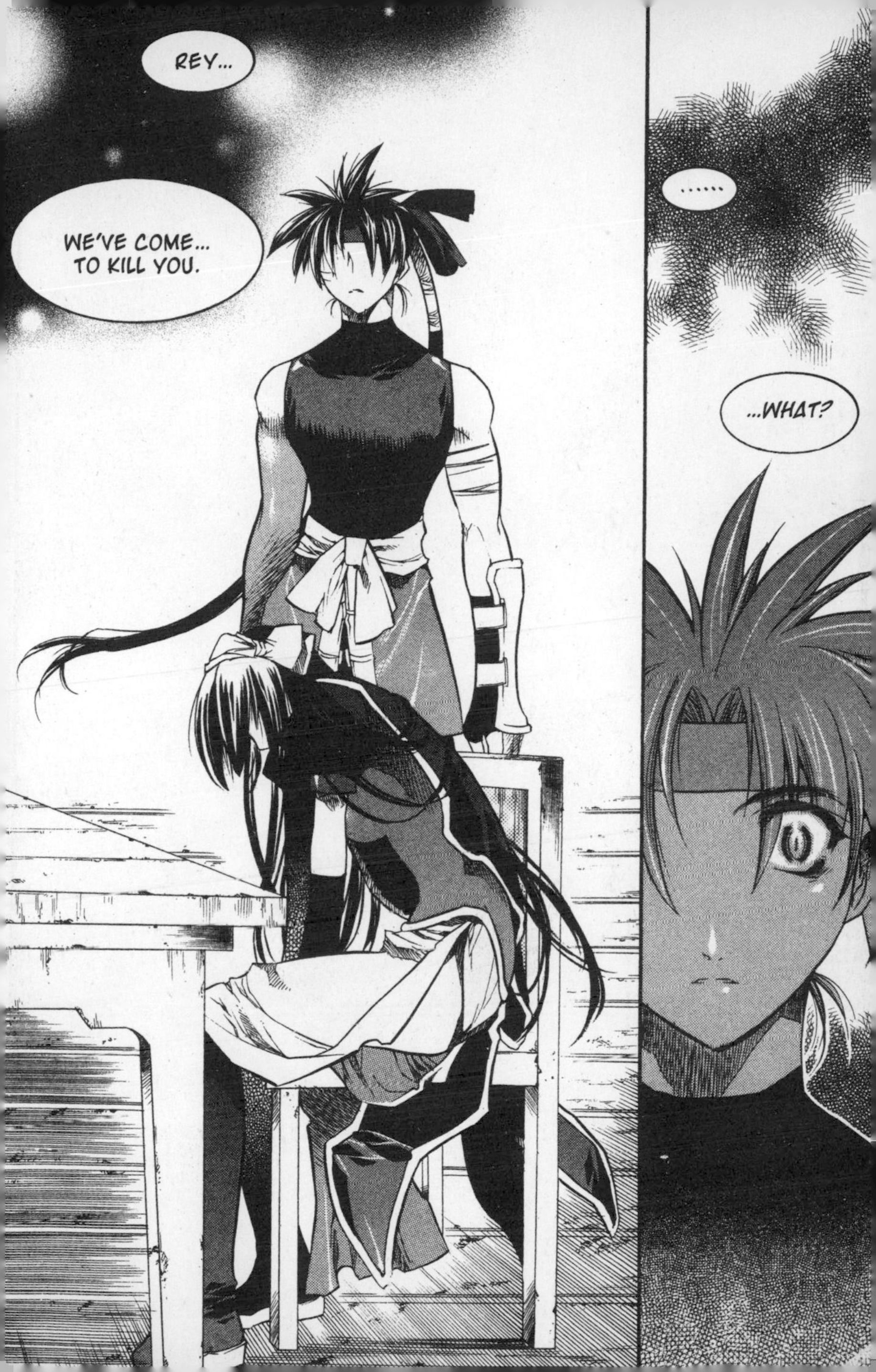
REY...
WE'VE COME... TO KILL YOU.
......
...WHAT?

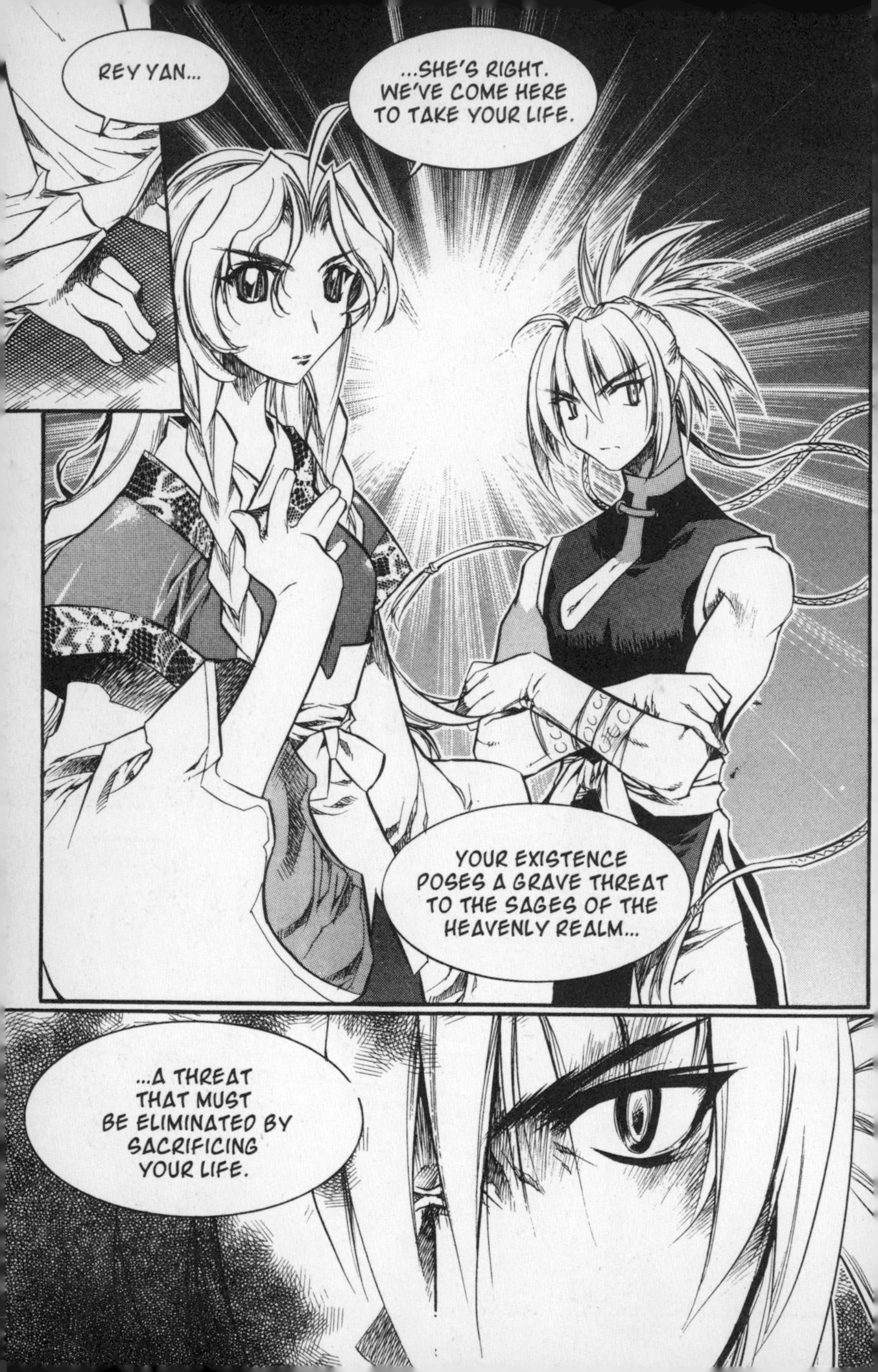
REY YAN...
...SHE'S RIGHT. WE'VE COME HERE TO TAKE YOUR LIFE.
YOUR EXISTENCE POSES A GRAVE THREAT TO THE SAGES OF THE HEAVENLY REALM...
...A THREAT THAT MUST BE ELIMINATED BY SACRIFICING YOUR LIFE.

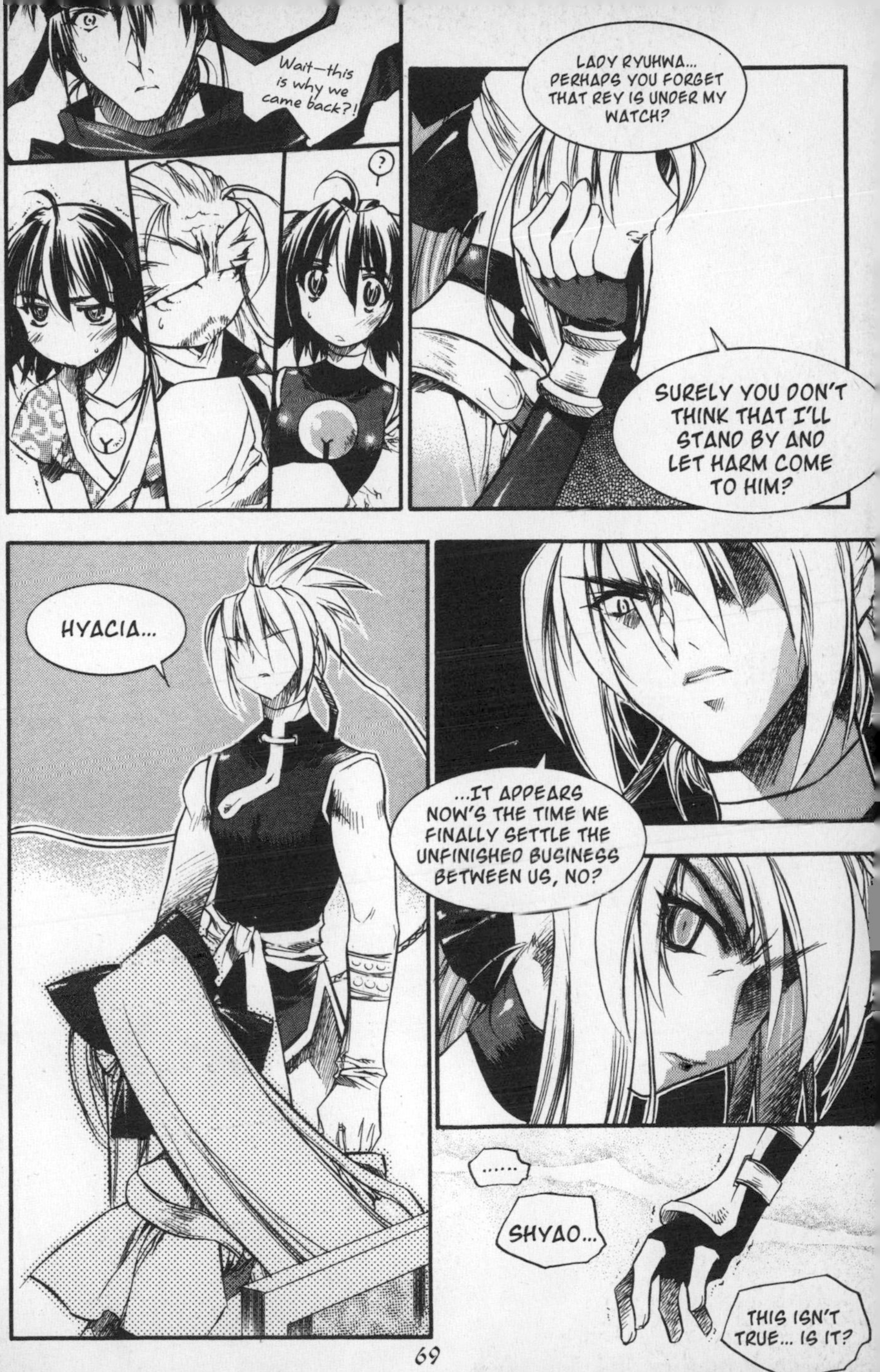
Wait—this is why we came back?!
?
LADY RYUHWA... PERHAPS YOU FORGET THAT REY IS UNDER MY WATCH?
SURELY YOU DON'T THINK THAT I'LL STAND BY AND LET HARM COME TO HIM?
HYACIA...
...IT APPEARS NOW'S THE TIME WE FINALLY SETTLE THE UNFINISHED BUSINESS BETWEEN US, NO?
......
SHYAO...
THIS ISN'T TRUE... IS IT?

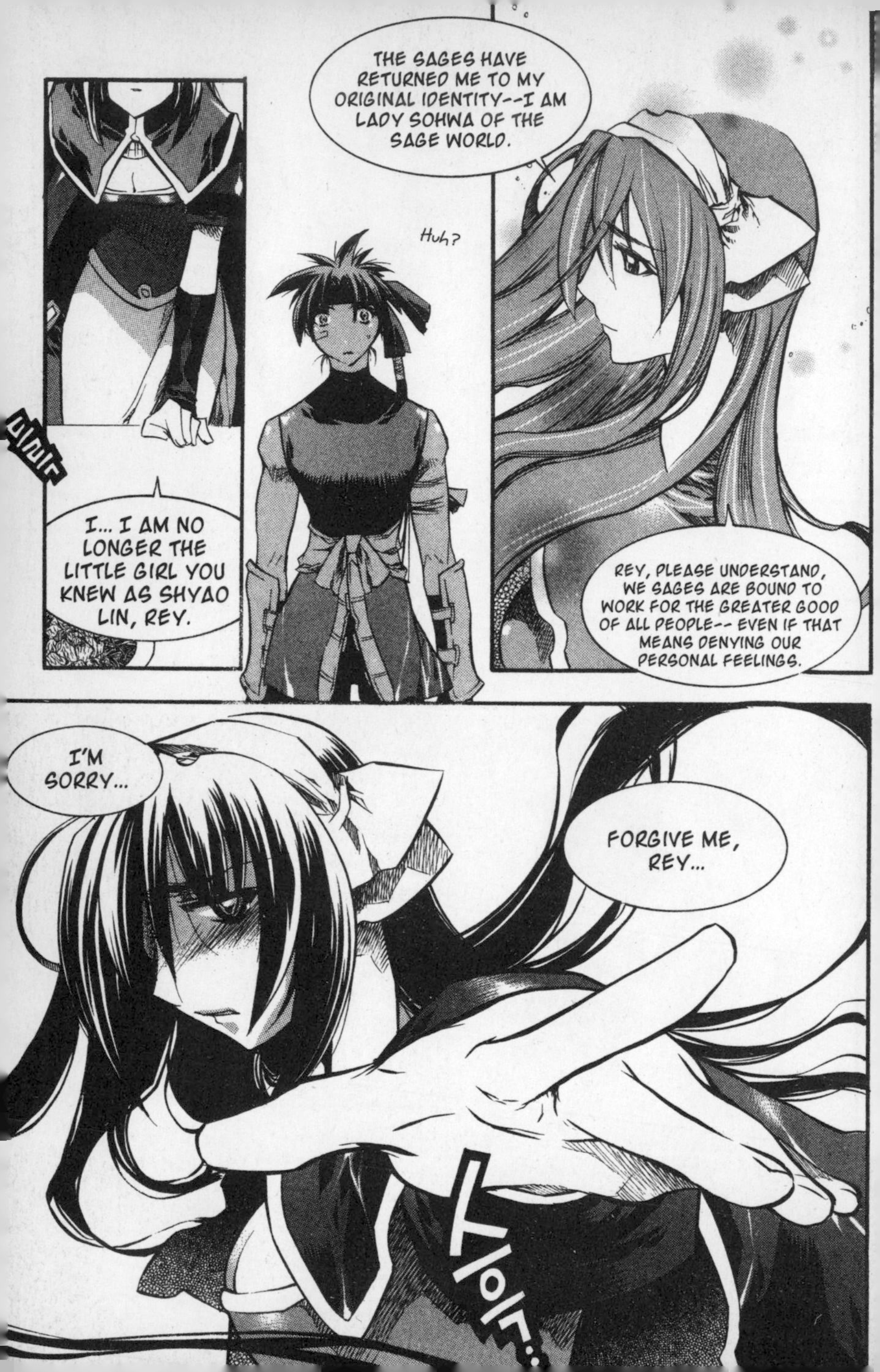

I... I AM NO LONGER THE LITTLE GIRL YOU KNEW AS SHYAO LIN, REY.
THE SAGES HAVE RETURNED ME TO MY ORIGINAL IDENTITY--I AM LADY SOHWA OF THE SAGE WORLD.
Huh?
REY, PLEASE UNDERSTAND, WE SAGES ARE BOUND TO WORK FOR THE GREATER GOOD OF ALL PEOPLE-- EVEN IF THAT MEANS DENYING OUR PERSONAL FEELINGS.
I'M SORRY...
FORGIVE ME, REY...

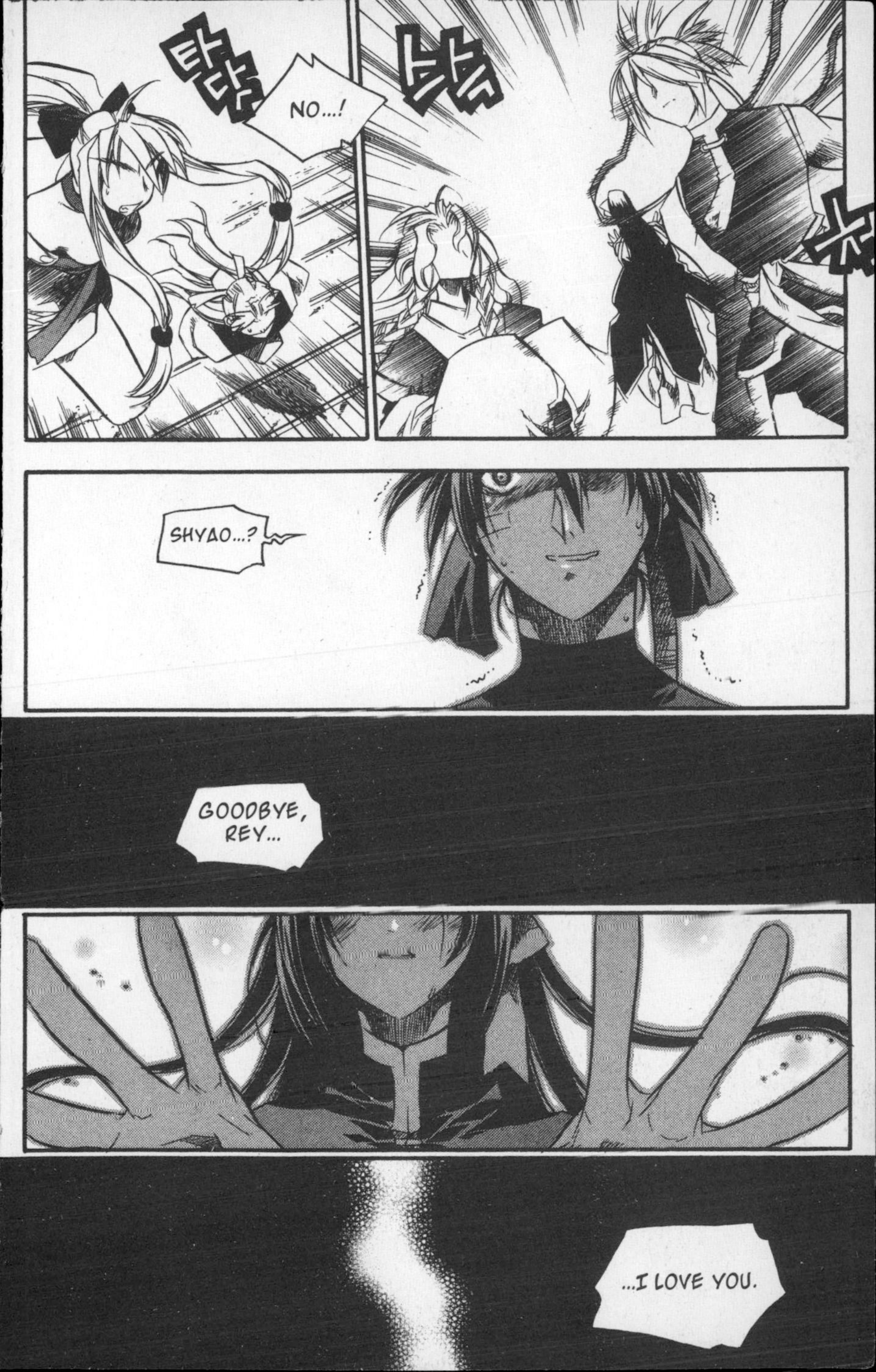
NO...!
SHYAO...?
GOODBYE, REY...
...I LOVE YOU.

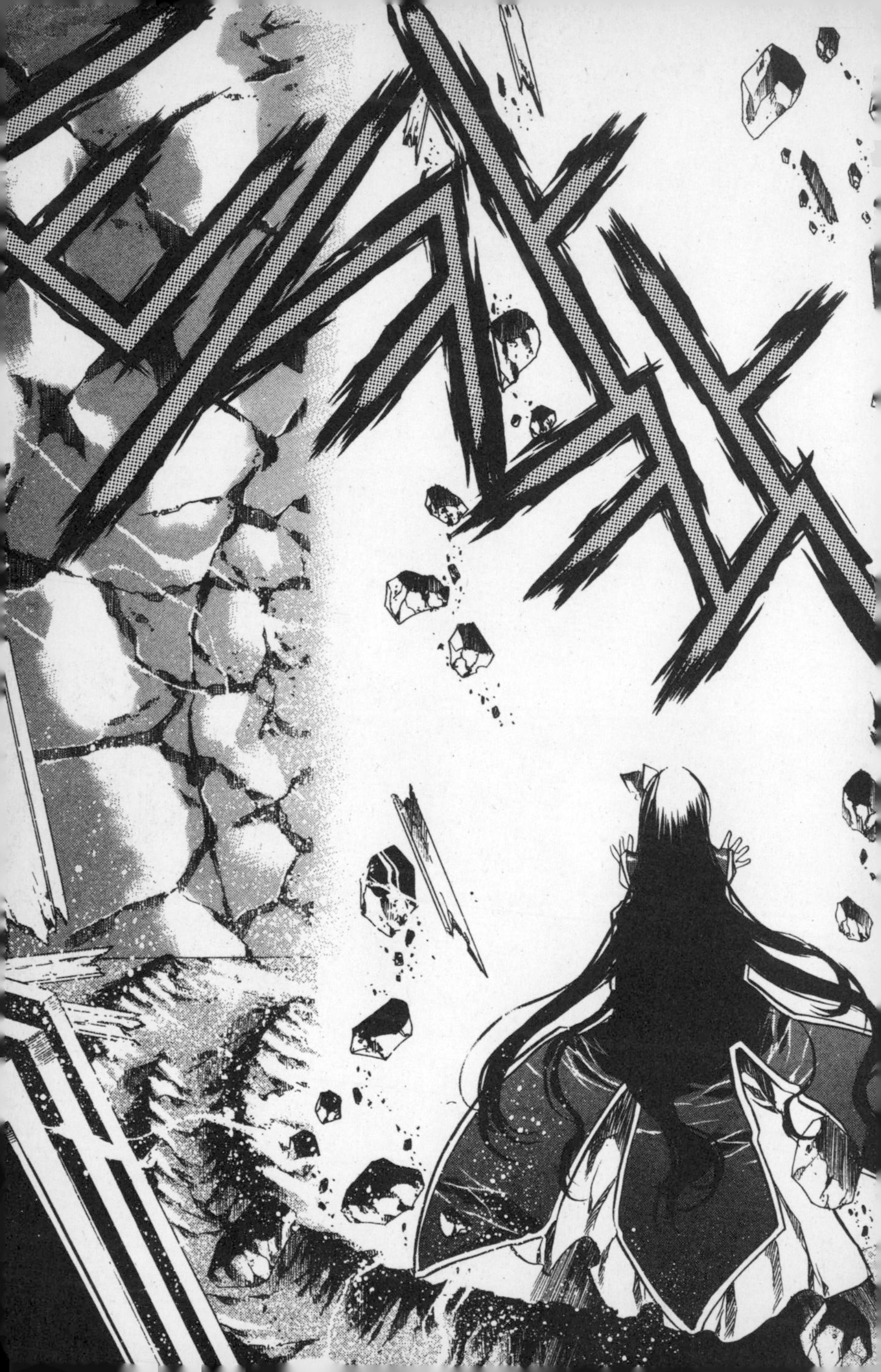

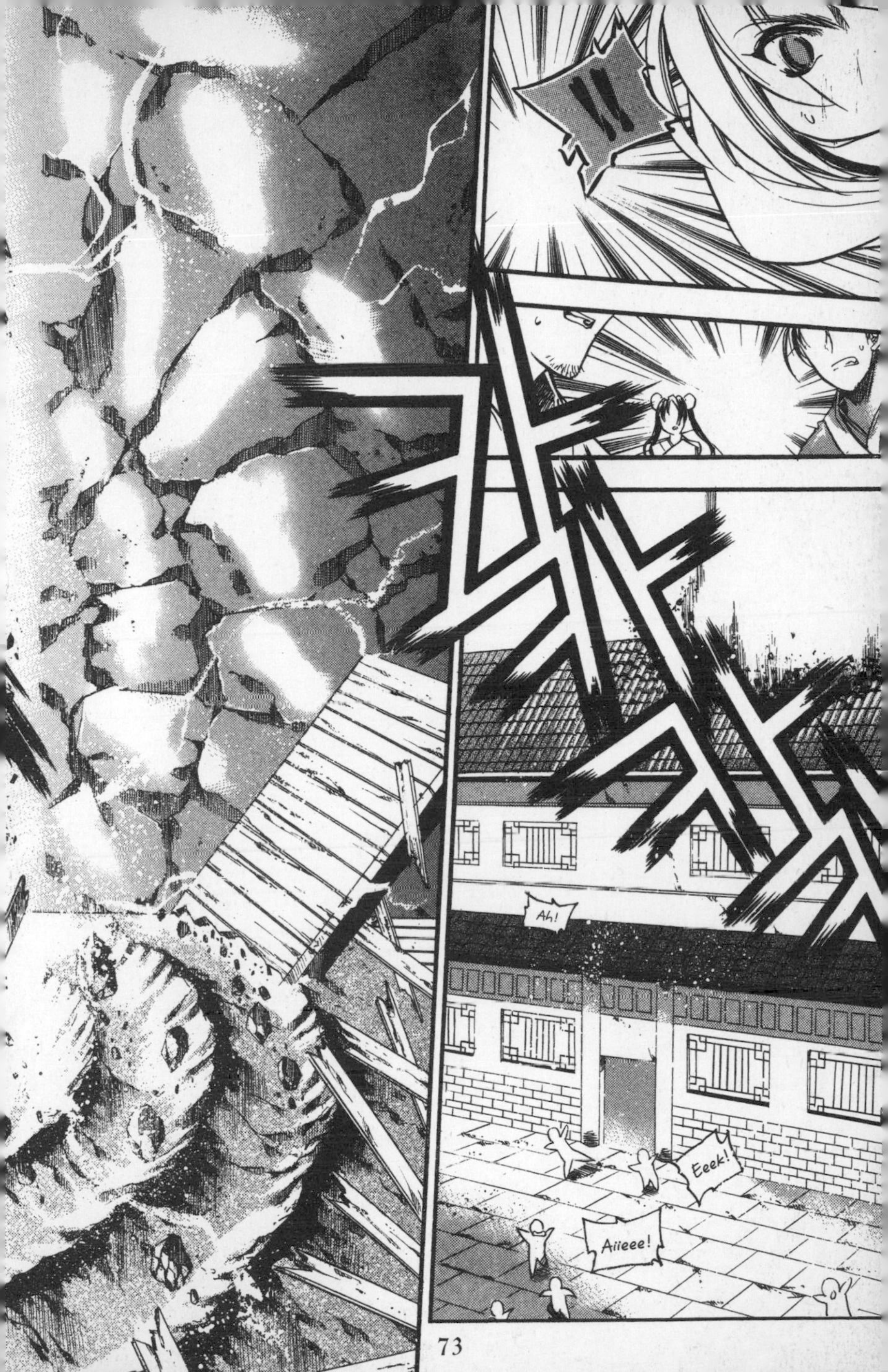
Ah!
Eeek!
Aiieee!

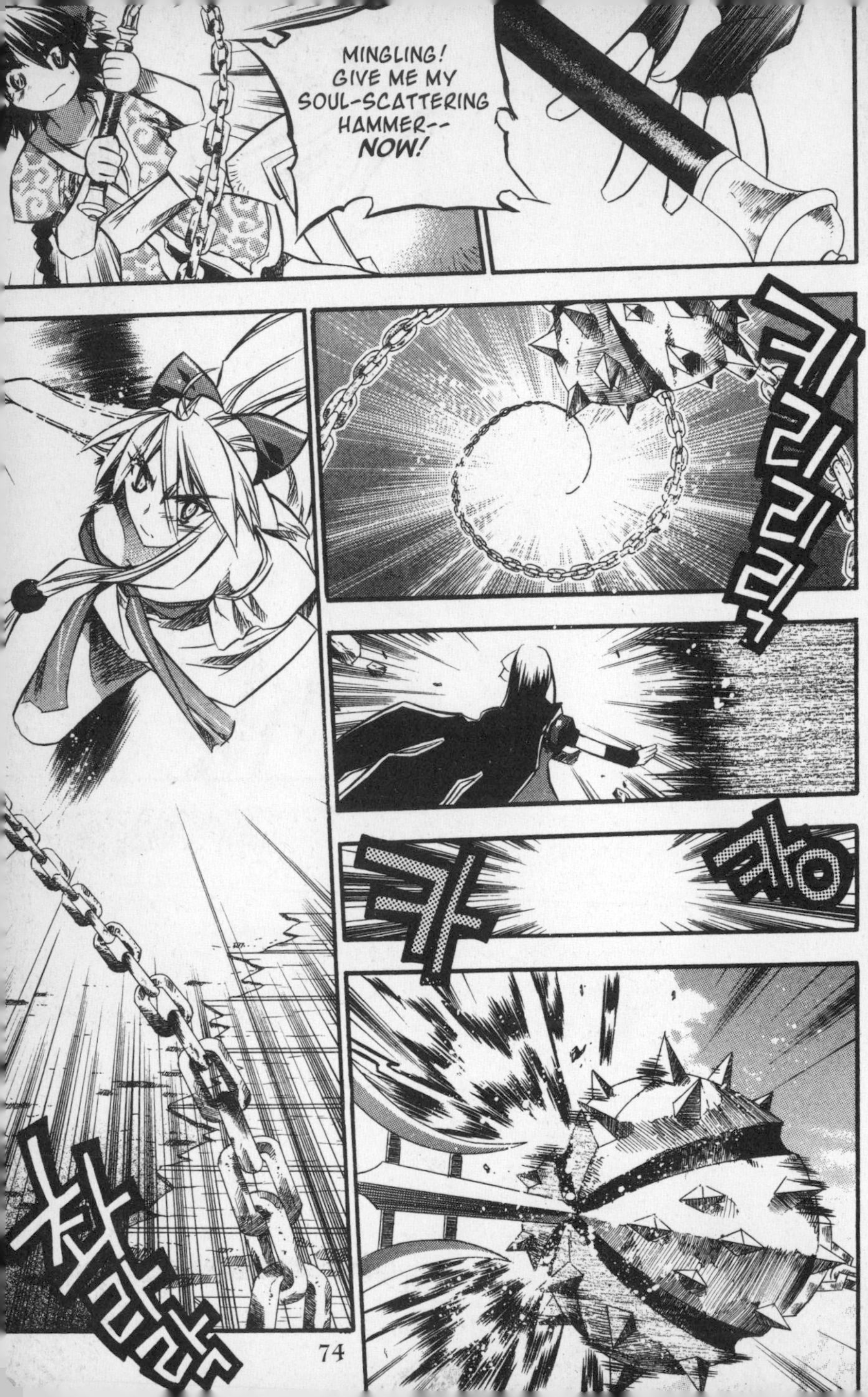
MINGLING! GIVE ME MY SOUL-SCATTERING HAMMER-- NOW!

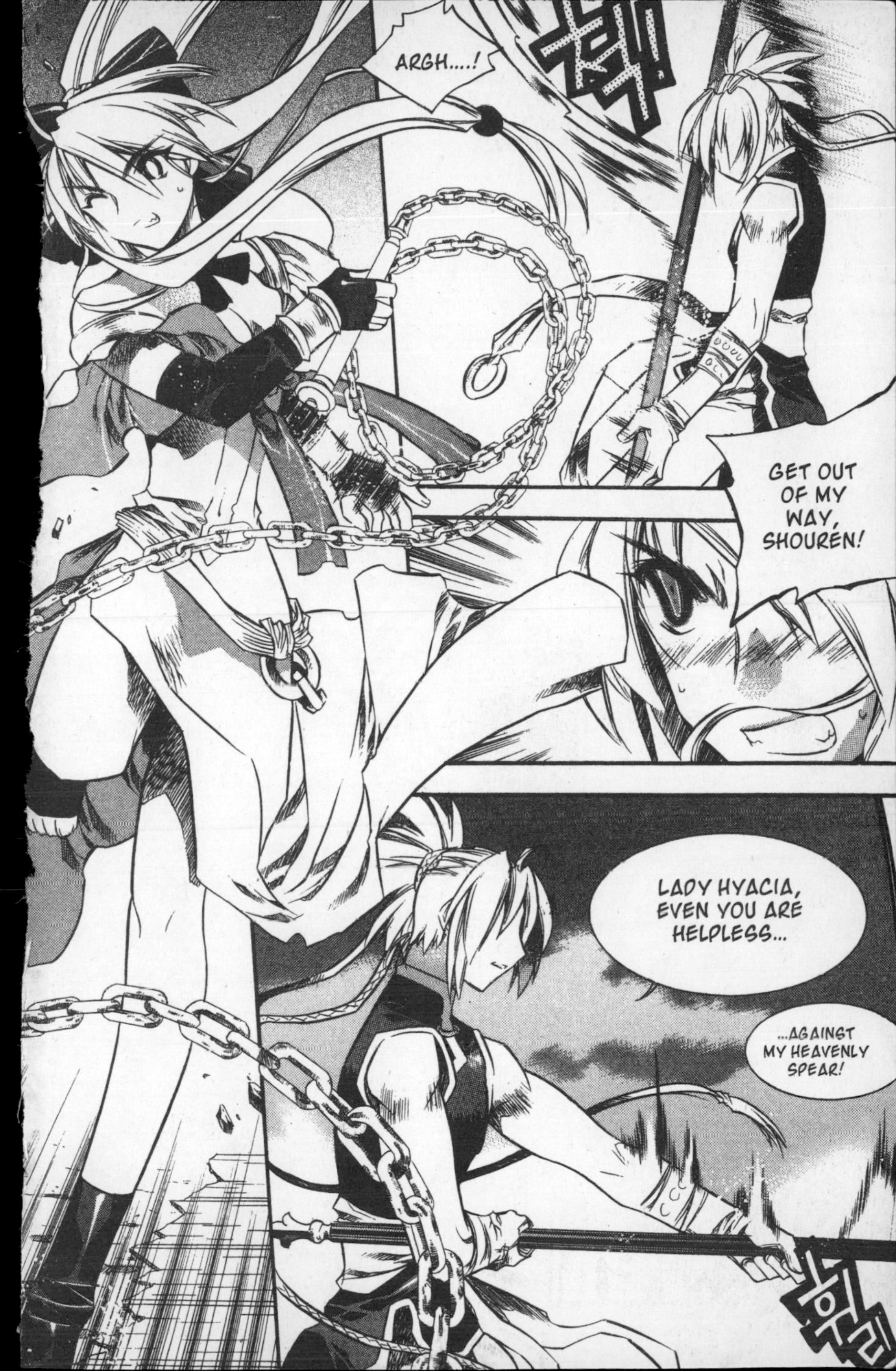
ARGH....!
GET OUT OF MY WAY, SHOUREN!
LADY HYACIA, EVEN YOU ARE HELPLESS...
...AGAINST MY HEAVENLY SPEAR!

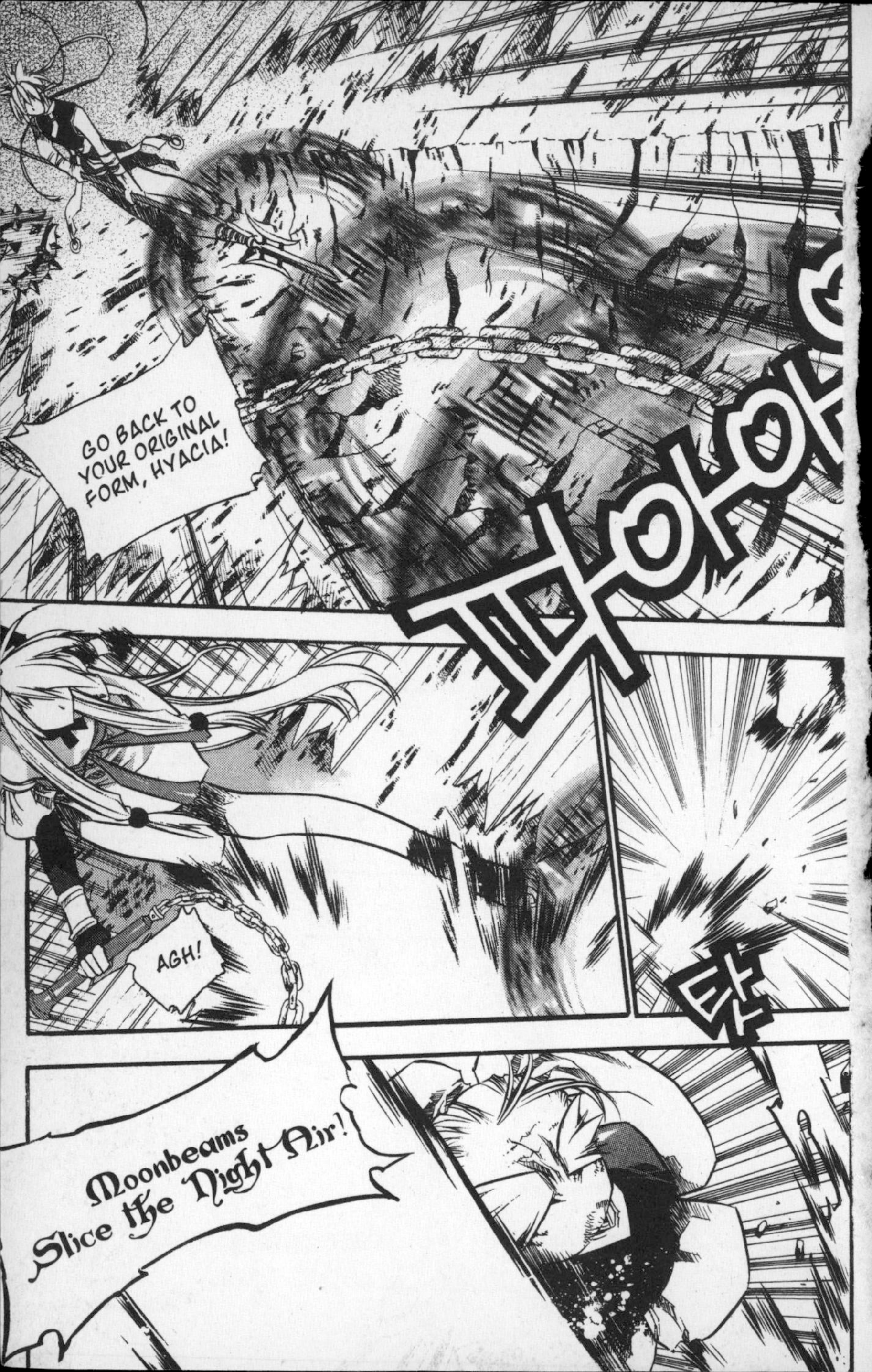
GO BACK TO YOUR ORIGINAL FORM, HYACIA!
AGH!
Moonbeams Slice the Night Air!

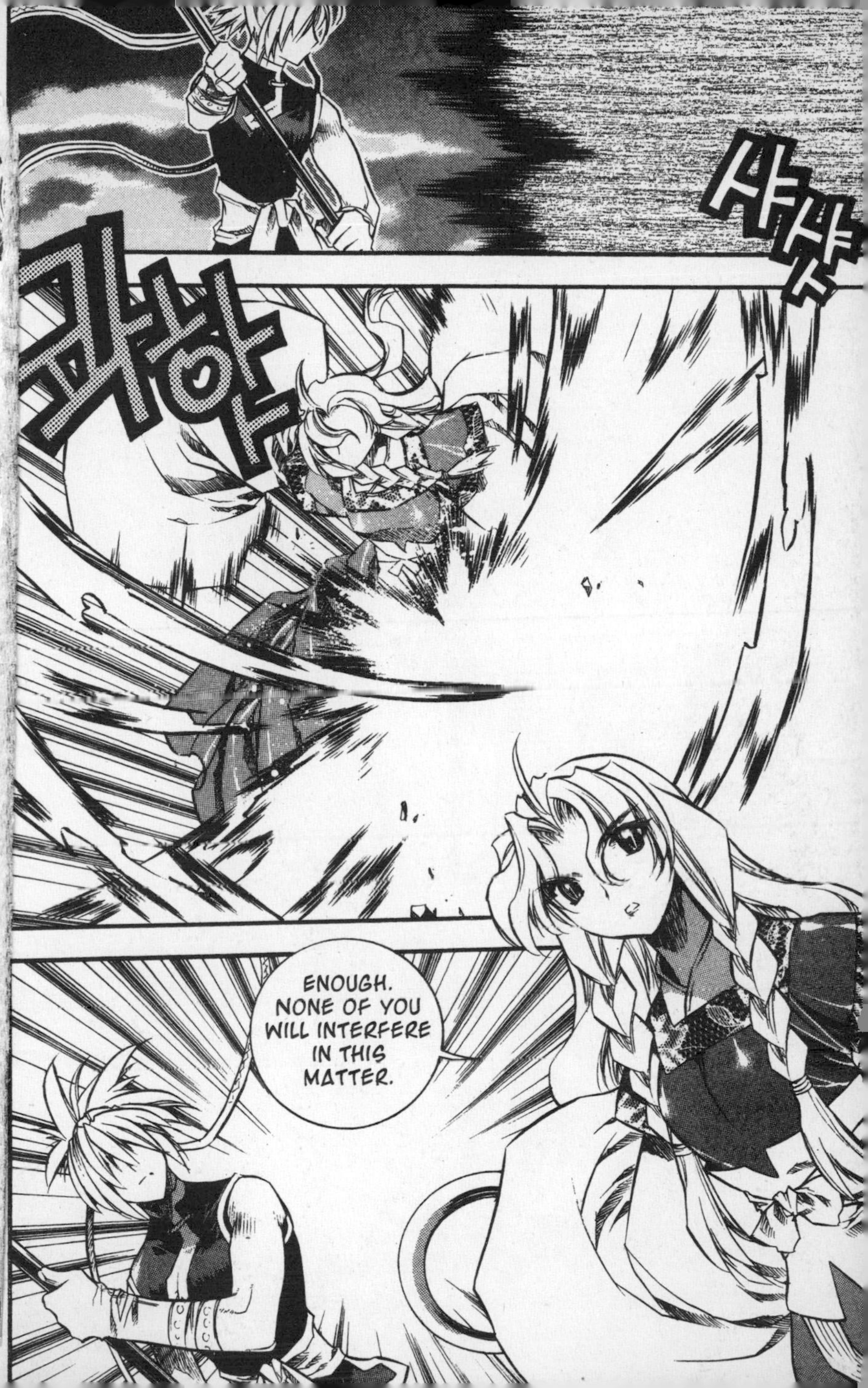
ENOUGH. NONE OF YOU WILL INTERFERE IN THIS MATTER.

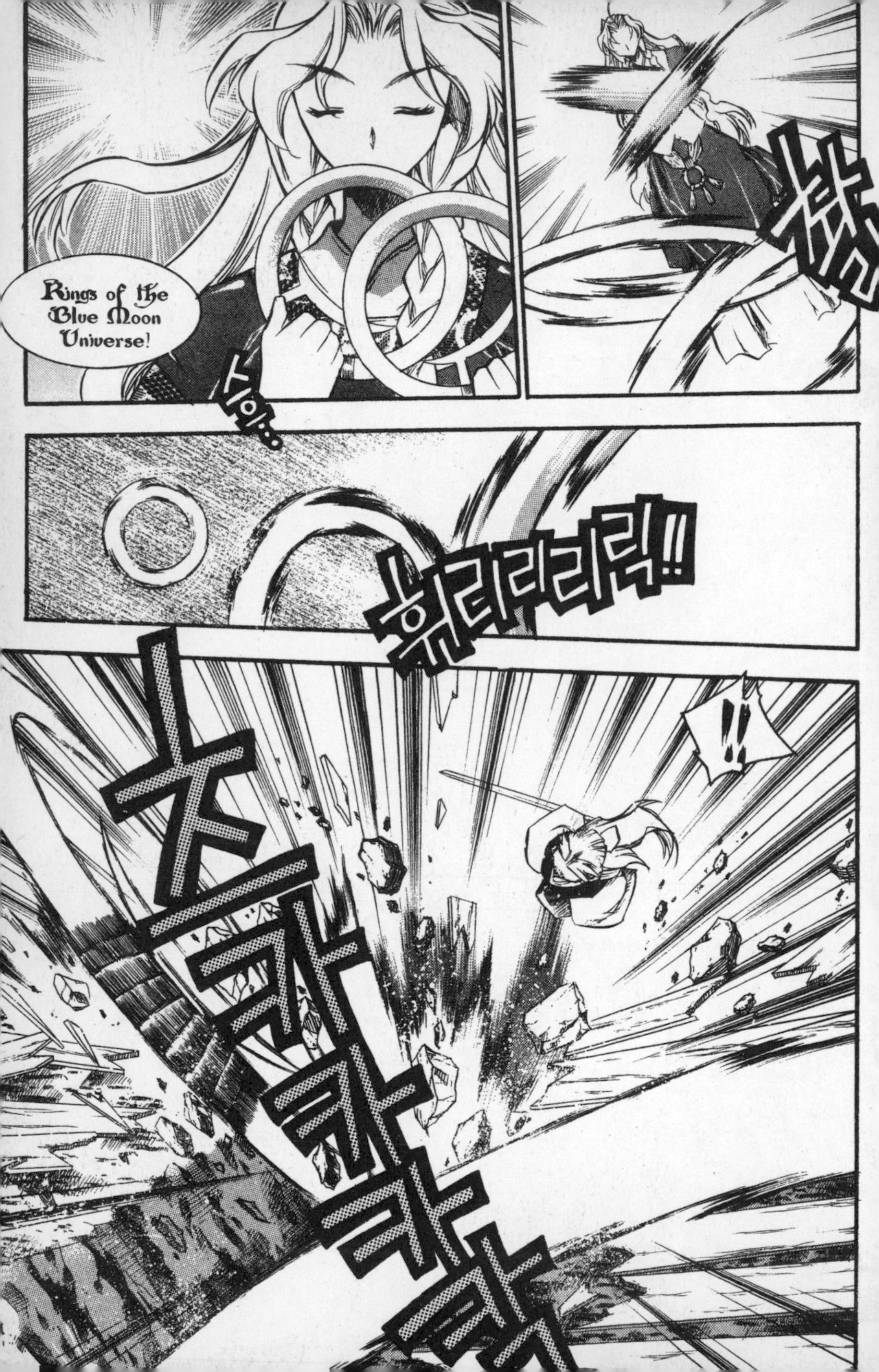
Rings of the Blue Moon Universe!
휘리리리릭!!
!!

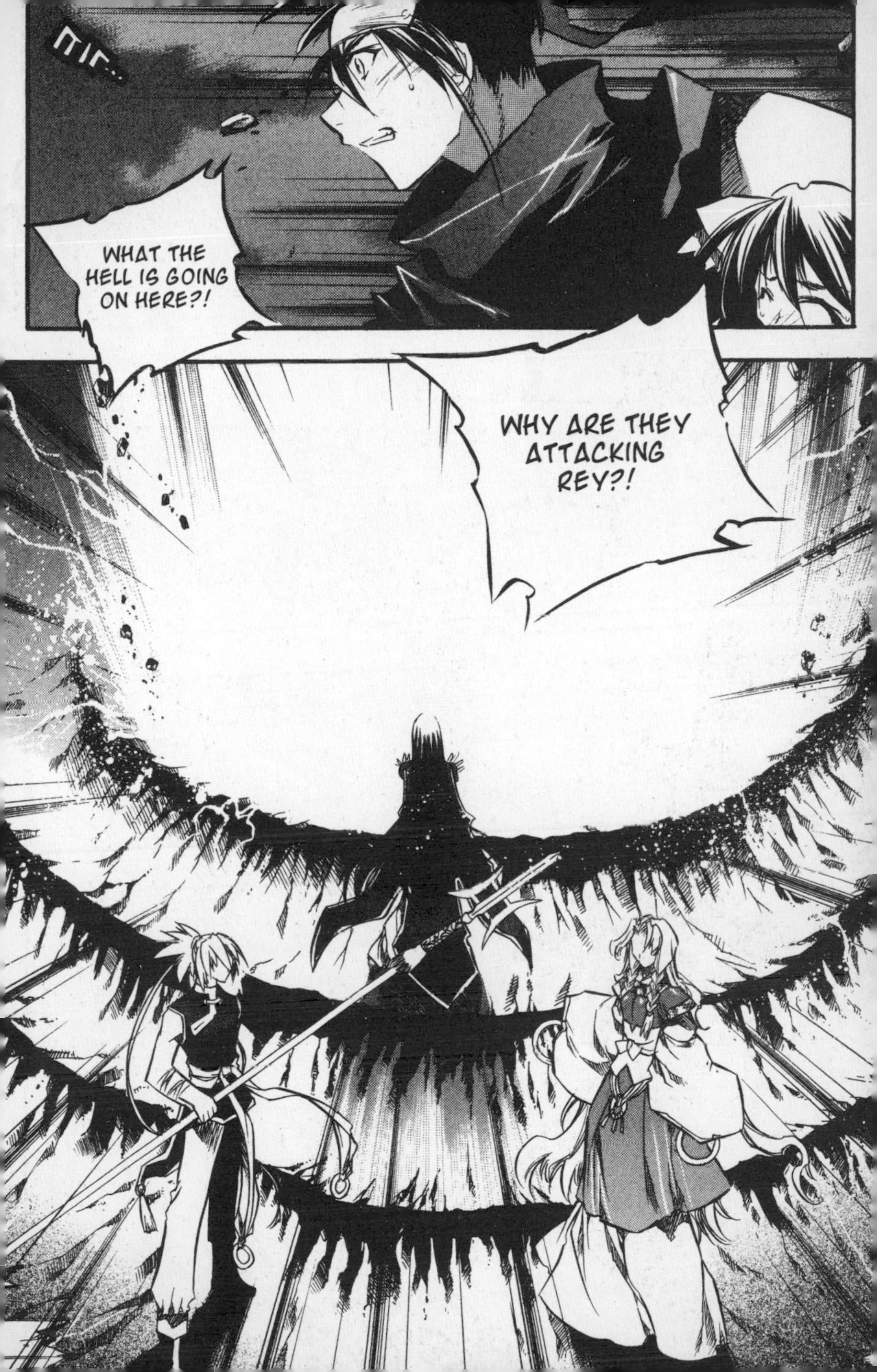
WHAT THE HELL IS GOING ON HERE?!
WHY ARE THEY ATTACKING REY?!

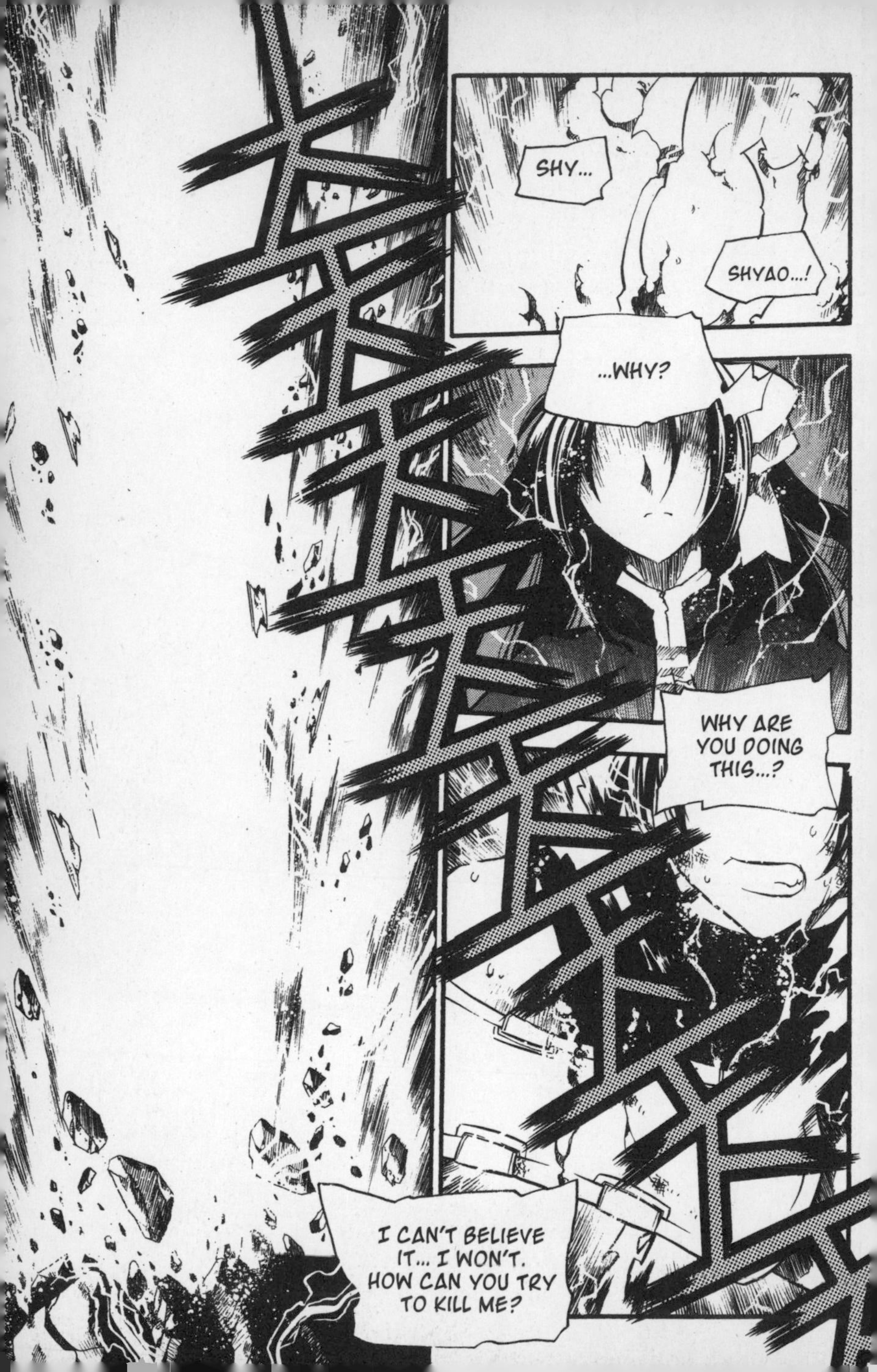
SHY...
SHYAO...!
...WHY?
WHY ARE YOU DOING THIS...?
I CAN'T BELIEVE IT... I WON'T. HOW CAN YOU TRY TO KILL ME?

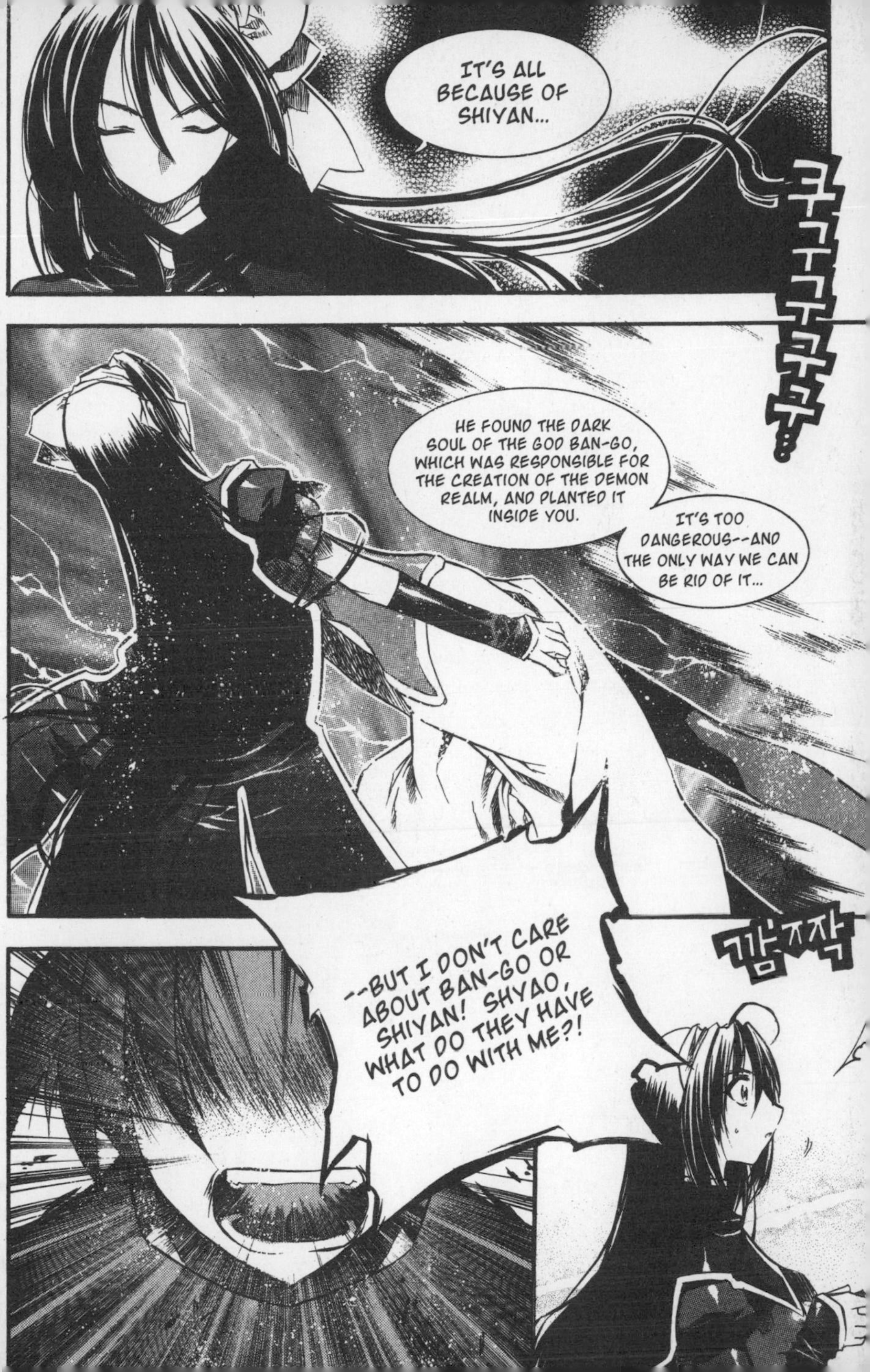
IT'S ALL BECAUSE OF SHIYAN...
쿠구구구구
HE FOUND THE DARK SOUL OF THE GOD BAN-GO, WHICH WAS RESPONSIBLE FOR THE CREATION OF THE DEMON REALM, AND PLANTED IT INSIDE YOU.
IT'S TOO DANGEROUS--AND THE ONLY WAY WE CAN BE RID OF IT...
깜짝
--BUT I DON'T CARE ABOUT BAN-GO OR SHIYAN! SHYAO, WHAT DO THEY HAVE TO DO WITH ME?!

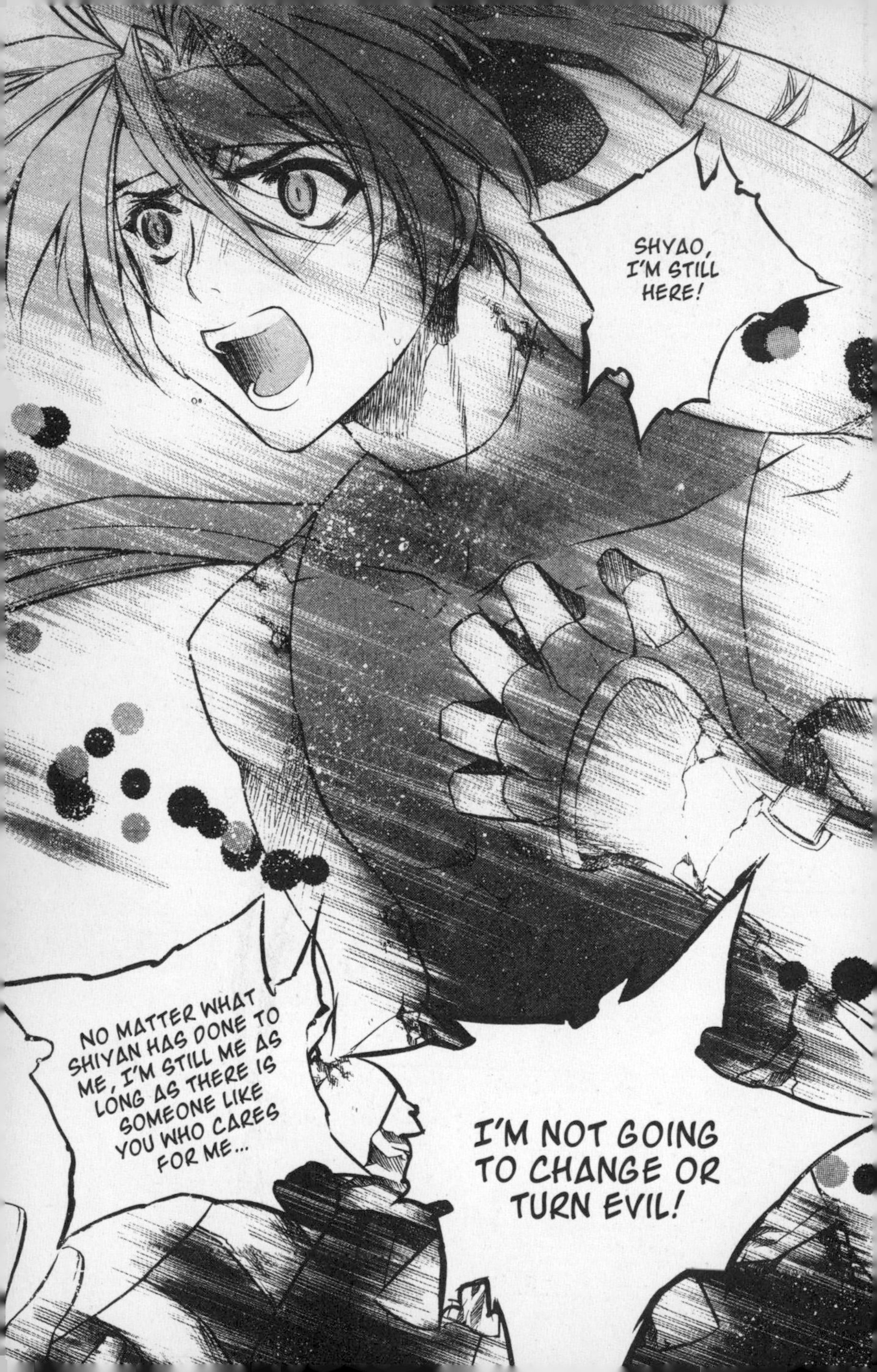
SHYAO, I'M STILL HERE!
NO MATTER WHAT SHIYAN HAS DONE TO ME, I'M STILL ME AS LONG AS THERE IS SOMEONE LIKE YOU WHO CARES FOR ME...
I'M NOT GOING TO CHANGE OR TURN EVIL!

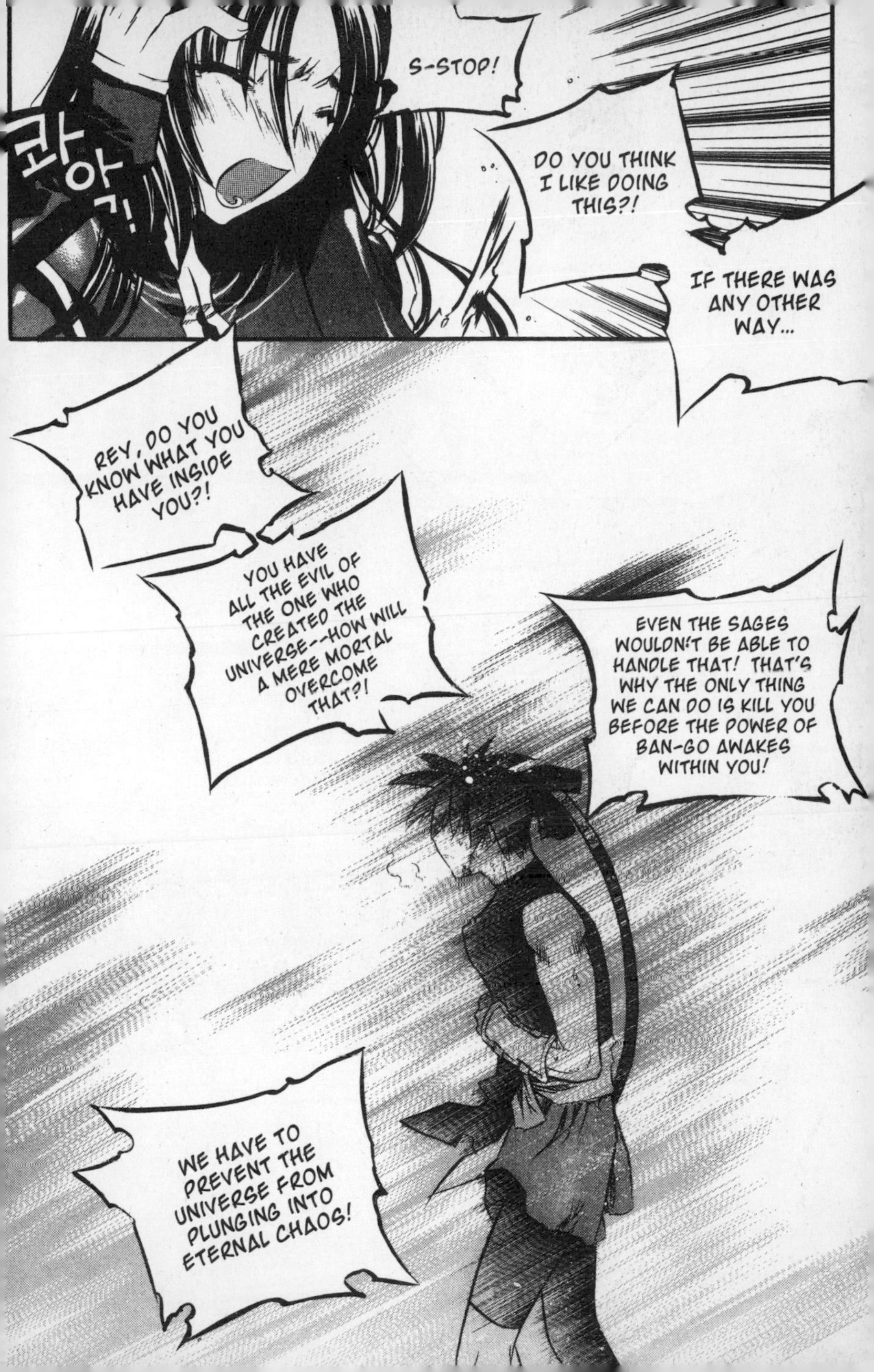
콰앙!
S-STOP!
DO YOU THINK I LIKE DOING THIS?!
IF THERE WAS ANY OTHER WAY...
REY, DO YOU KNOW WHAT YOU HAVE INSIDE YOU?!
YOU HAVE ALL THE EVIL OF THE ONE WHO CREATED THE UNIVERSE--HOW WILL A MERE MORTAL OVERCOME THAT?!
EVEN THE SAGES WOULDN'T BE ABLE TO HANDLE THAT! THAT'S WHY THE ONLY THING WE CAN DO IS KILL YOU BEFORE THE POWER OF BAN-GO AWAKES WITHIN YOU!
WE HAVE TO PREVENT THE UNIVERSE FROM PLUNGING INTO ETERNAL CHAOS!

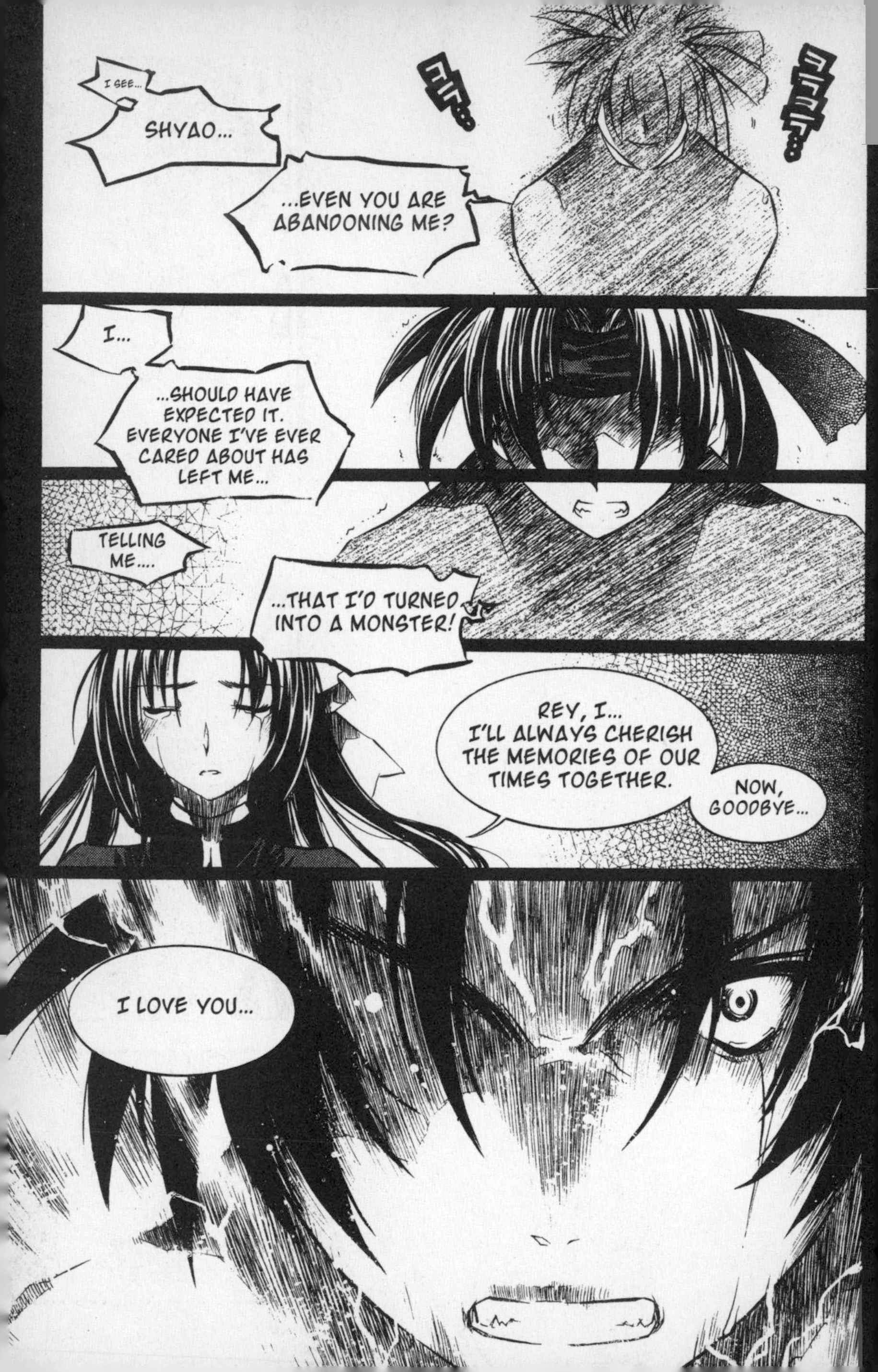
I SEE...
SHYAO...
...EVEN YOU ARE ABANDONING ME?
I...
...SHOULD HAVE EXPECTED IT. EVERYONE I'VE EVER CARED ABOUT HAS LEFT ME...
TELLING ME....
...THAT I'D TURNED INTO A MONSTER!
REY, I... I'LL ALWAYS CHERISH THE MEMORIES OF OUR TIMES TOGETHER.
NOW, GOODBYE...
I LOVE YOU...

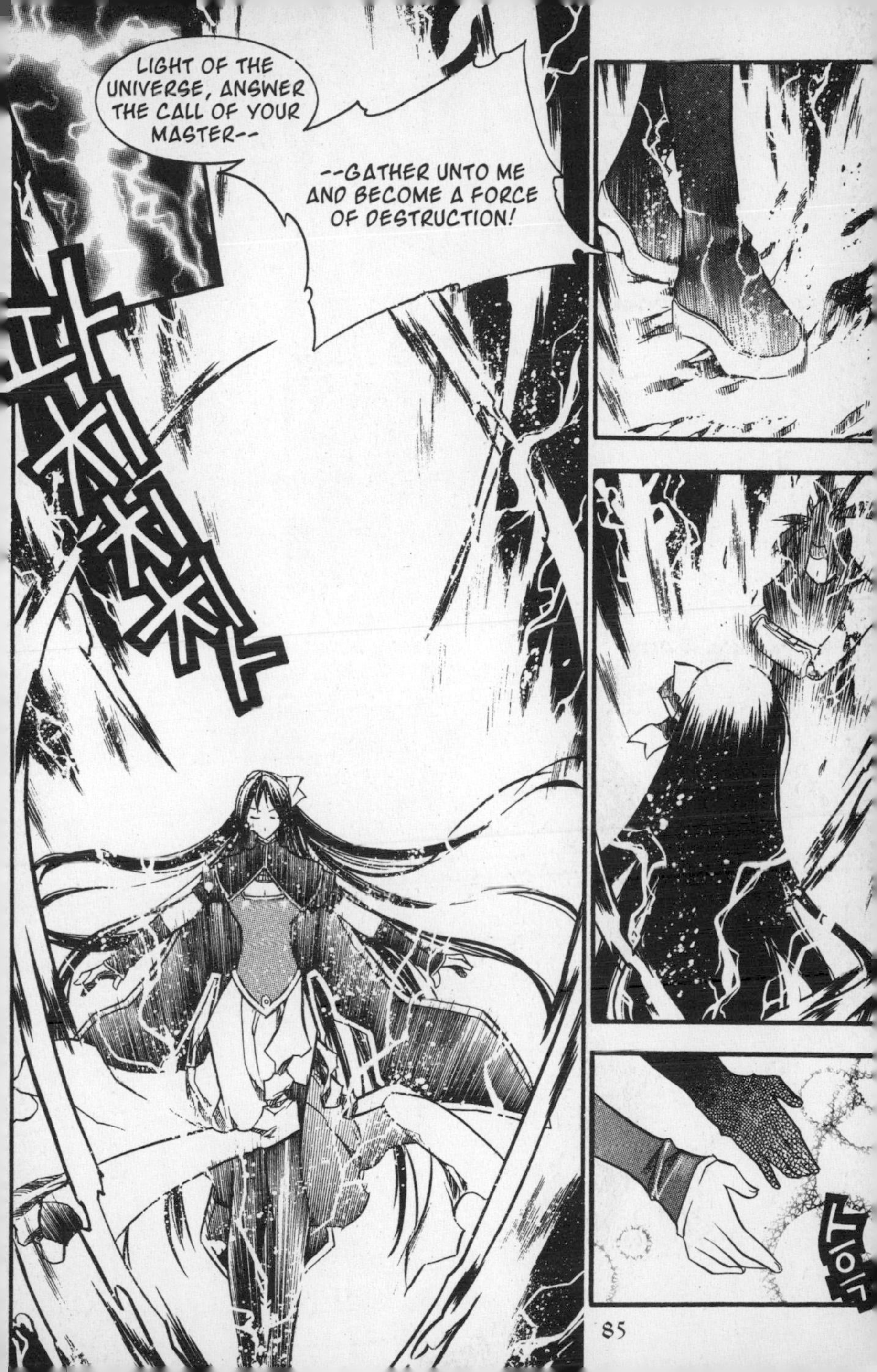
LIGHT OF THE UNIVERSE, ANSWER THE CALL OF YOUR MASTER--
--GATHER UNTO ME AND BECOME A FORCE OF DESTRUCTION!

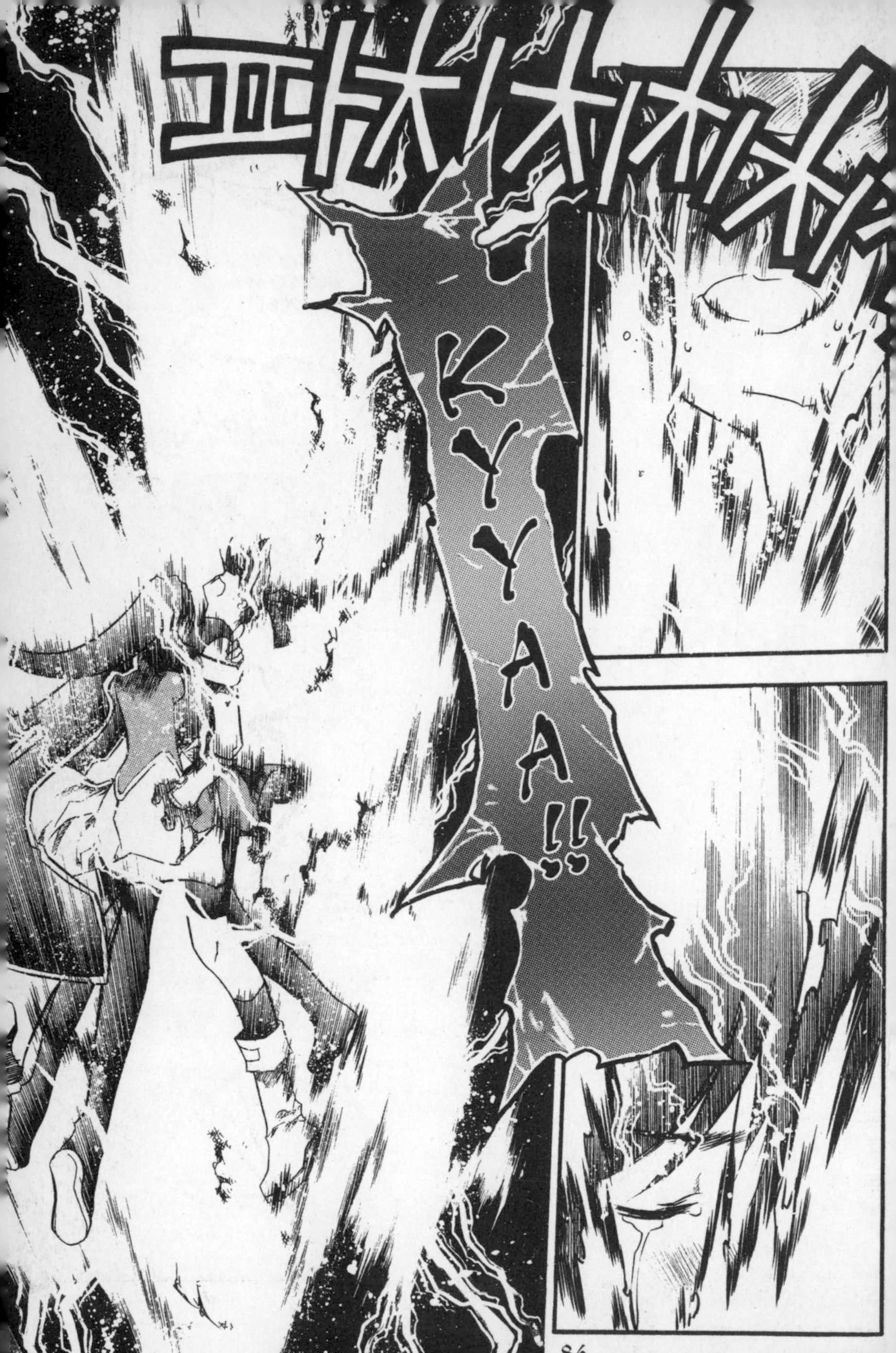
KYYAA!!

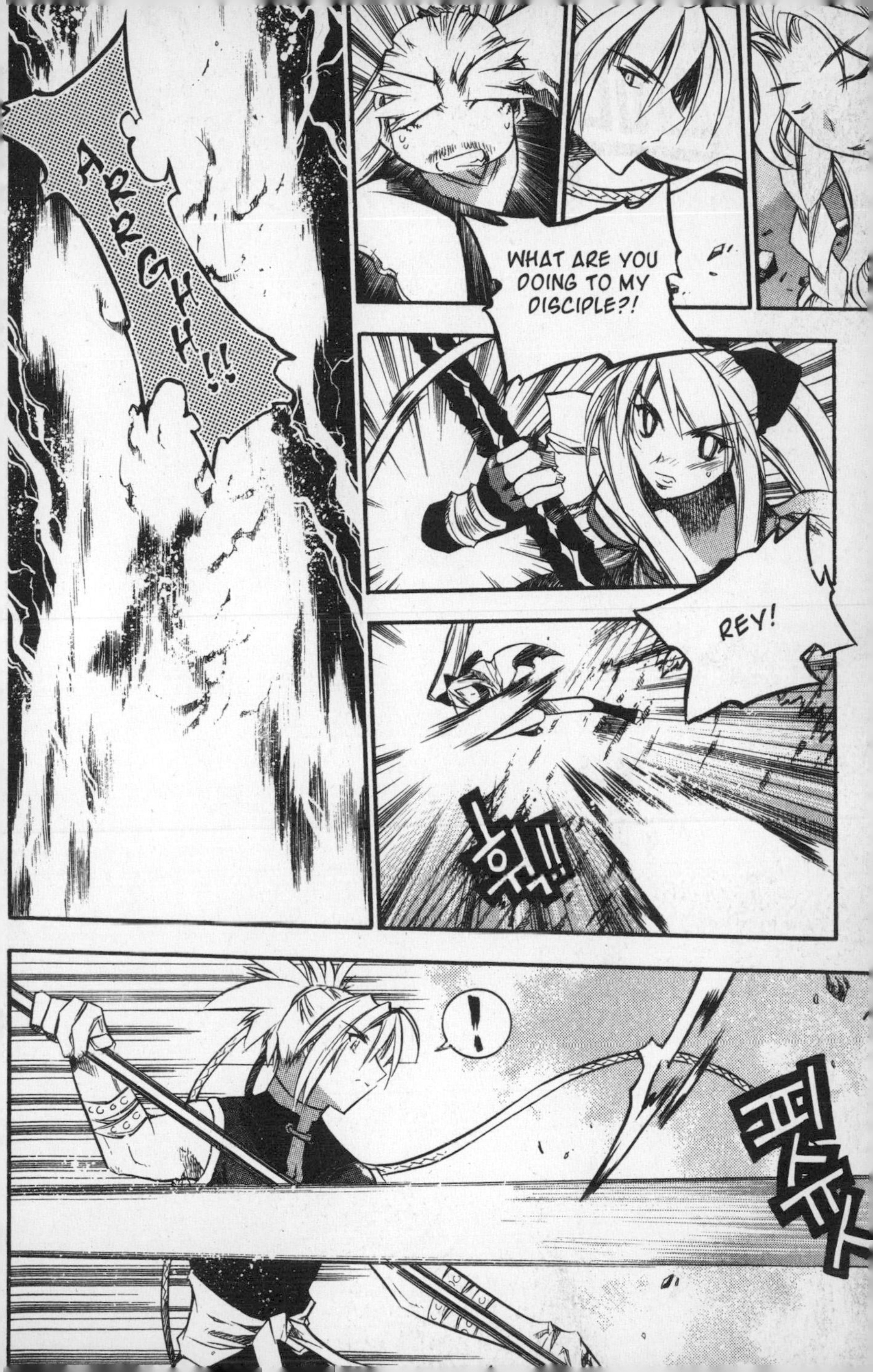
ARRGH!!
WHAT ARE YOU DOING TO MY DISCIPLE?!
REY!
!

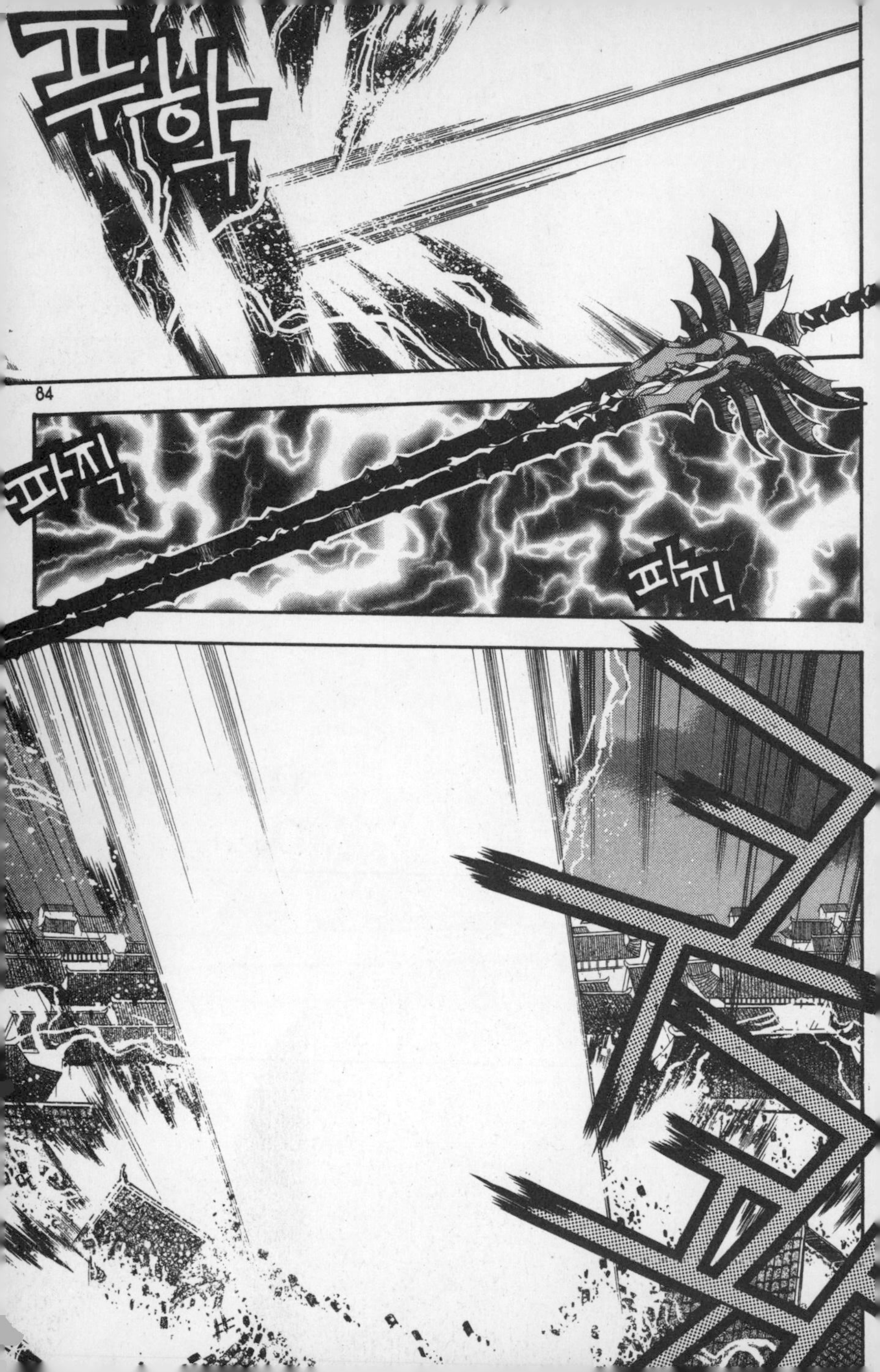
푸확
파직
파직

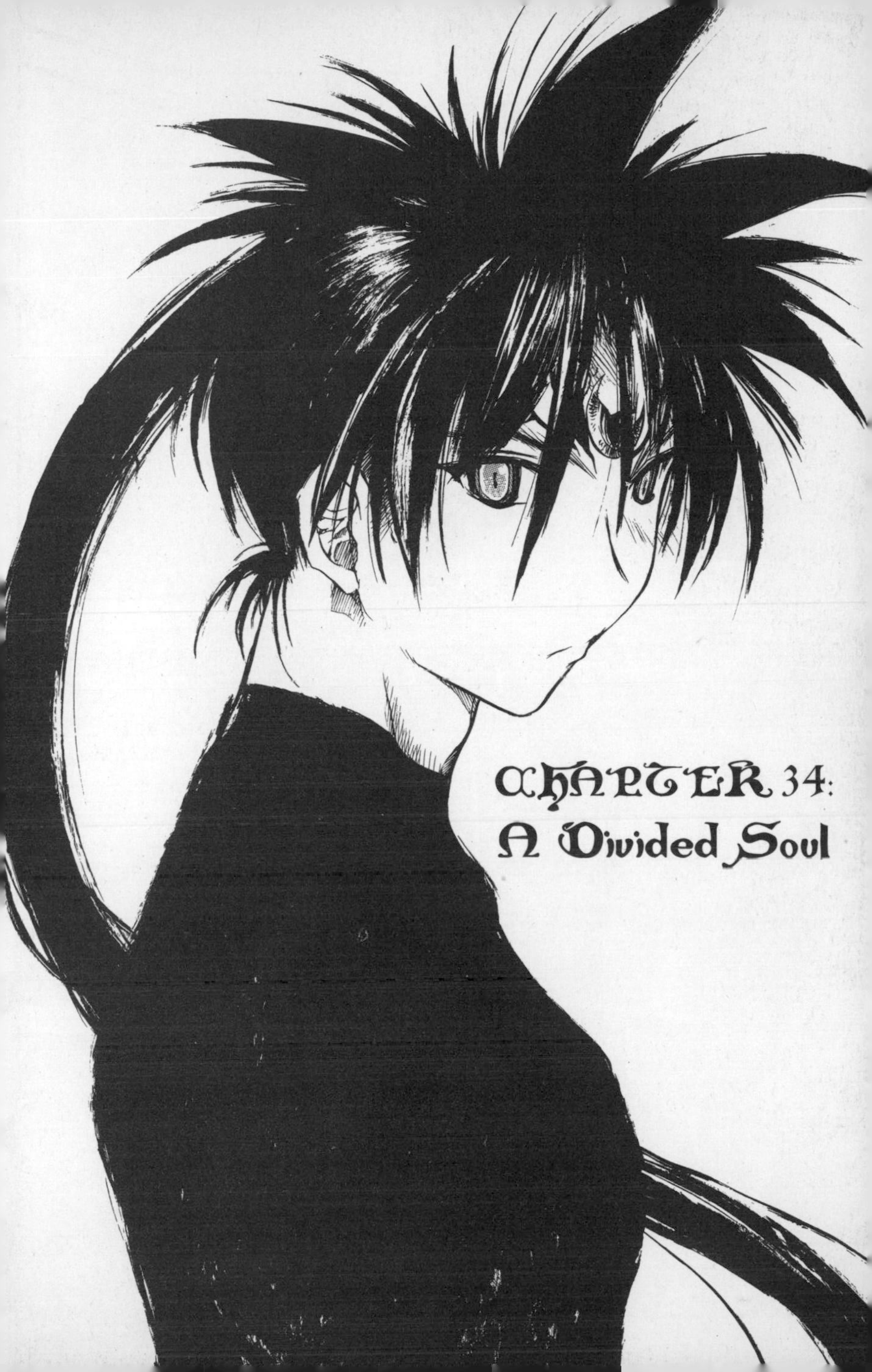

CHAPTER 34: A Divided Soul

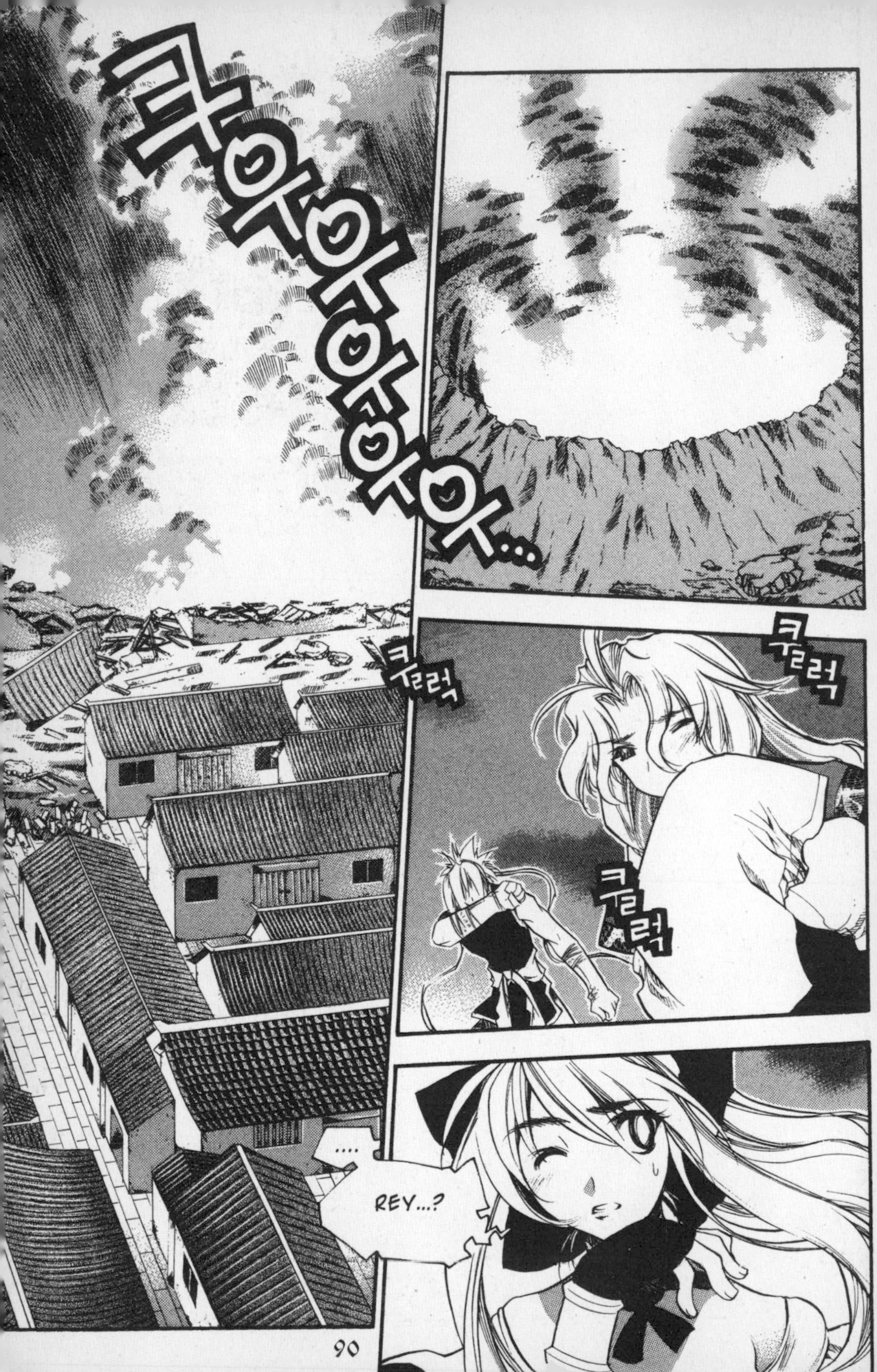
쿠우우우우우...
쿠르럭
쿠르럭
쿠르럭
....
REY...?

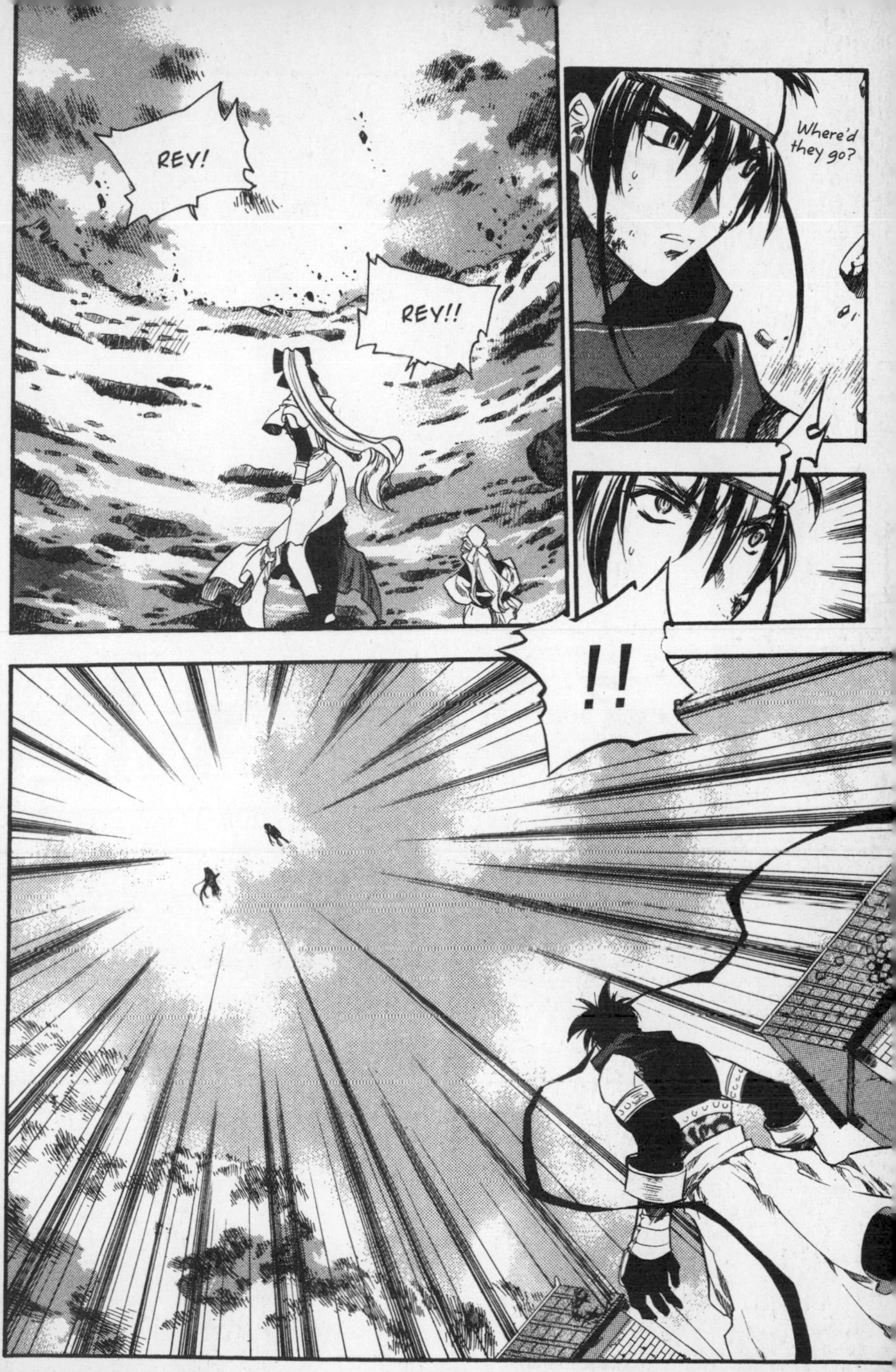
REY!
REY!!
Where'd they go?
!!

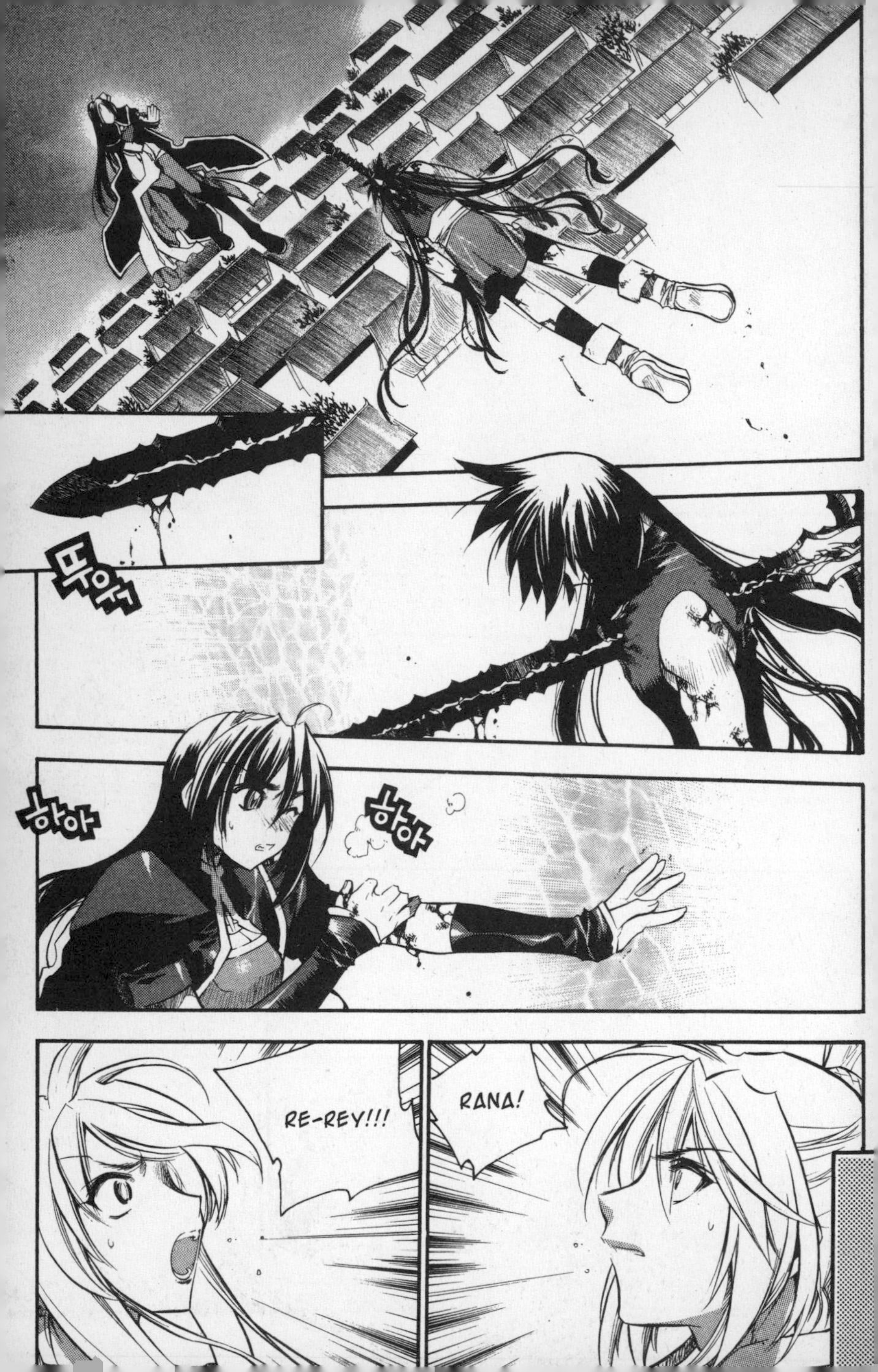

부악
하아
하아
RE-REY!!!
RANA!

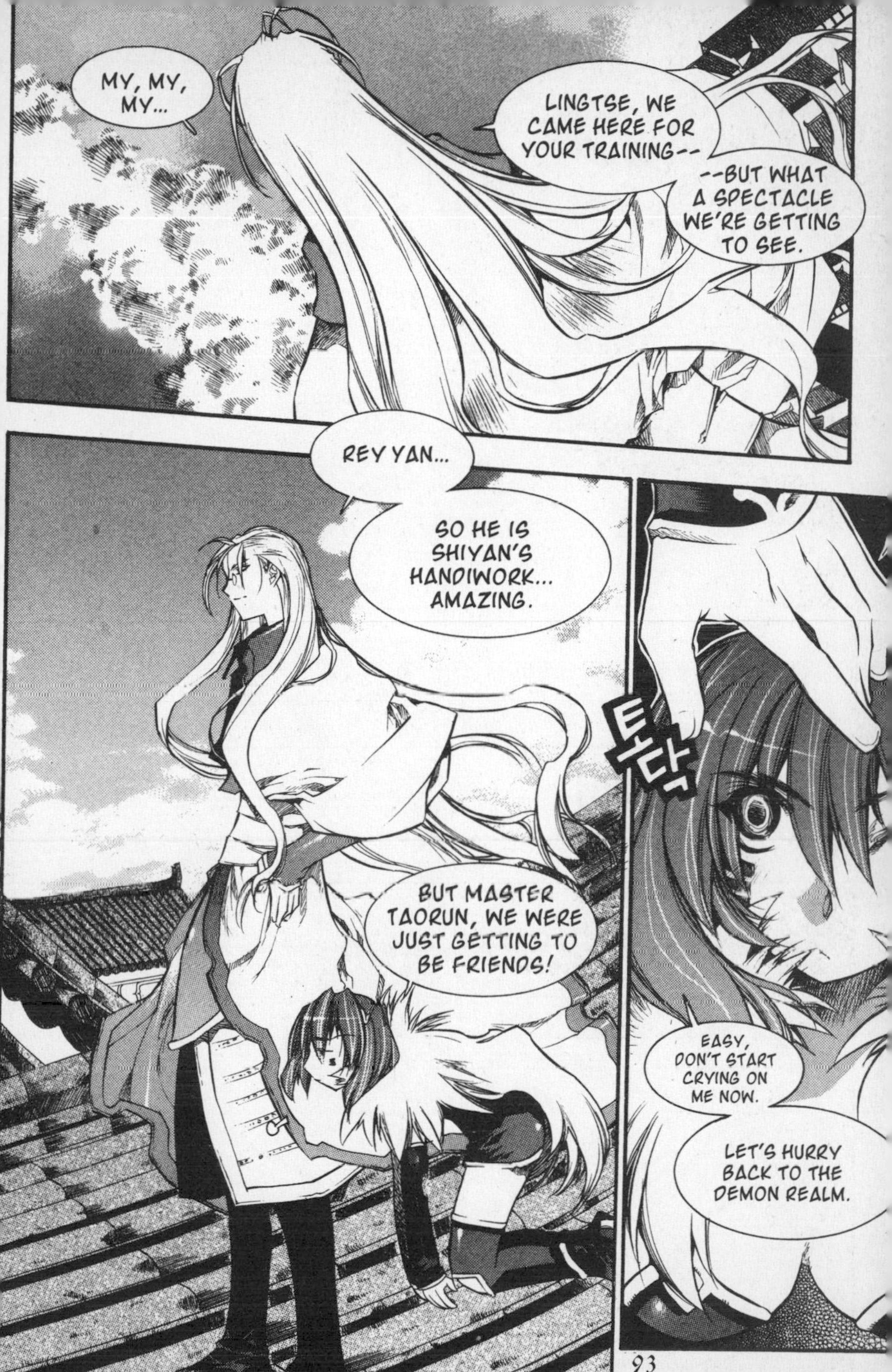
MY, MY, MY...
LINGTSE, WE CAME HERE FOR YOUR TRAINING--
--BUT WHAT A SPECTACLE WE'RE GETTING TO SEE.
REY YAN...
SO HE IS SHIYAN'S HANDIWORK... AMAZING.
BUT MASTER TAORUN, WE WERE JUST GETTING TO BE FRIENDS!
토닥
EASY, DON'T START CRYING ON ME NOW.
LET'S HURRY BACK TO THE DEMON REALM.

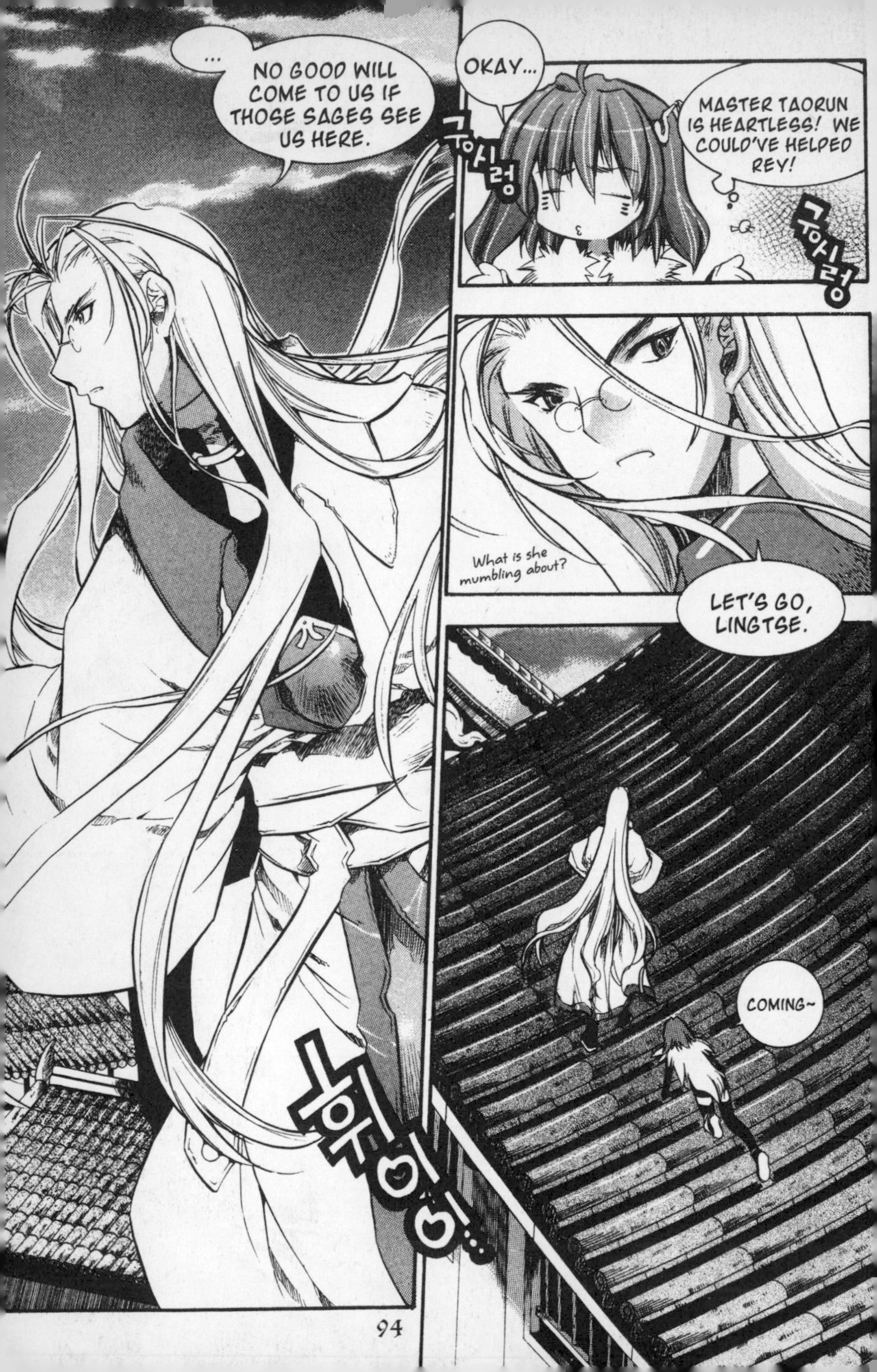
...
NO GOOD WILL COME TO US IF THOSE SAGES SEE US HERE.
휘이잉...
OKAY...
궁시렁
MASTER TAORUN IS HEARTLESS! WE COULD'VE HELPED REY!
궁시렁
What is she mumbling about?
LET'S GO, LINGTSE.
COMING~

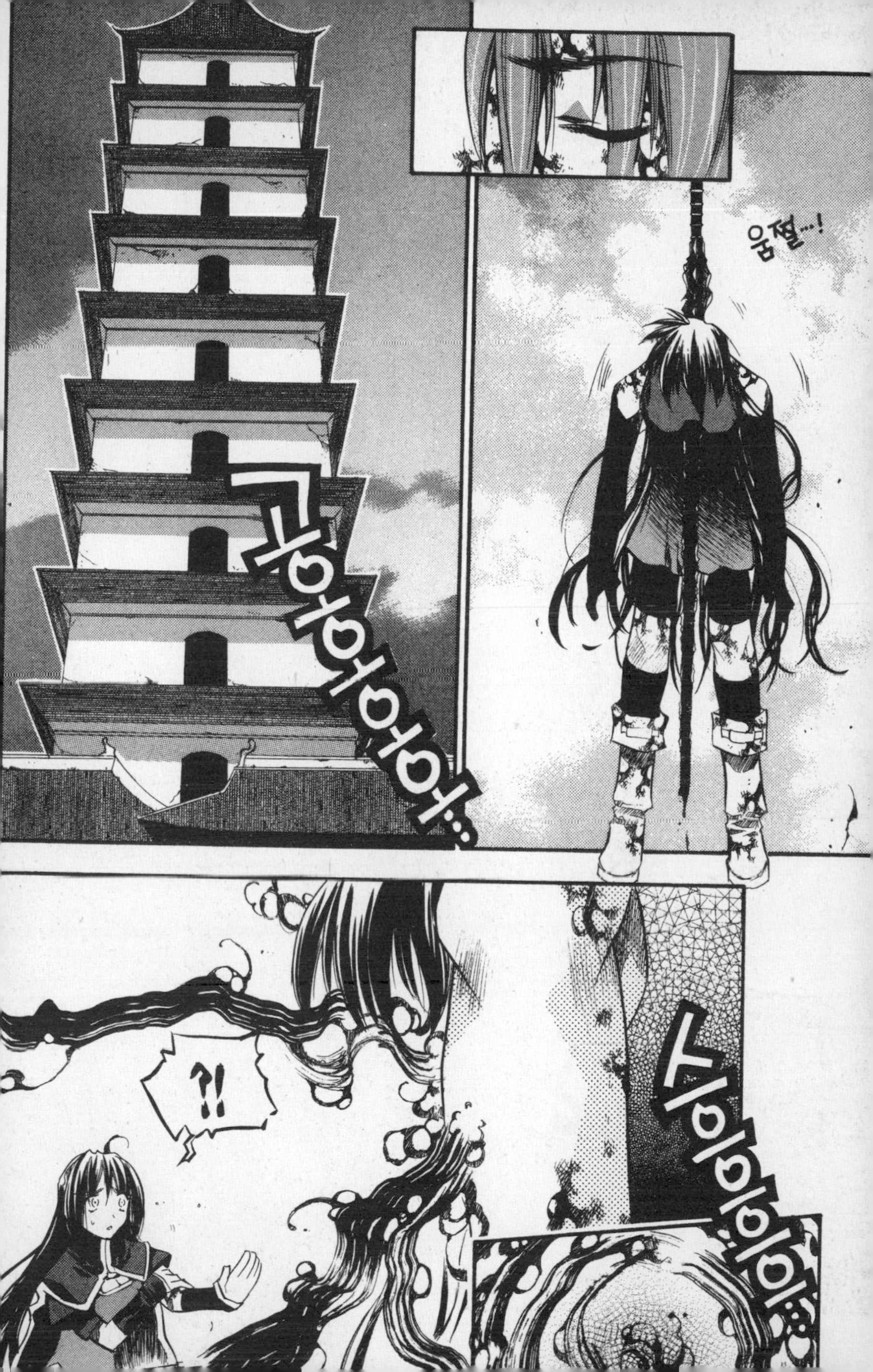
그아아아아…
움찔…!
?!
시이이이이…

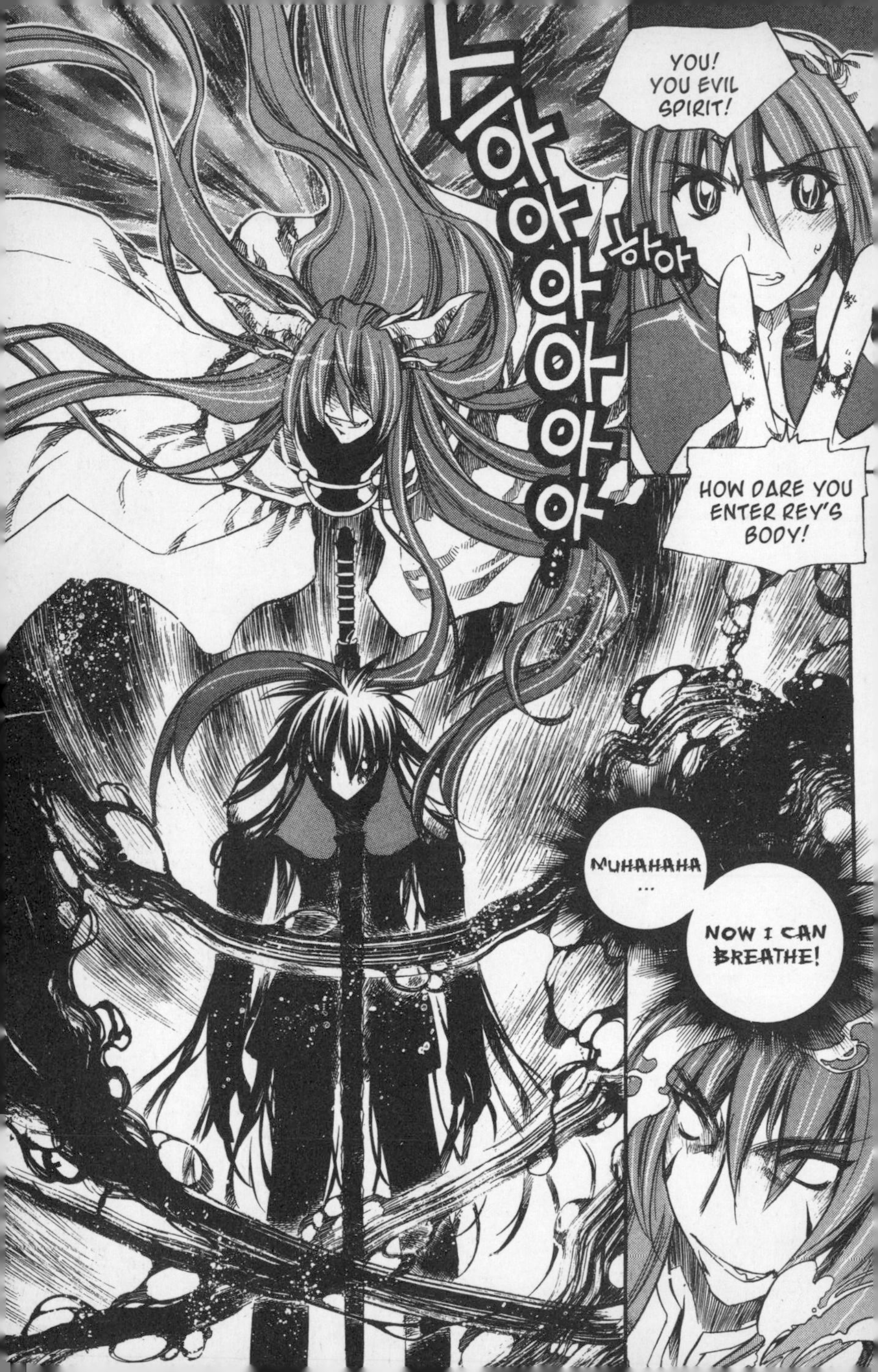

야야야야야야...
하야
YOU! YOU EVIL SPIRIT!
HOW DARE YOU ENTER REY'S BODY!
MUHAHAHA ...
NOW I CAN BREATHE!

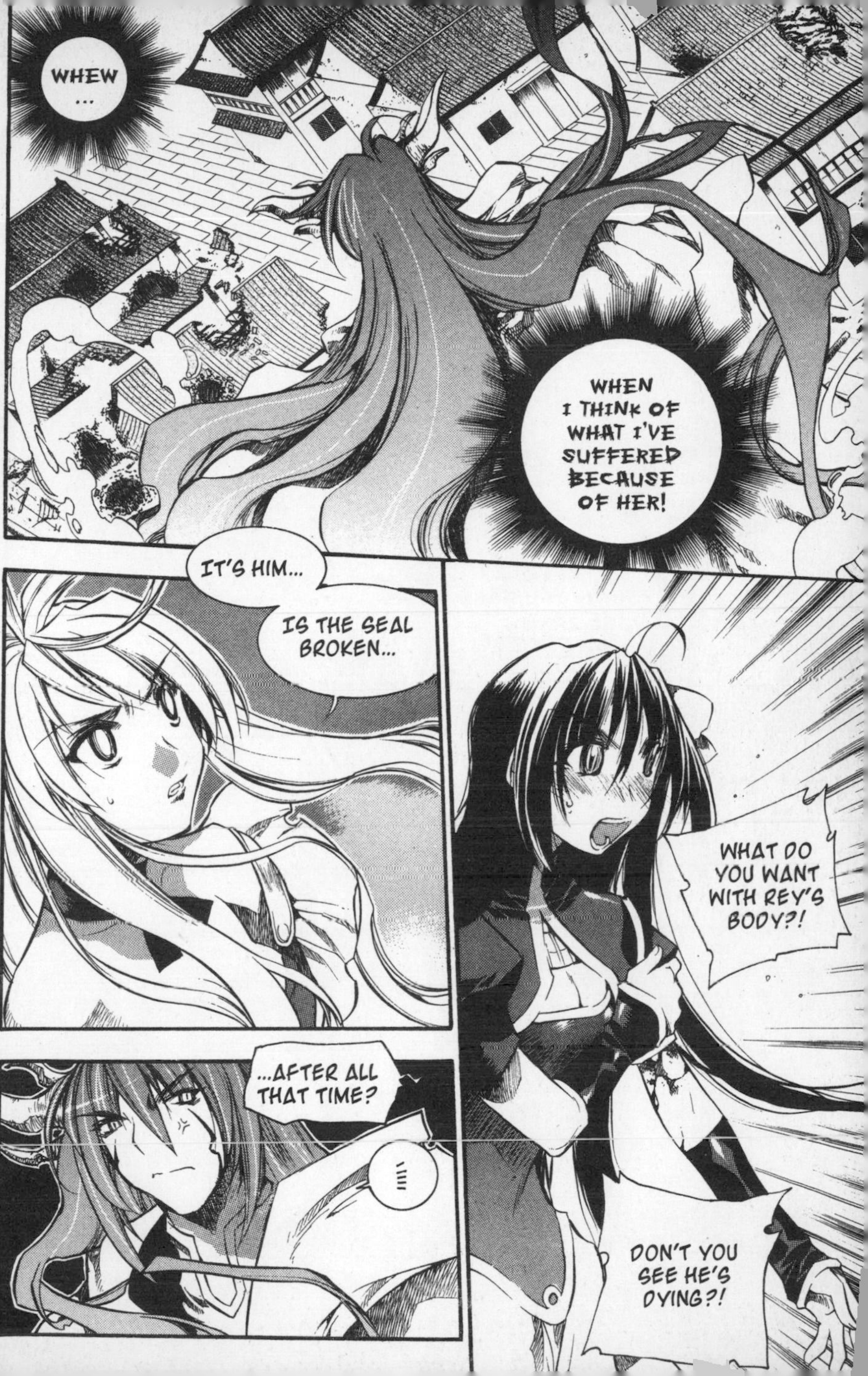
WHEW ...
WHEN I THINK OF WHAT I'VE SUFFERED BECAUSE OF HER!
IT'S HIM...
IS THE SEAL BROKEN...
...AFTER ALL THAT TIME?
WHAT DO YOU WANT WITH REY'S BODY?!
DON'T YOU SEE HE'S DYING?!

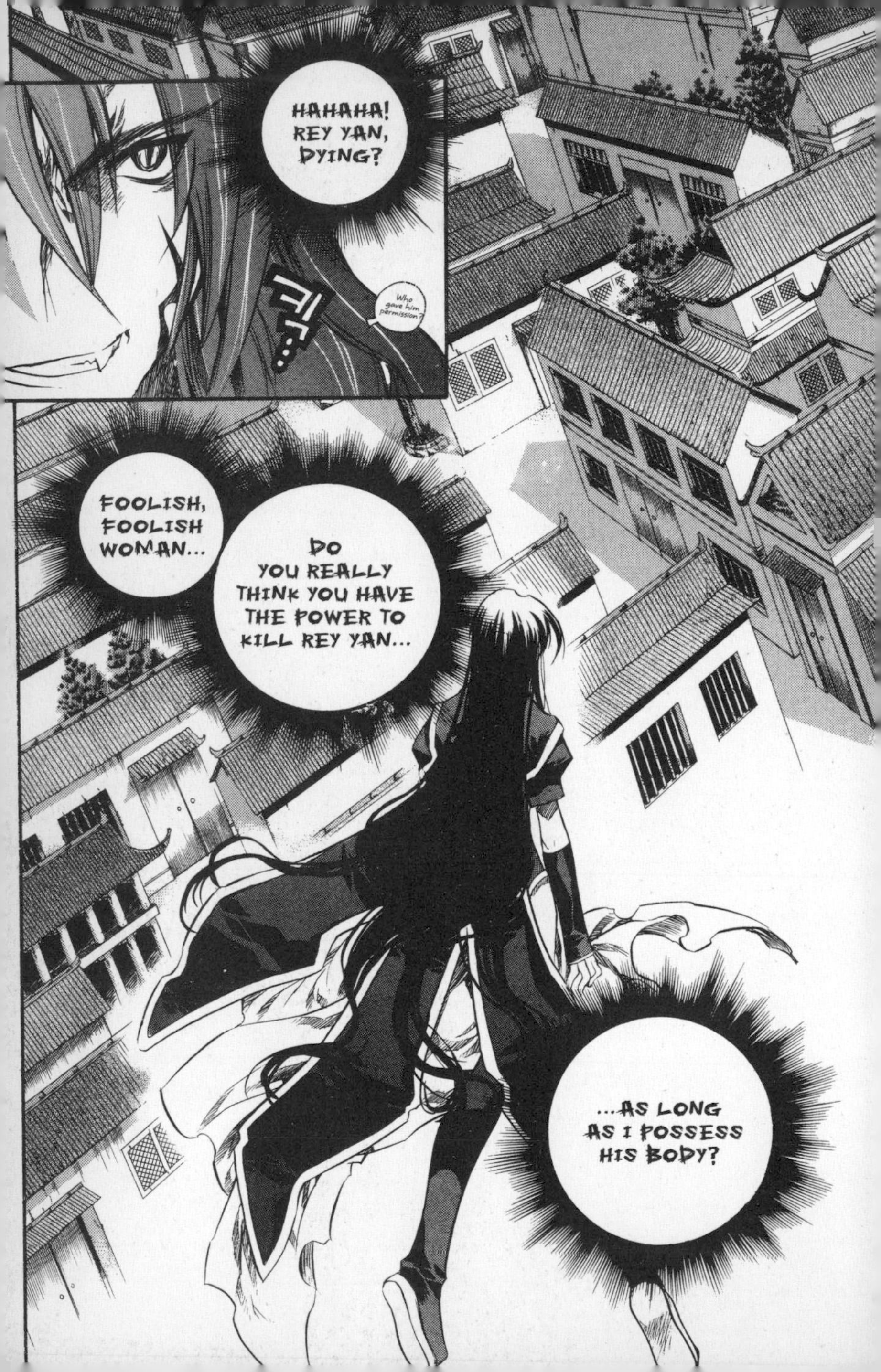
HAHAHA! REY YAN, DYING?
Who gave him permission?
FOOLISH, FOOLISH WOMAN...
DO YOU REALLY THINK YOU HAVE THE POWER TO KILL REY YAN...
...AS LONG AS I POSSESS HIS BODY?

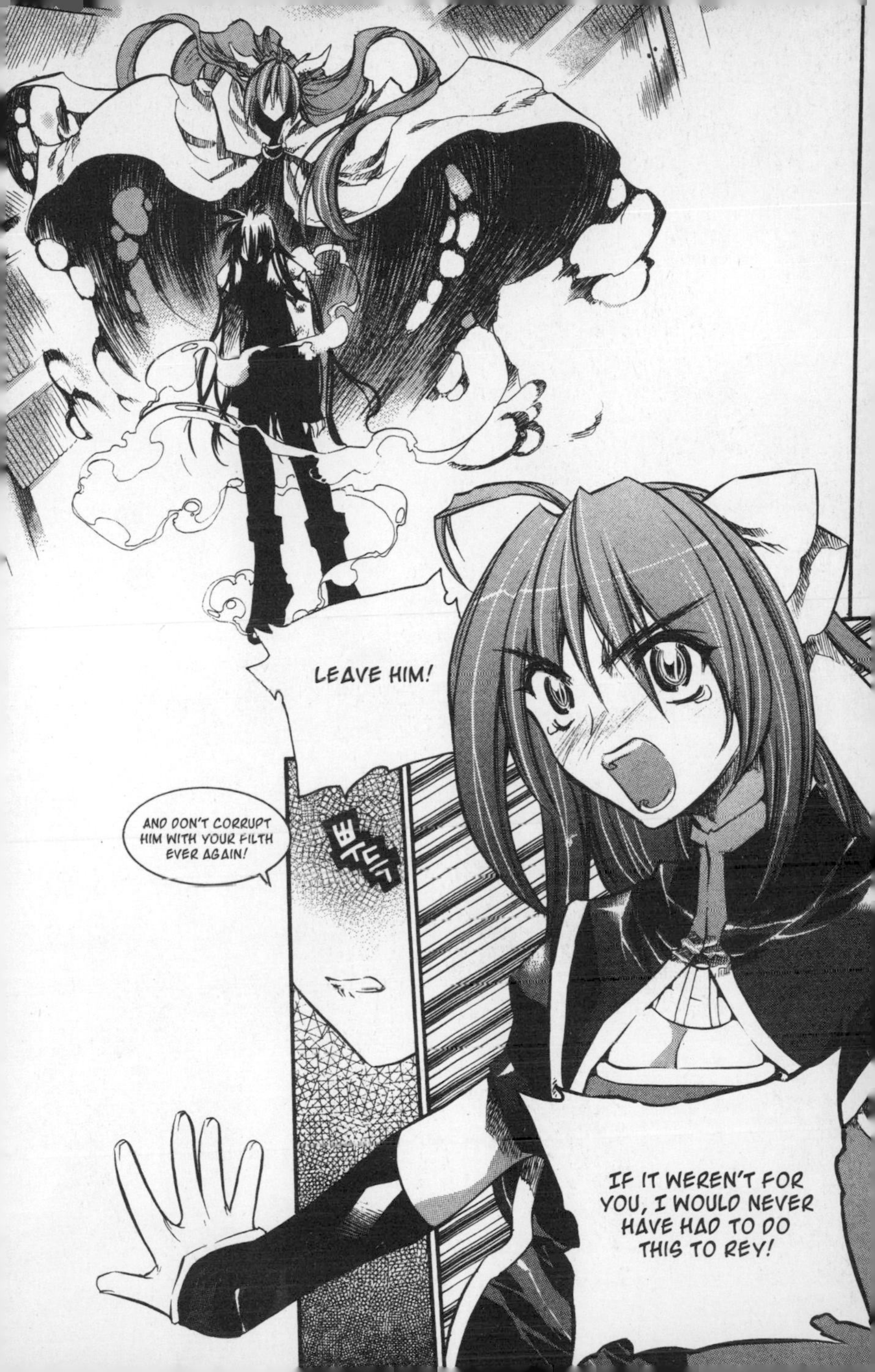
LEAVE HIM!
AND DON'T CORRUPT HIM WITH YOUR FILTH EVER AGAIN!
IF IT WEREN'T FOR YOU, I WOULD NEVER HAVE HAD TO DO THIS TO REY!

I'D ARGUE THAT WHAT YOU'VE DONE TO REY IS WORSE THAN DEATH!
GIVE ME A BREAK...
IT WAS YOU WHO BETRAYED HIM.
HE TRUSTED YOU, AND YOU CRUSHED HIS HEART.

I CAN ONLY DOMINATE HIM WHEN HE'S SUFFERED TREMENDOUS PHYSICAL OR MENTAL DAMAGE...
THANKS TO YOU, I HAVE HIM FULLY IN MY CONTROL A LOT SOONER THAN I THOUGHT I WOULD...
I...
REY...?
I OWE YOU, LADY SOHWA, MY DEEPEST GRATITUDE FOR MAKING MY EMERGENCE POSSIBLE.

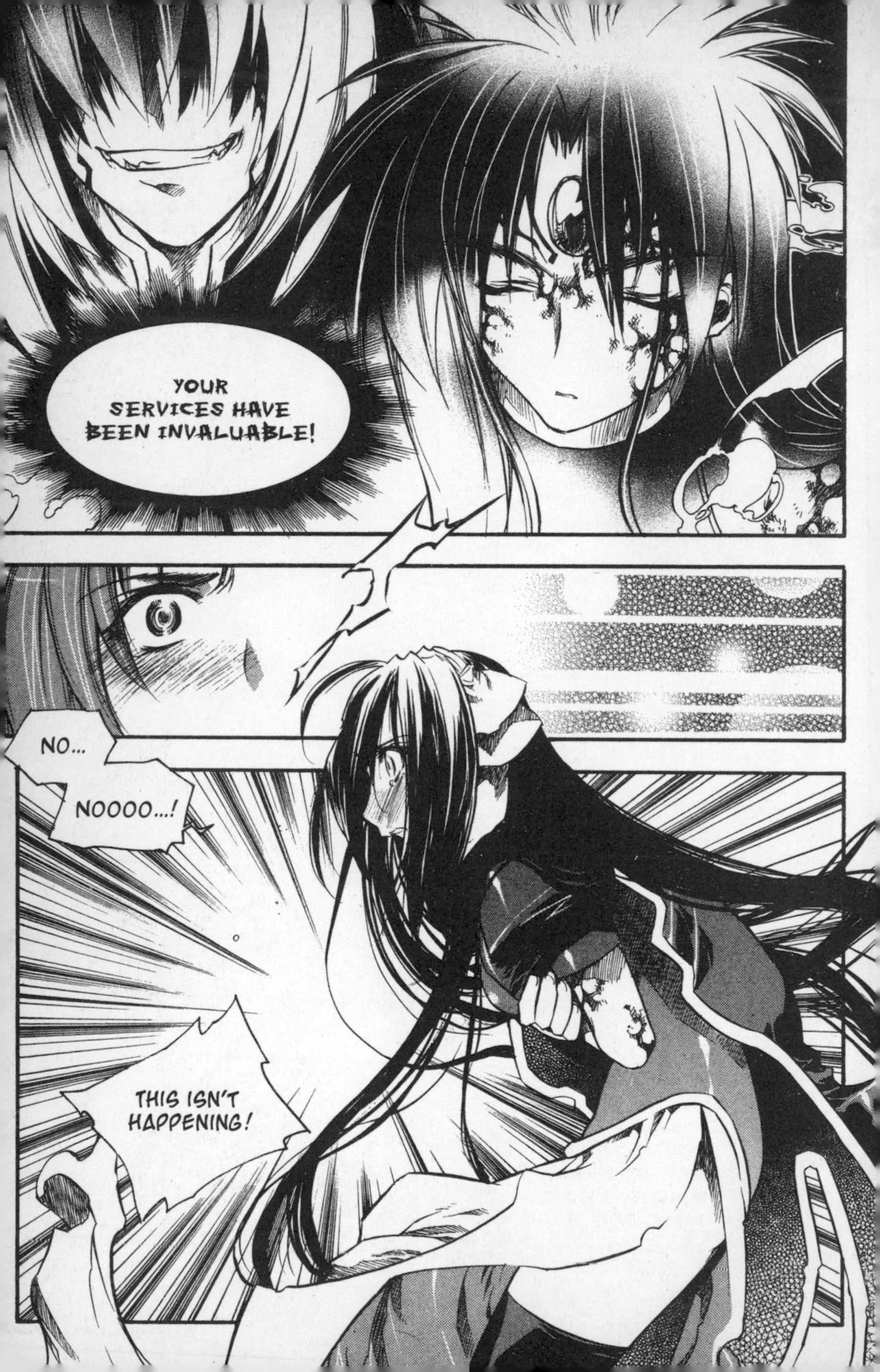
YOUR SERVICES HAVE BEEN INVALUABLE!
NO...
NOOOO...!
THIS ISN'T HAPPENING!

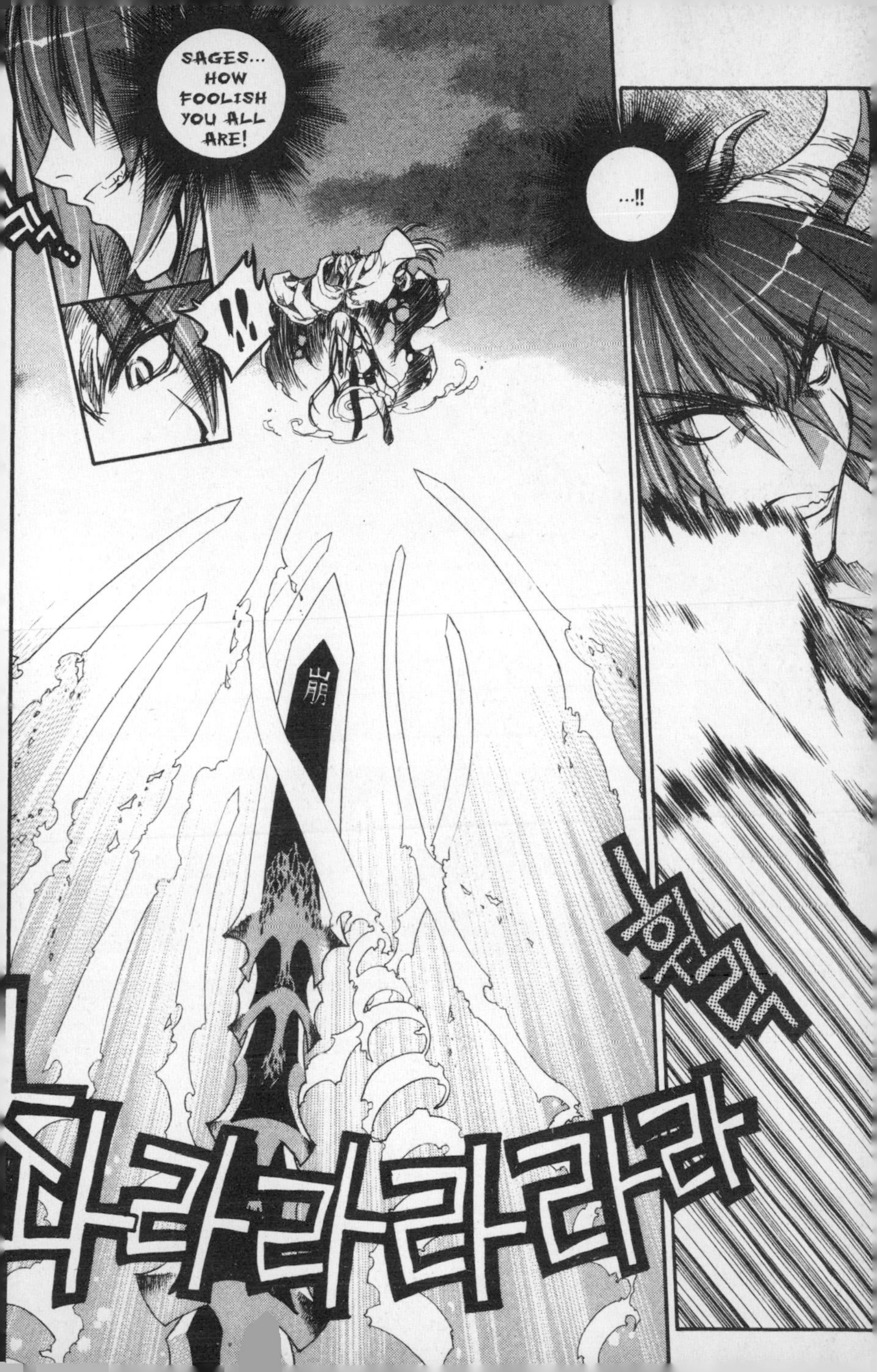
SAGES... HOW FOOLISH YOU ALL ARE!
!!
...!!
崩

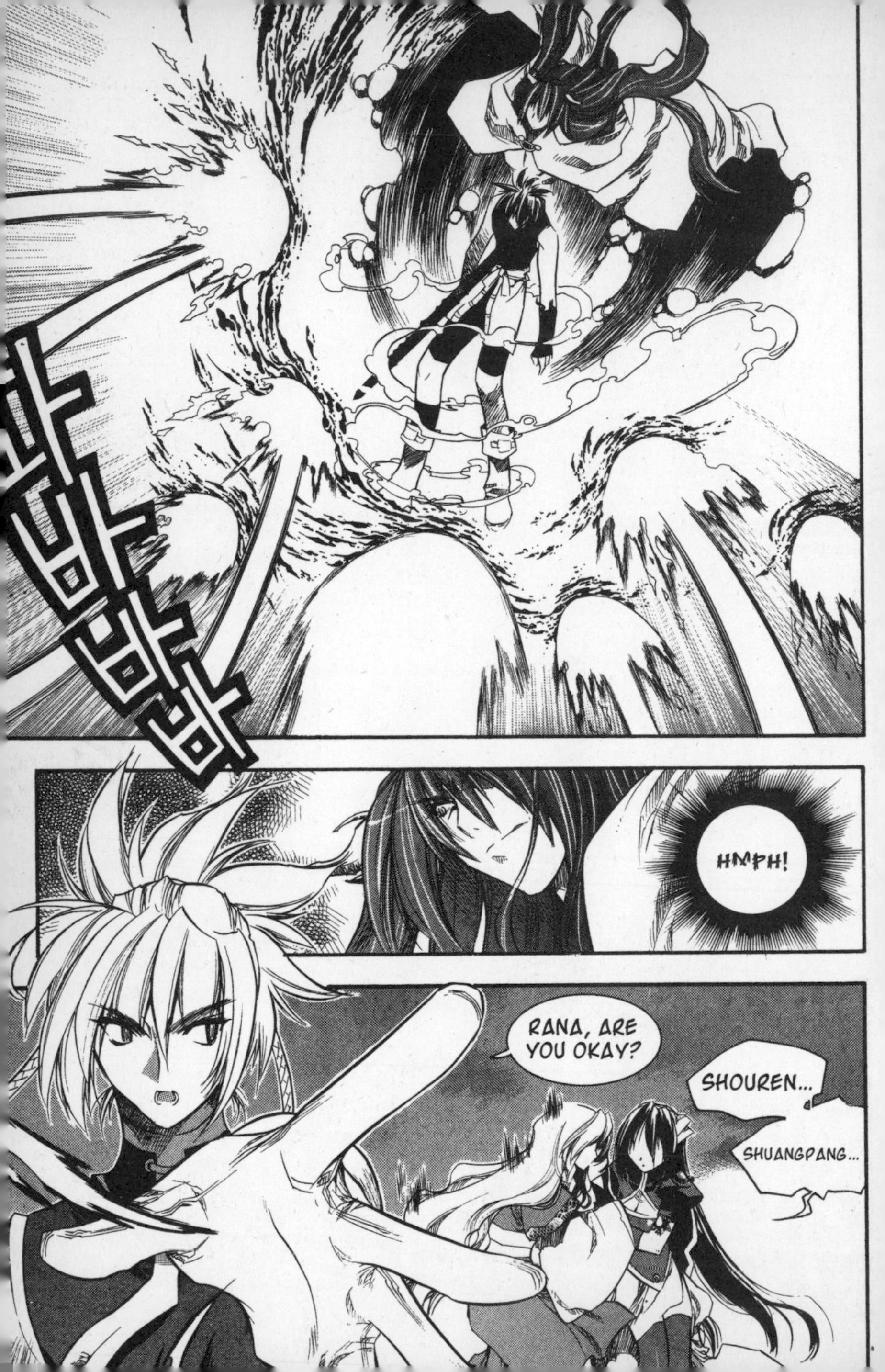
HMPH!
RANA, ARE YOU OKAY?
SHOUREN...
SHUANGPANG...

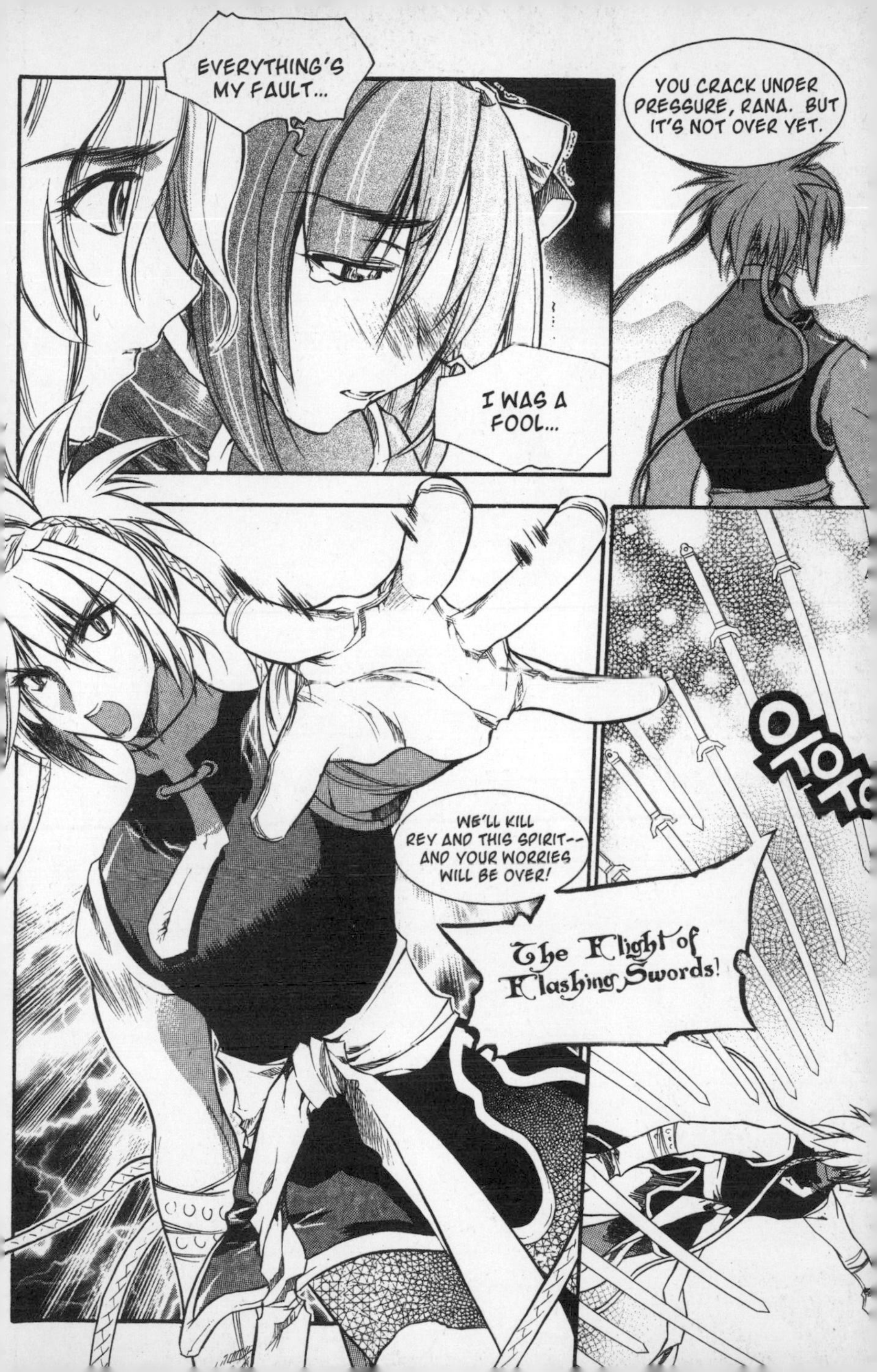
EVERYTHING'S MY FAULT...
I WAS A FOOL...
YOU CRACK UNDER PRESSURE, RANA. BUT IT'S NOT OVER YET.
WE'LL KILL REY AND THIS SPIRIT--AND YOUR WORRIES WILL BE OVER!
The Flight of Flashing Swords!

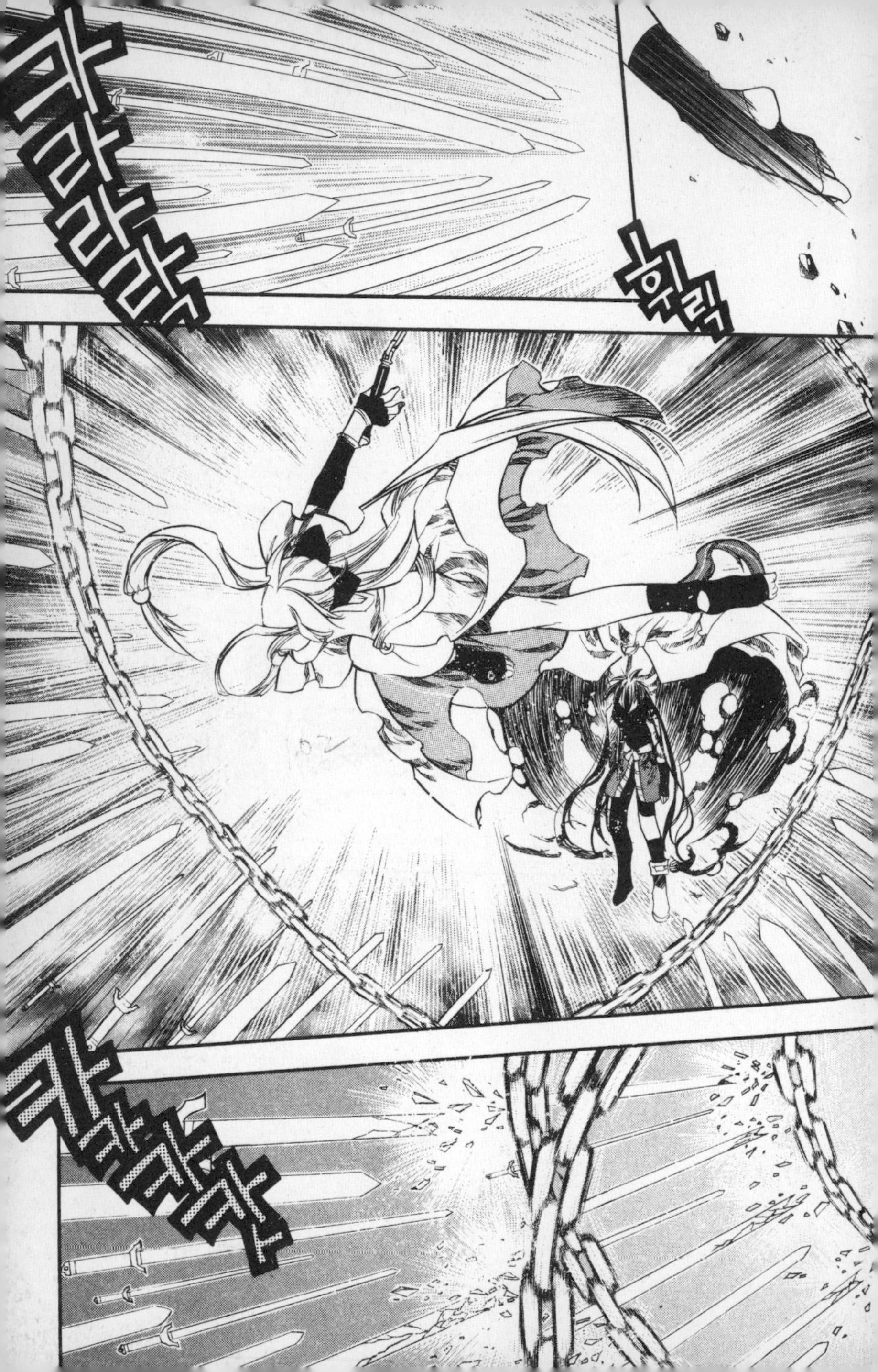
카라라랑
휘릭

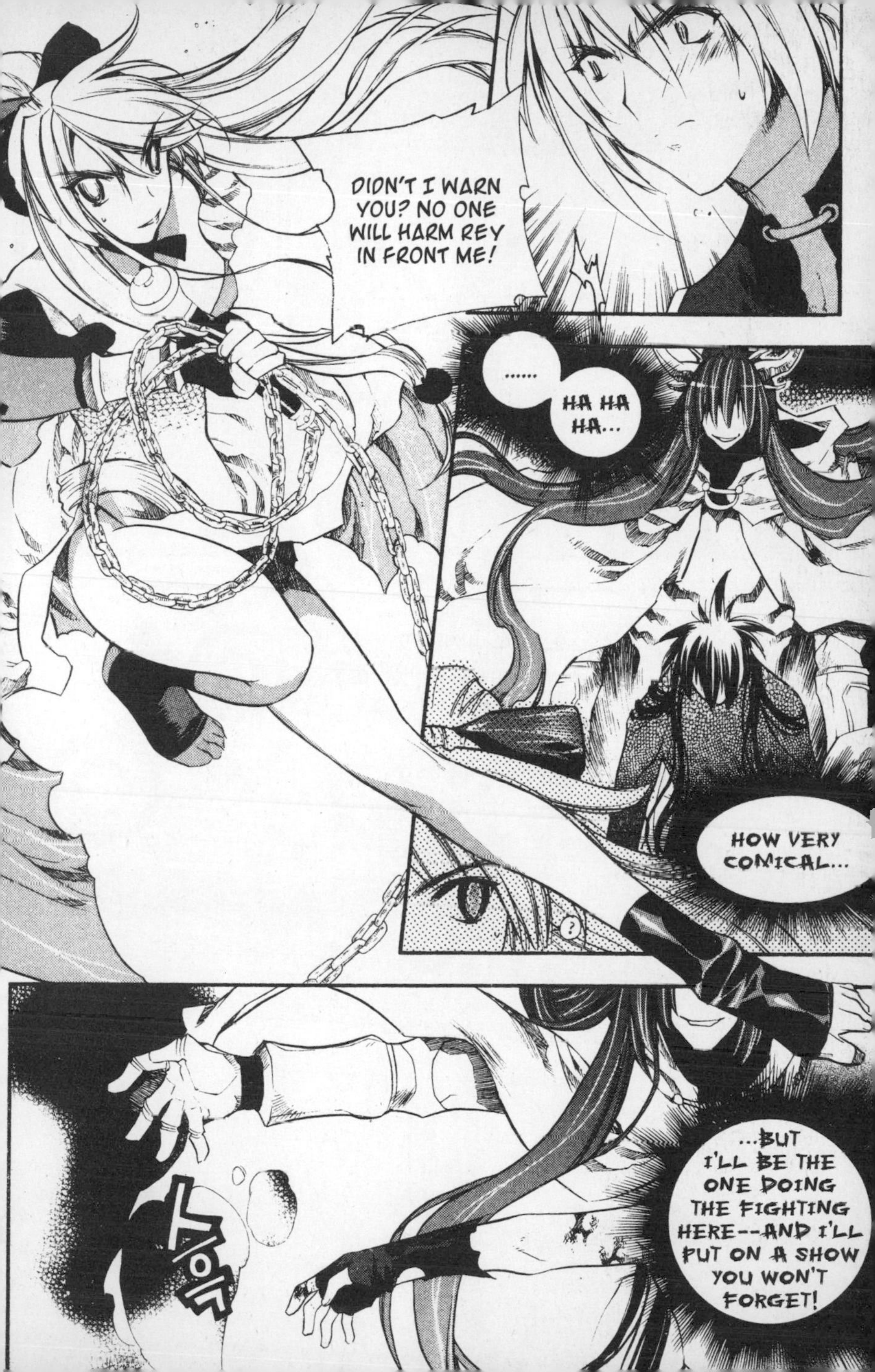
DIDN'T I WARN YOU? NO ONE WILL HARM REY IN FRONT ME!
......
HA HA HA...
HOW VERY COMICAL...
?
...BUT I'LL BE THE ONE DOING THE FIGHTING HERE--AND I'LL PUT ON A SHOW YOU WON'T FORGET!

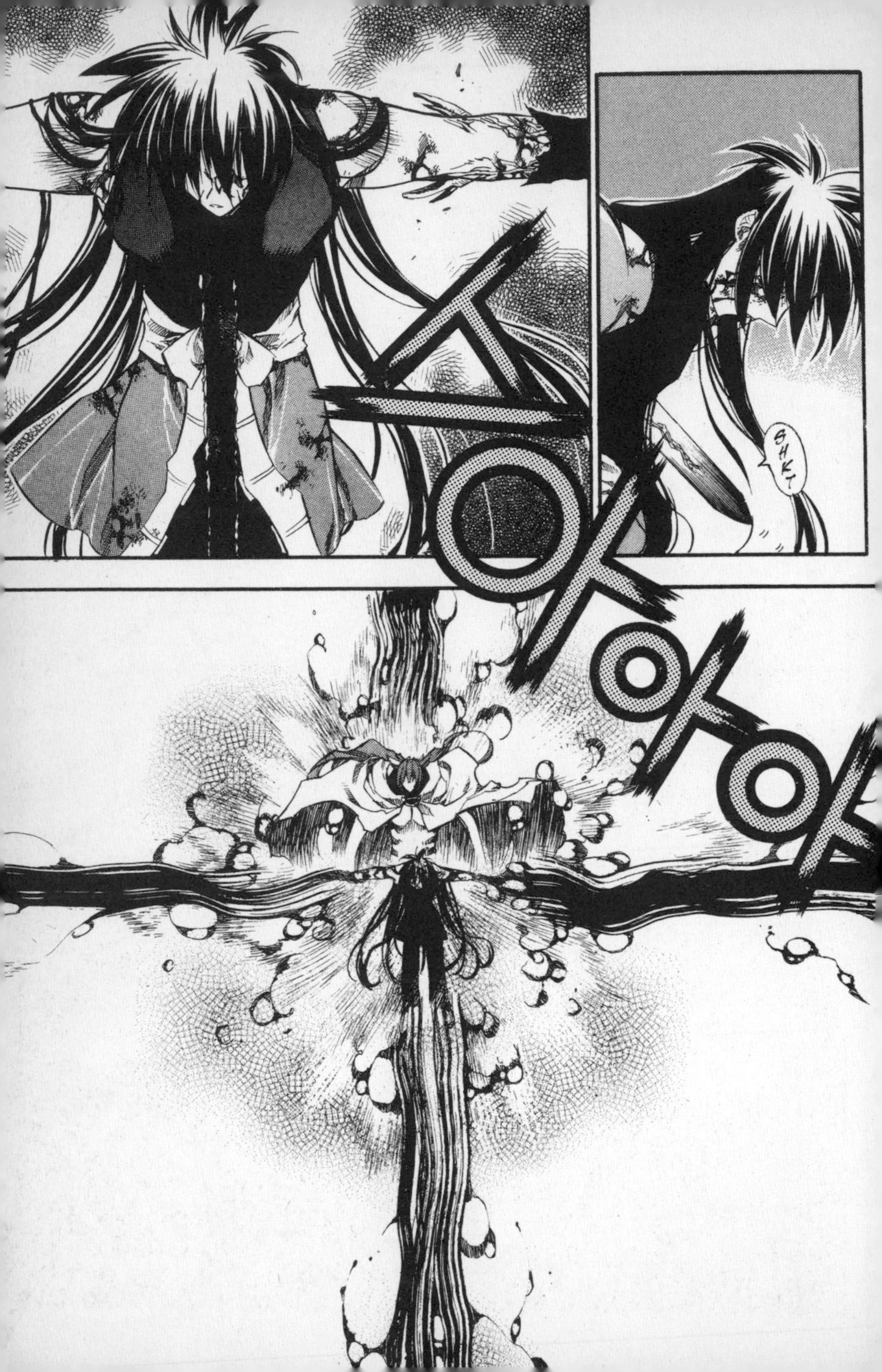
SHKT

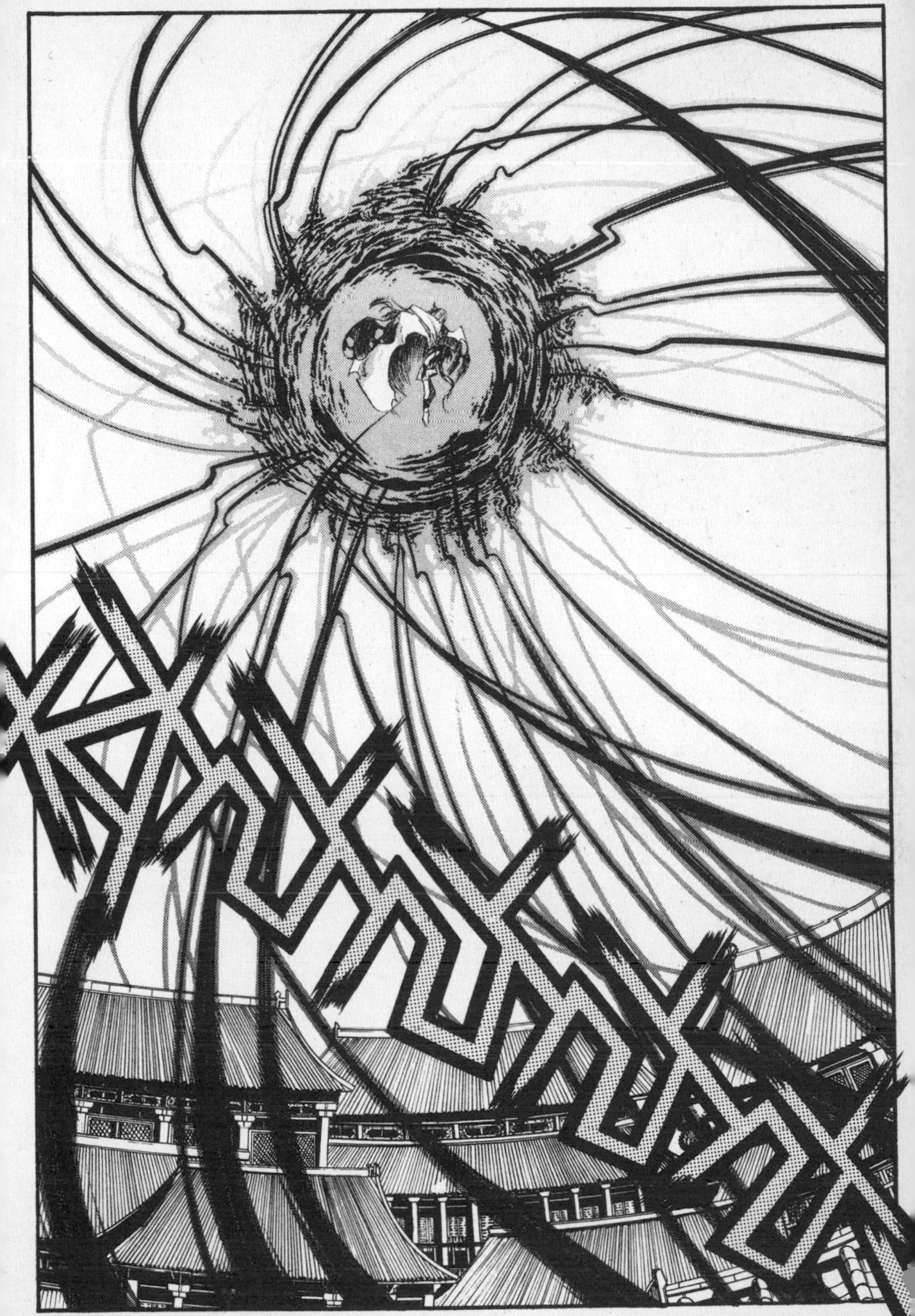

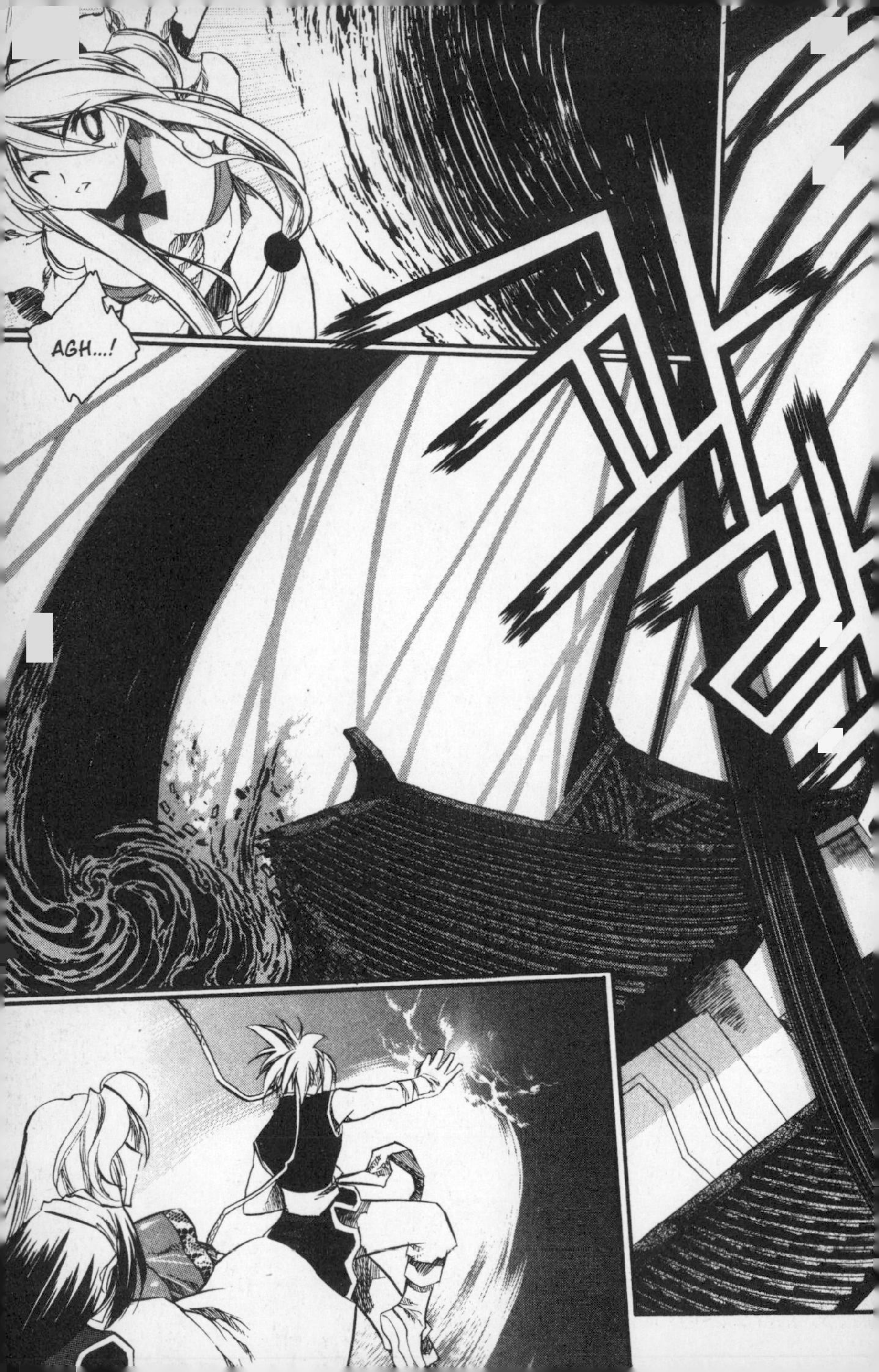
AGH...!

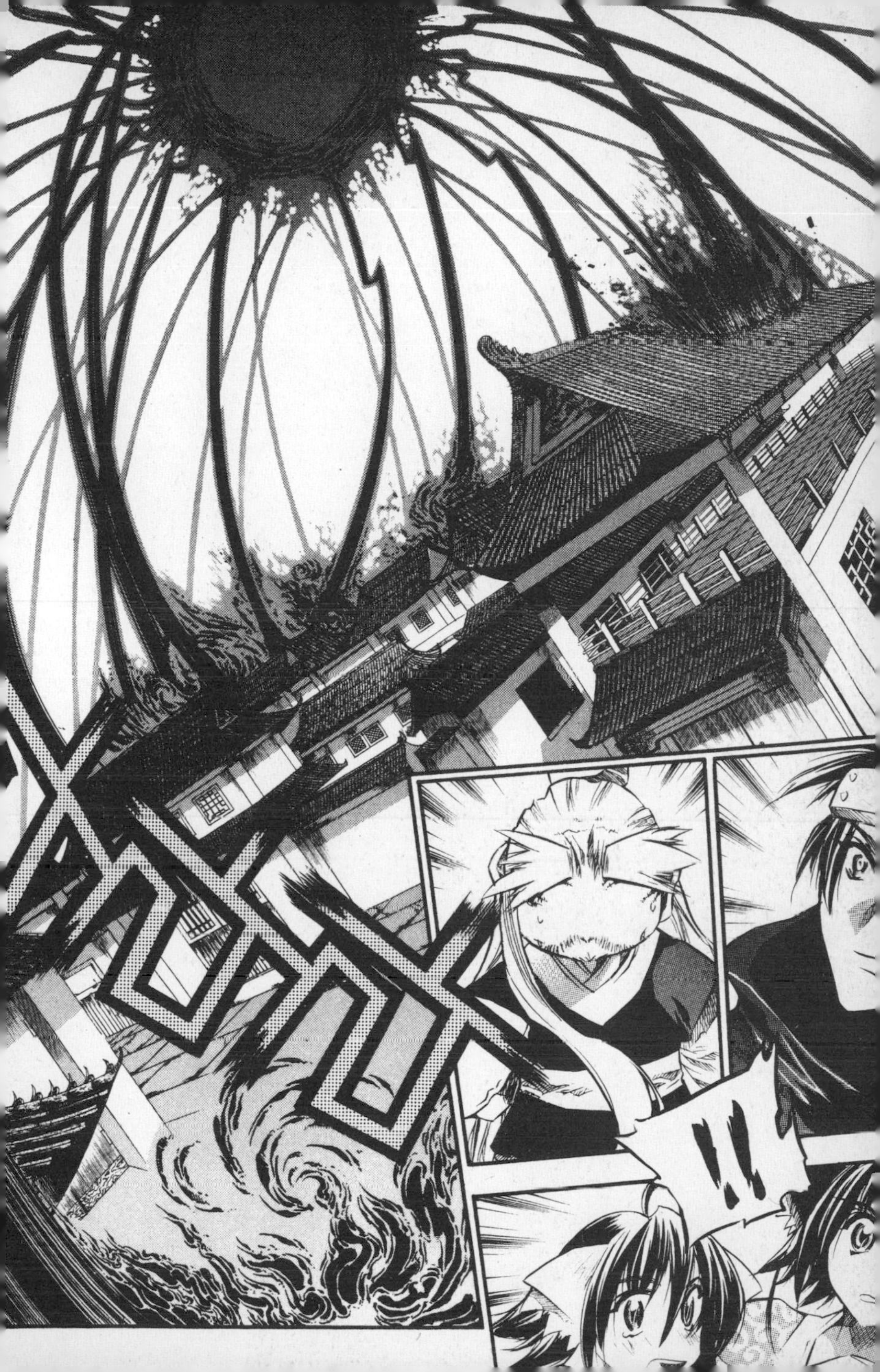
!!

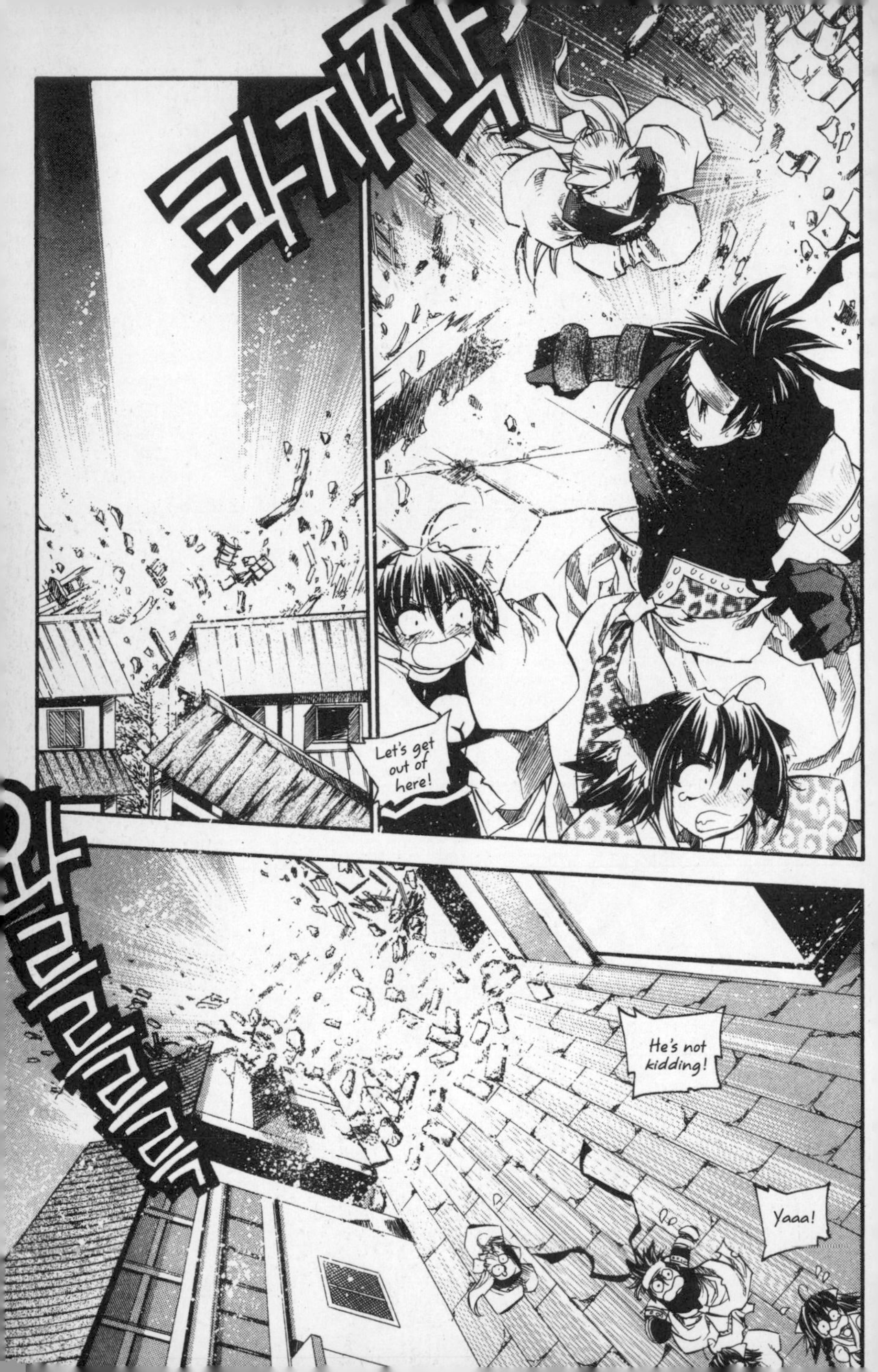
Let's get out of here!
He's not kidding!
Yaaa!

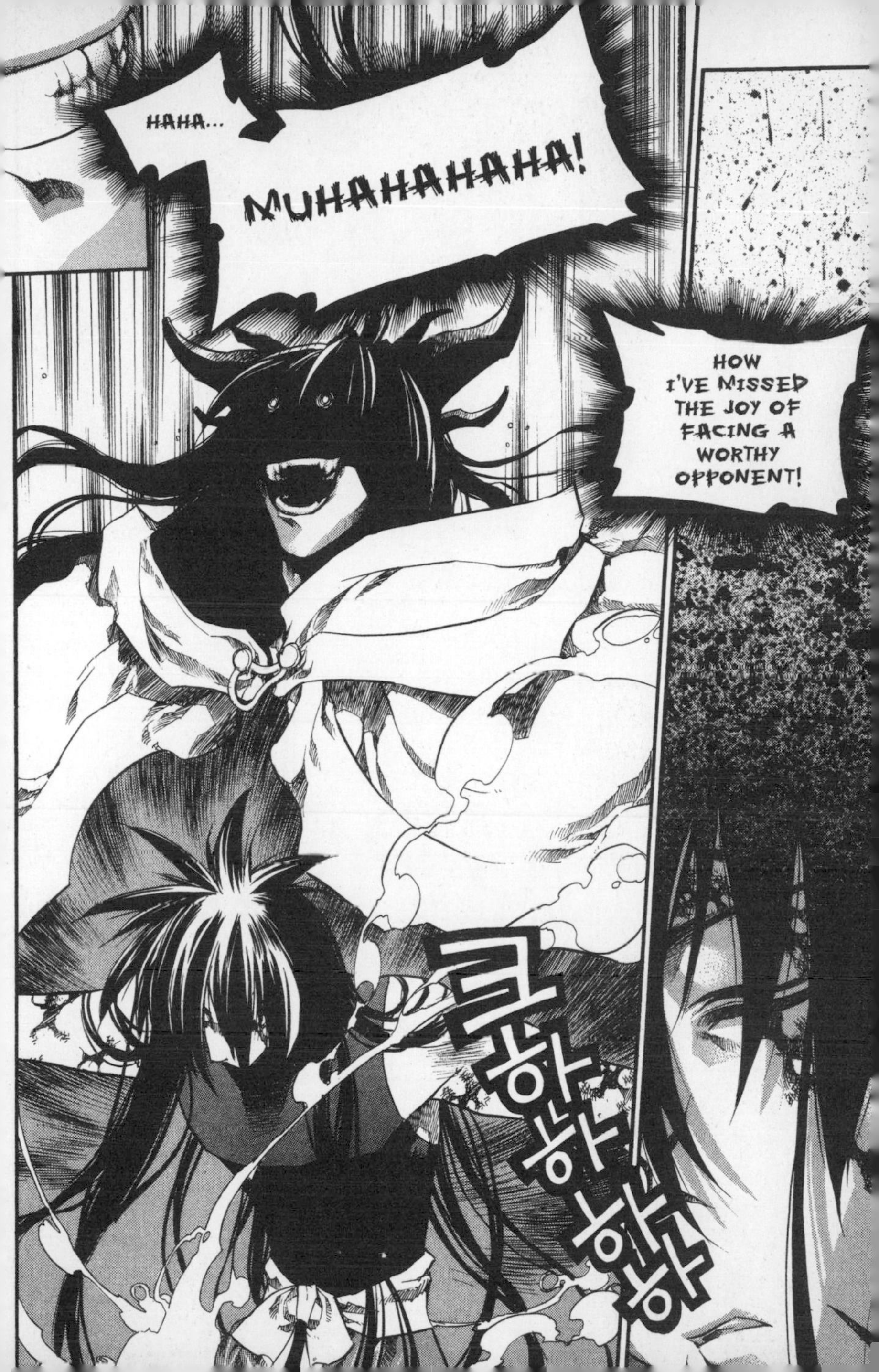
HAHA...
MUHAHAHAHA!
HOW I'VE MISSED THE JOY OF FACING A WORTHY OPPONENT!

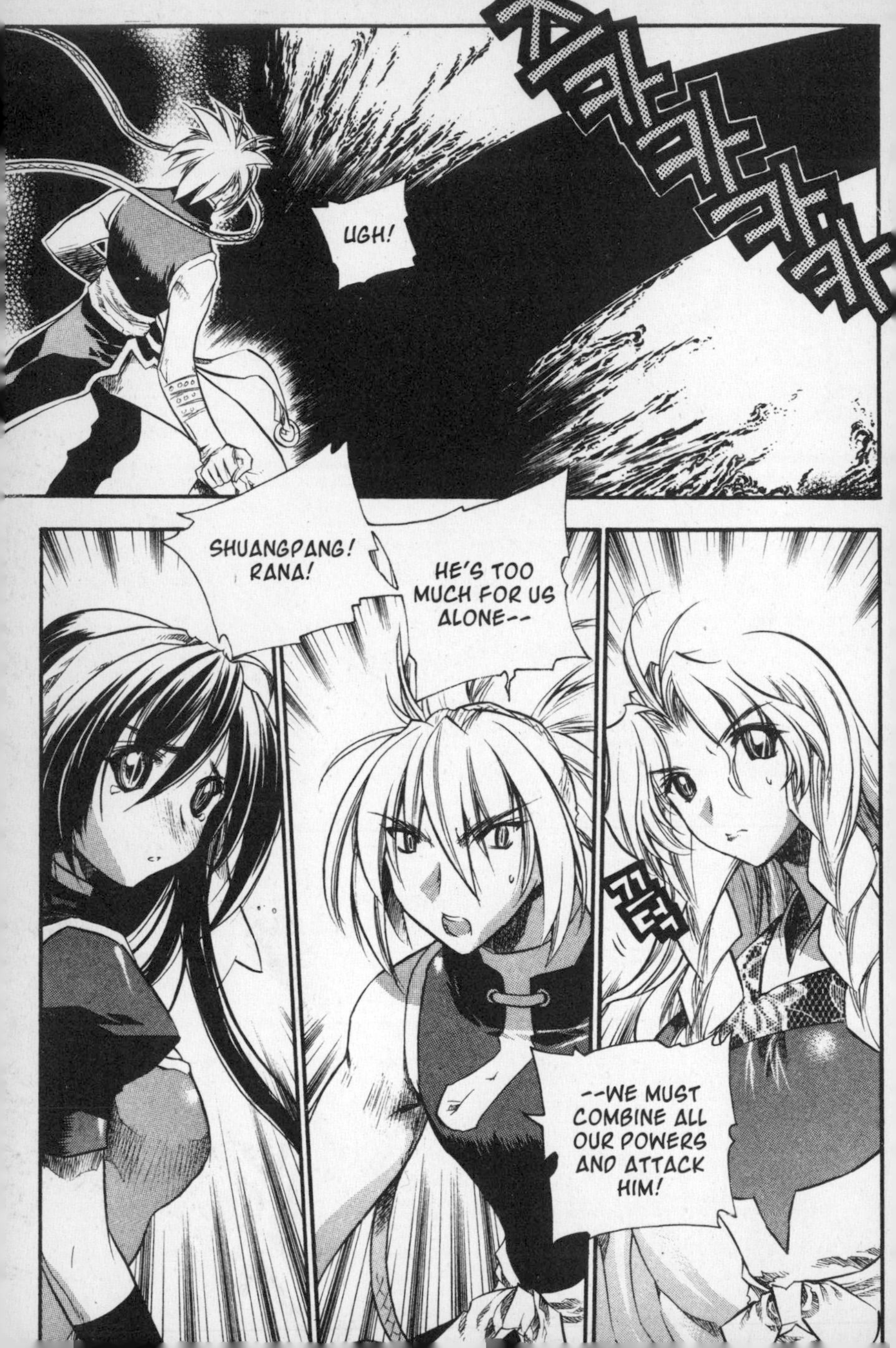
UGH!
SHUANGPANG! RANA!
HE'S TOO MUCH FOR US ALONE--
--WE MUST COMBINE ALL OUR POWERS AND ATTACK HIM!

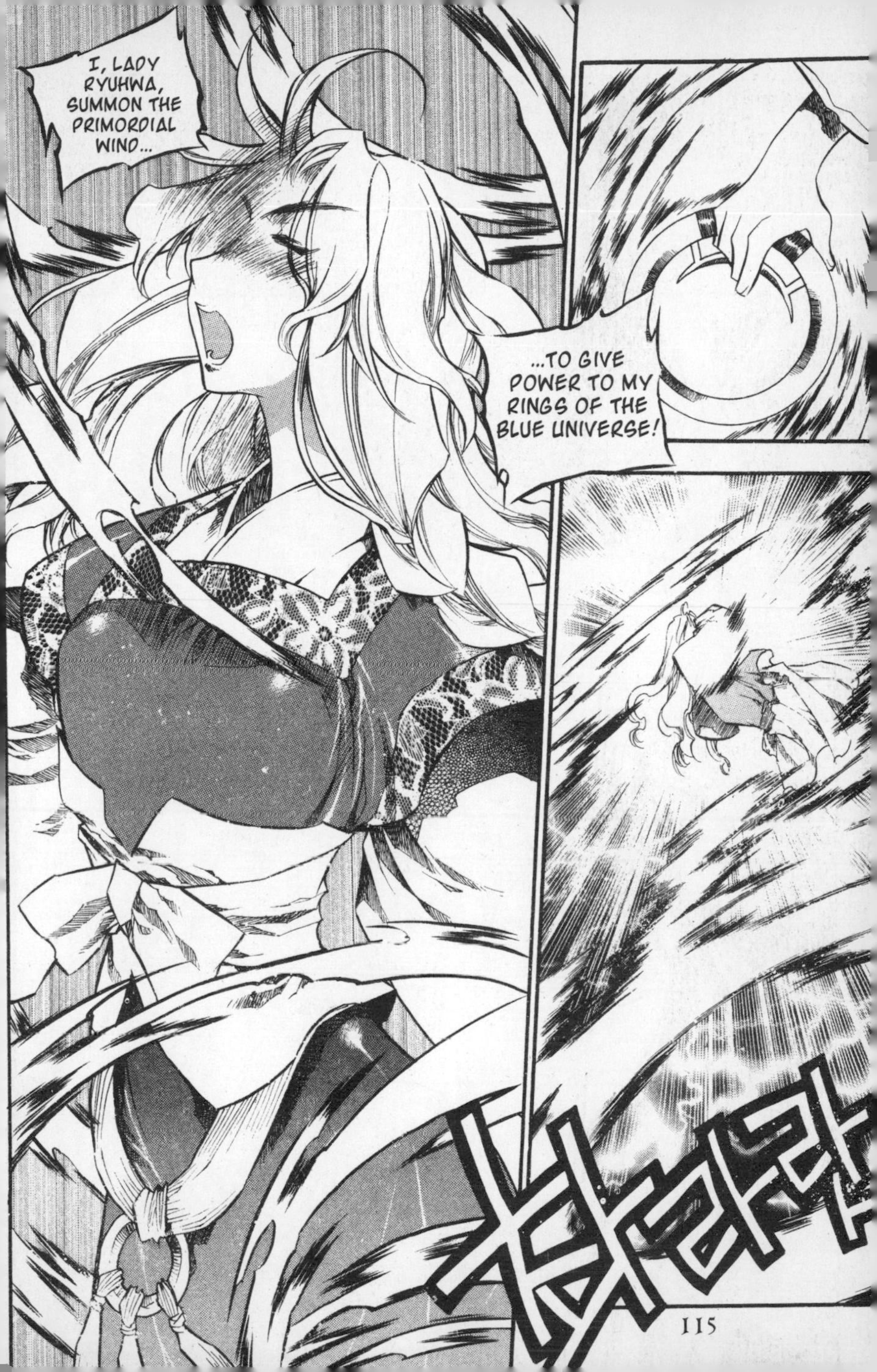
I, LADY RYUHWA, SUMMON THE PRIMORDIAL WIND...
...TO GIVE POWER TO MY RINGS OF THE BLUE UNIVERSE!

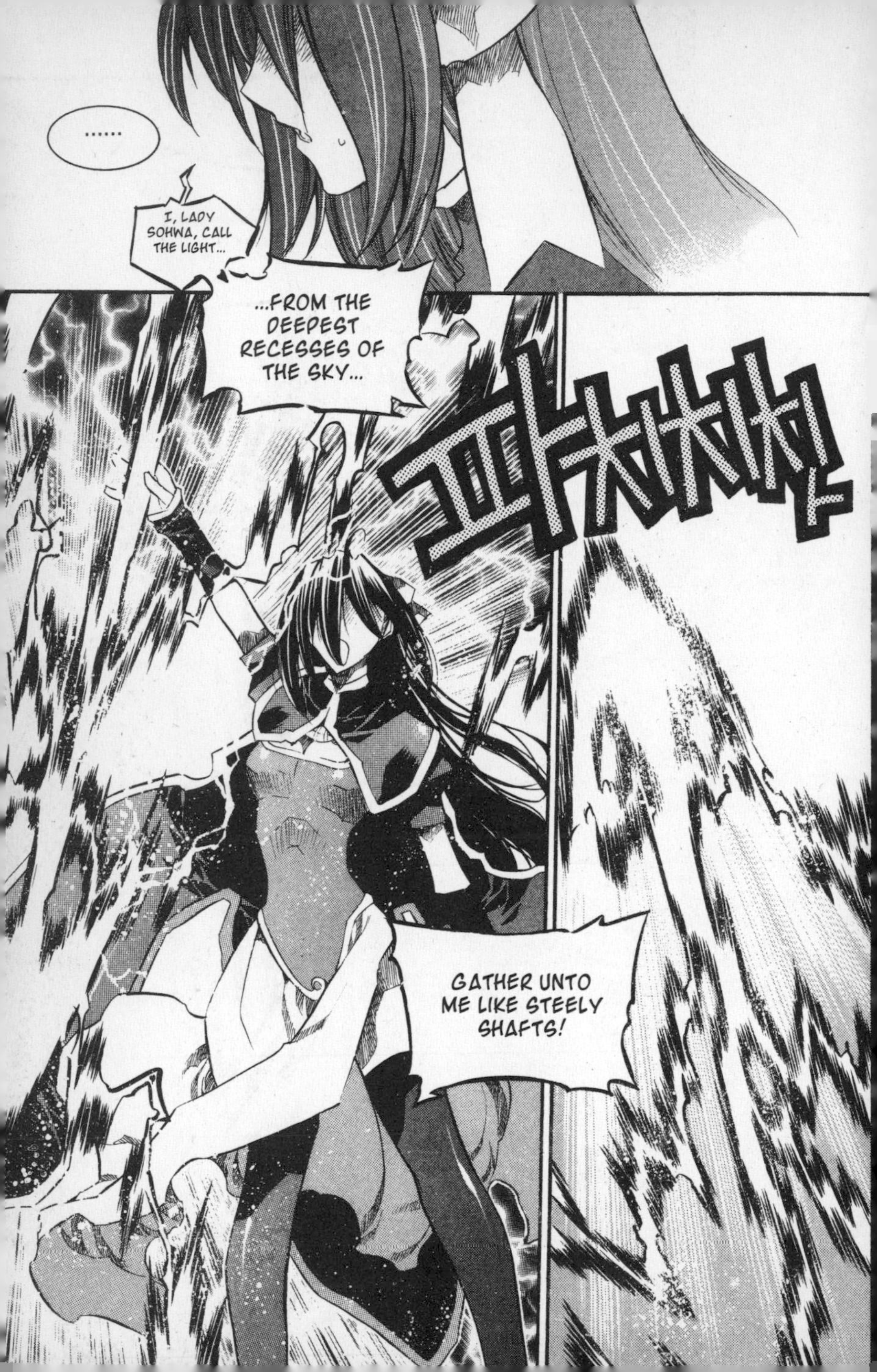
......
I, LADY SOHWA, CALL THE LIGHT...
...FROM THE DEEPEST RECESSES OF THE SKY...
GATHER UNTO ME LIKE STEELY SHAFTS!

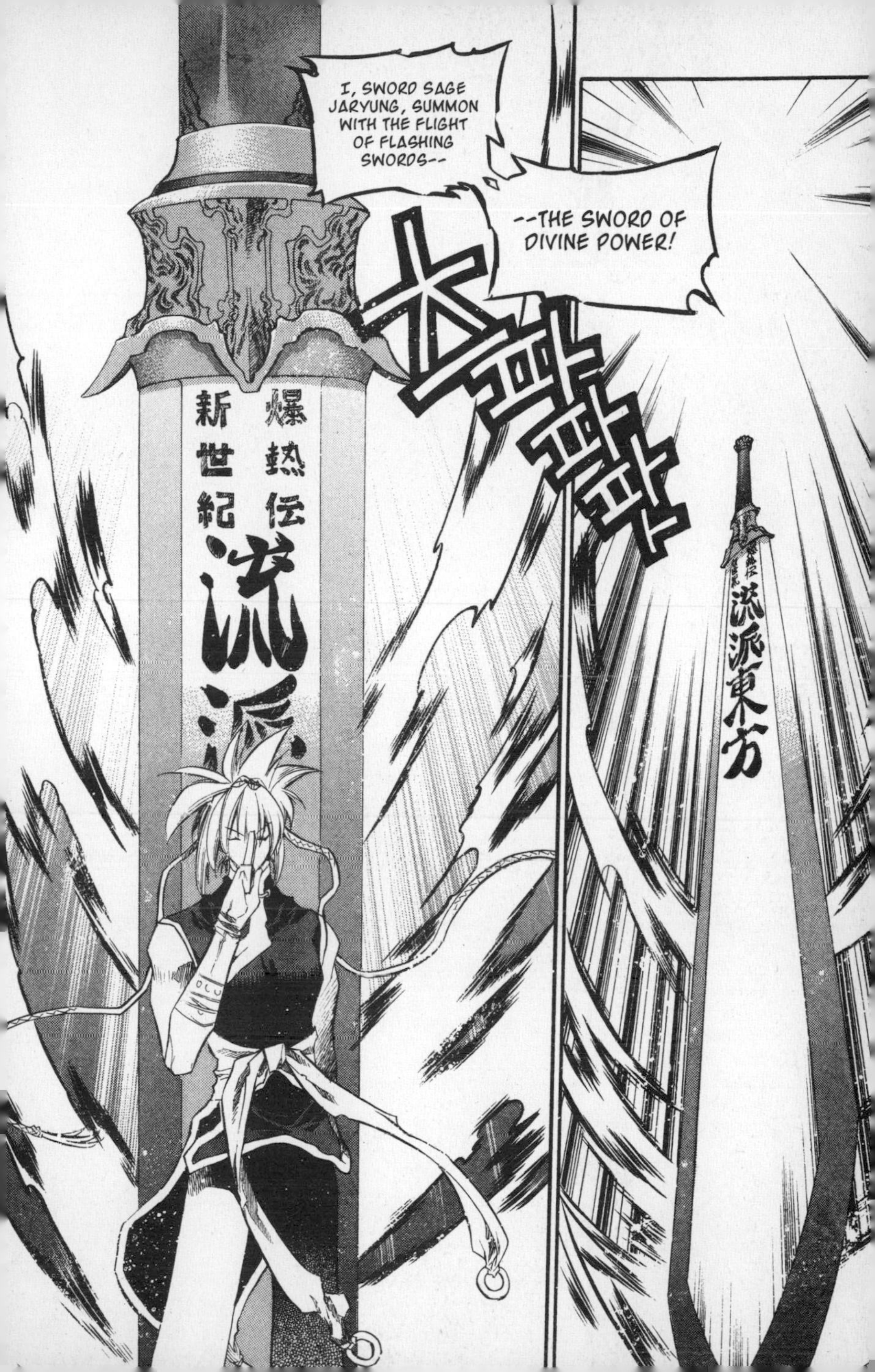

I, SWORD SAGE JARYUNG, SUMMON WITH THE FLIGHT OF FLASHING SWORDS--
--THE SWORD OF DIVINE POWER!
爆熱伝
新世紀
流派
流派東方

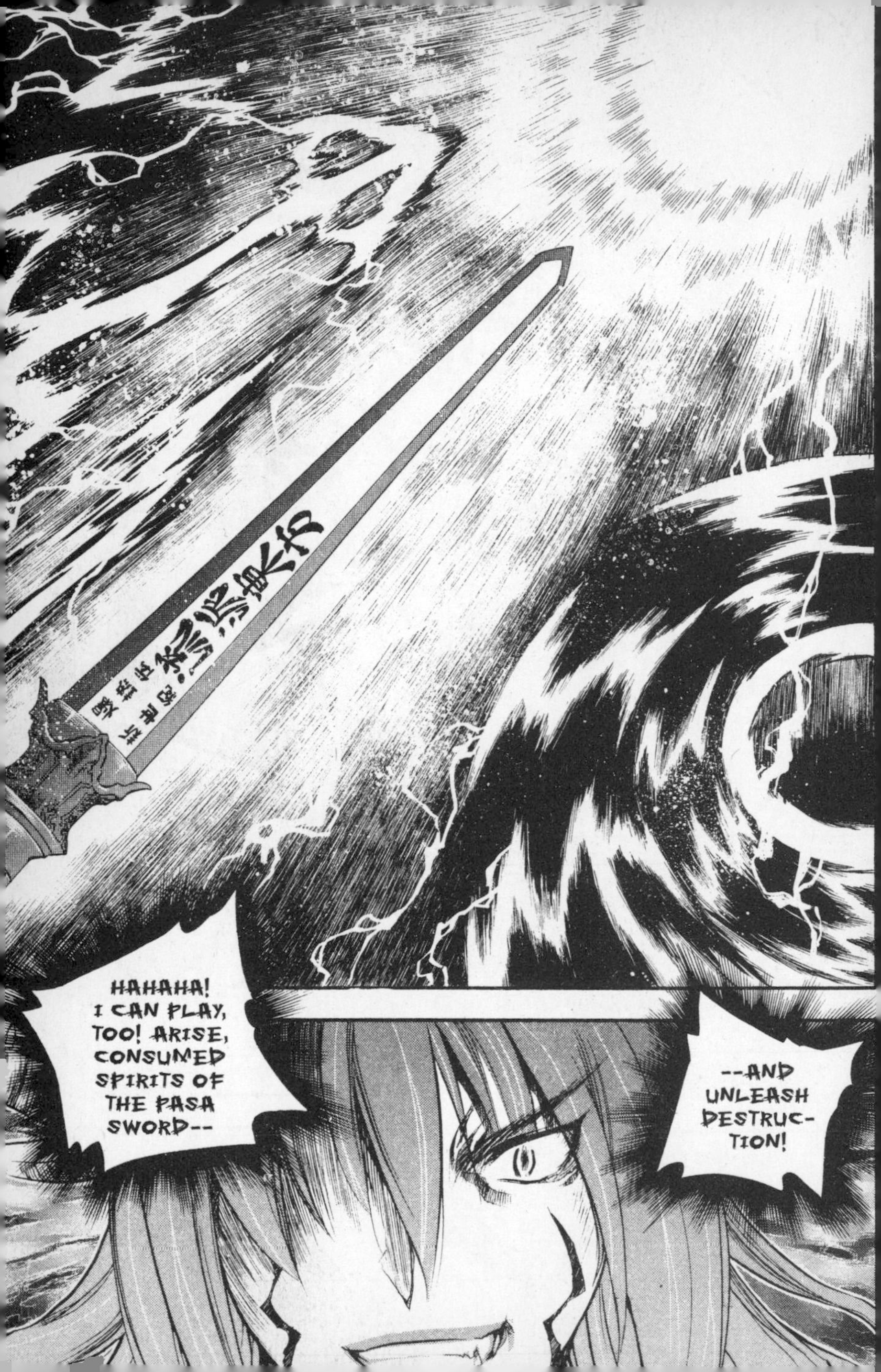
HAHAHA! I CAN PLAY, TOO! ARISE, CONSUMED SPIRITS OF THE PASA SWORD--
--AND UNLEASH DESTRUC-TION!

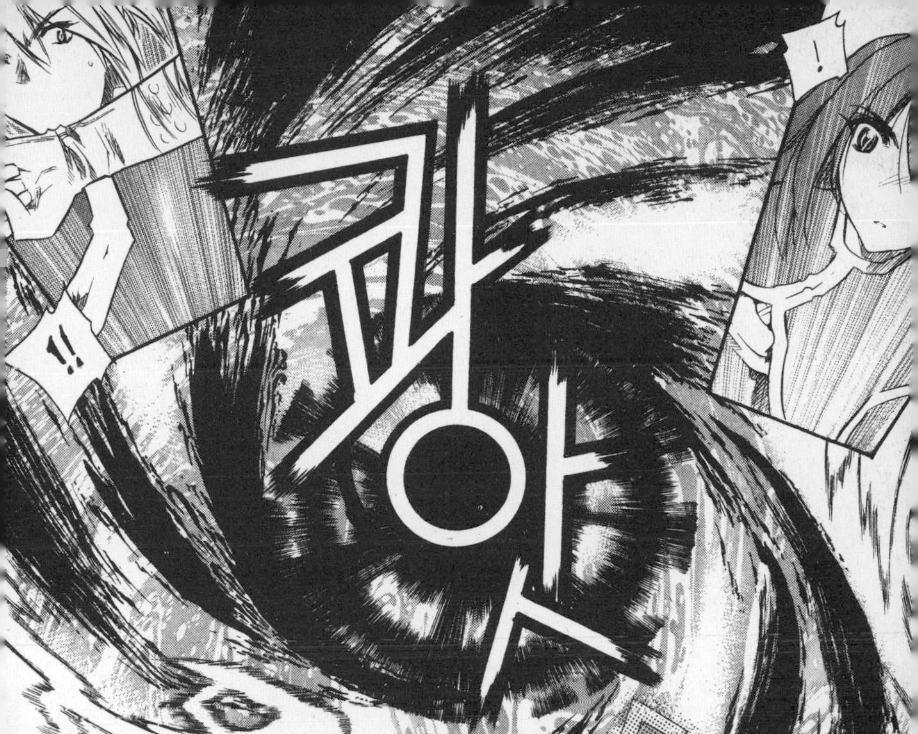
!!
콰앗
!
?!
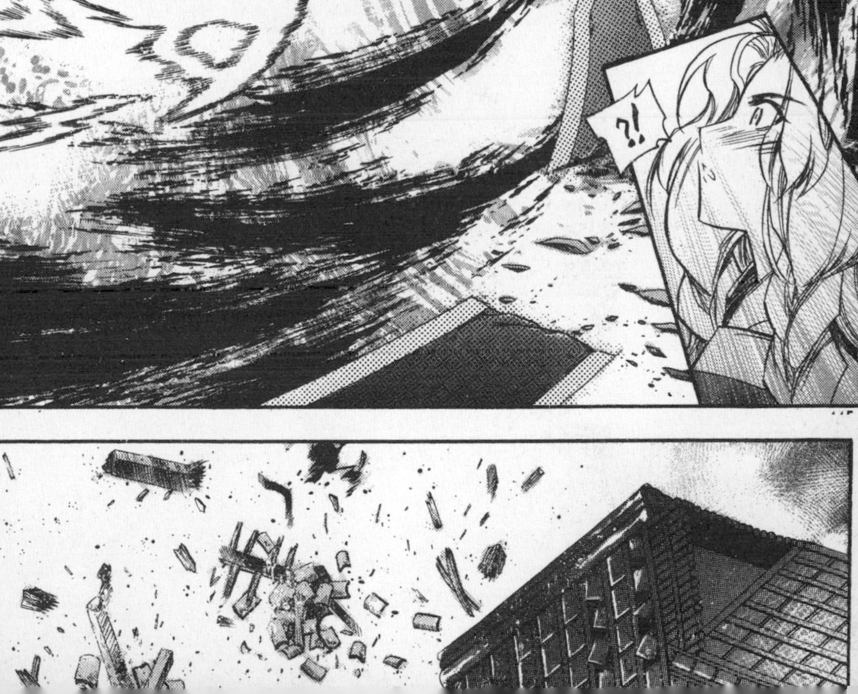

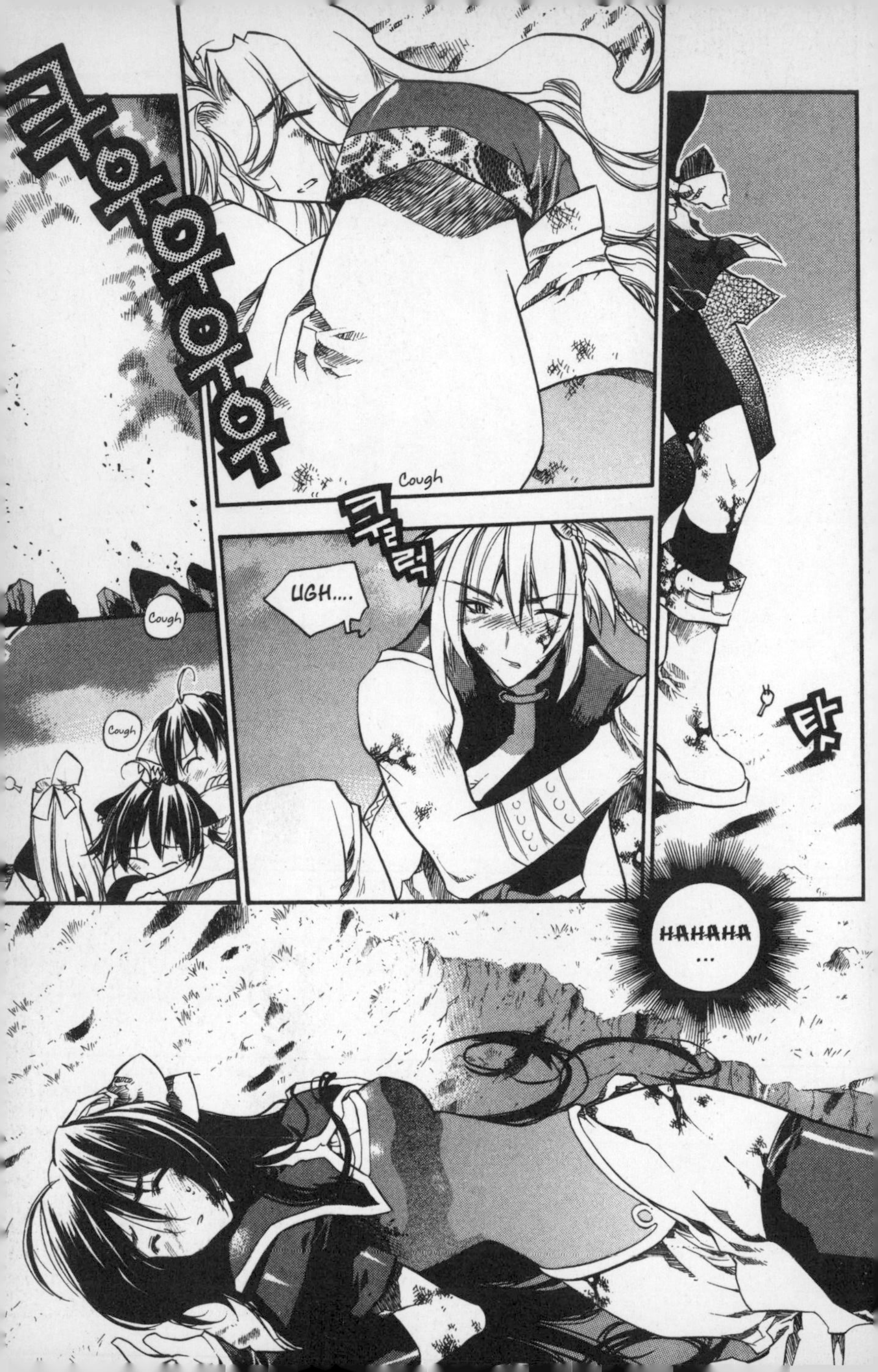
캬아아아아악
Cough
쿨럭
Cough
Cough
UGH....
탓
HAHAHA
...

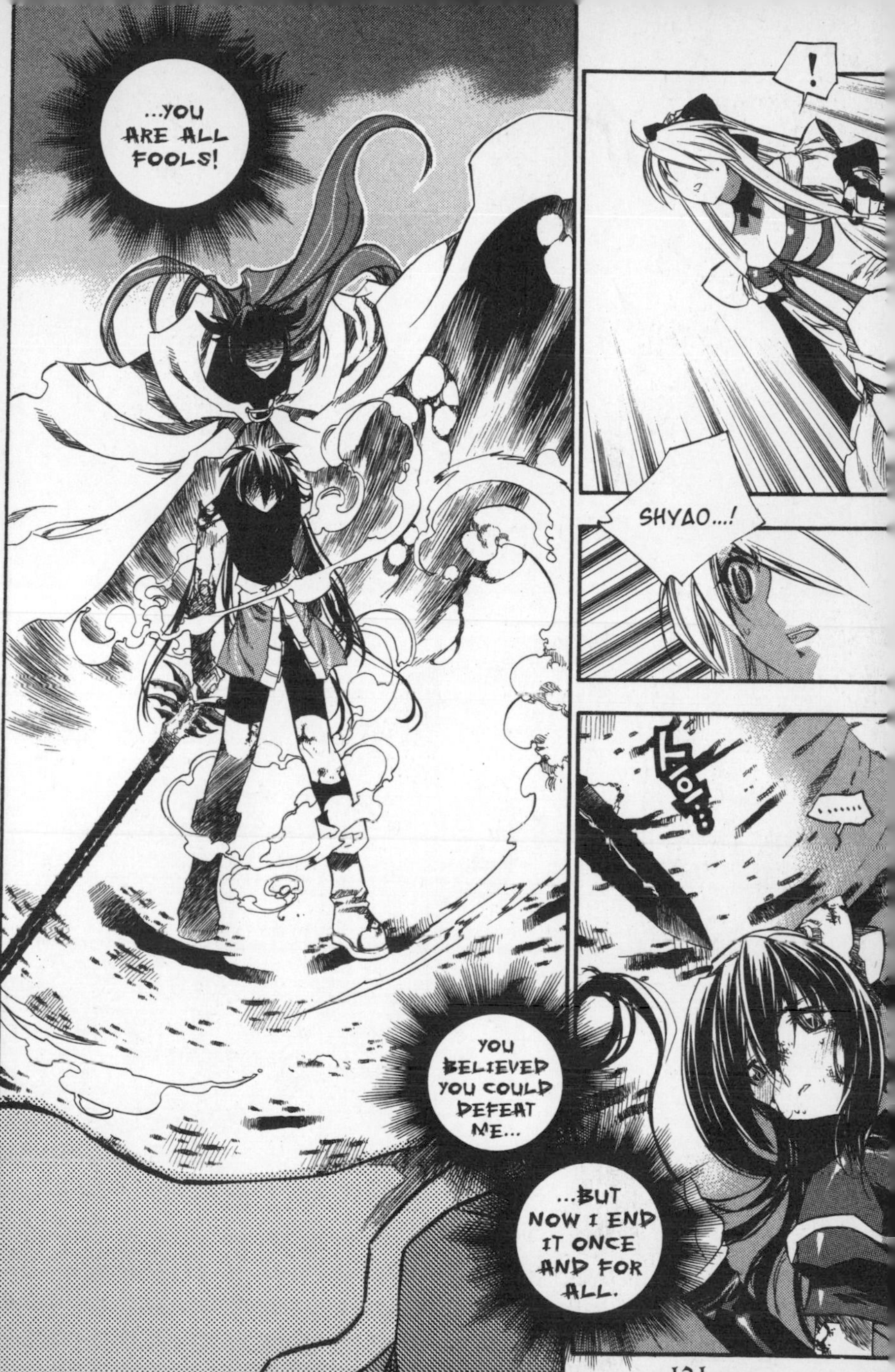
...YOU ARE ALL FOOLS!
YOU BELIEVED YOU COULD DEFEAT ME...
...BUT NOW I END IT ONCE AND FOR ALL.
!
SHYAO...!
......

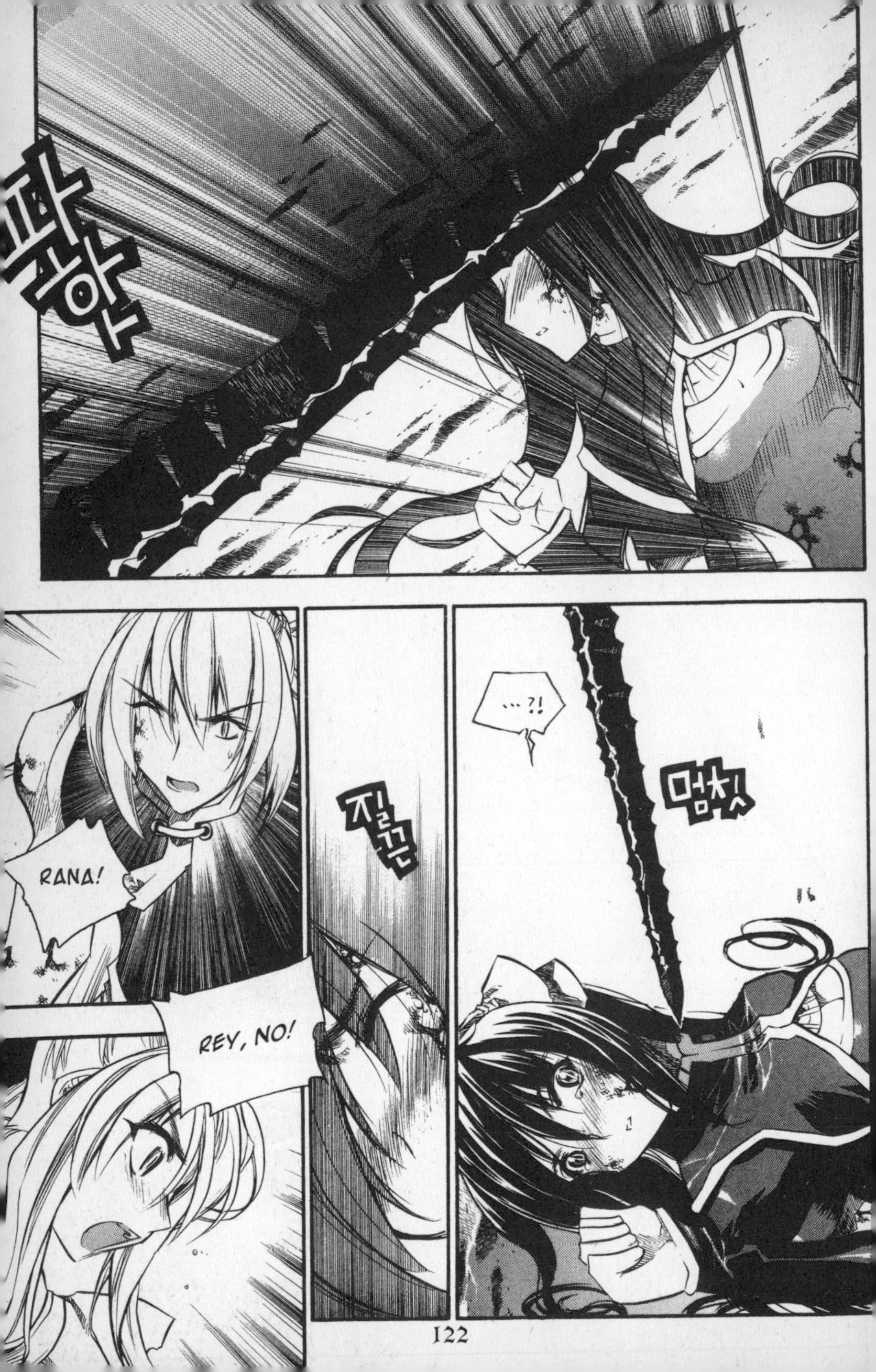

파앙
RANA!
REY, NO!
질끈
...?!
멈칫

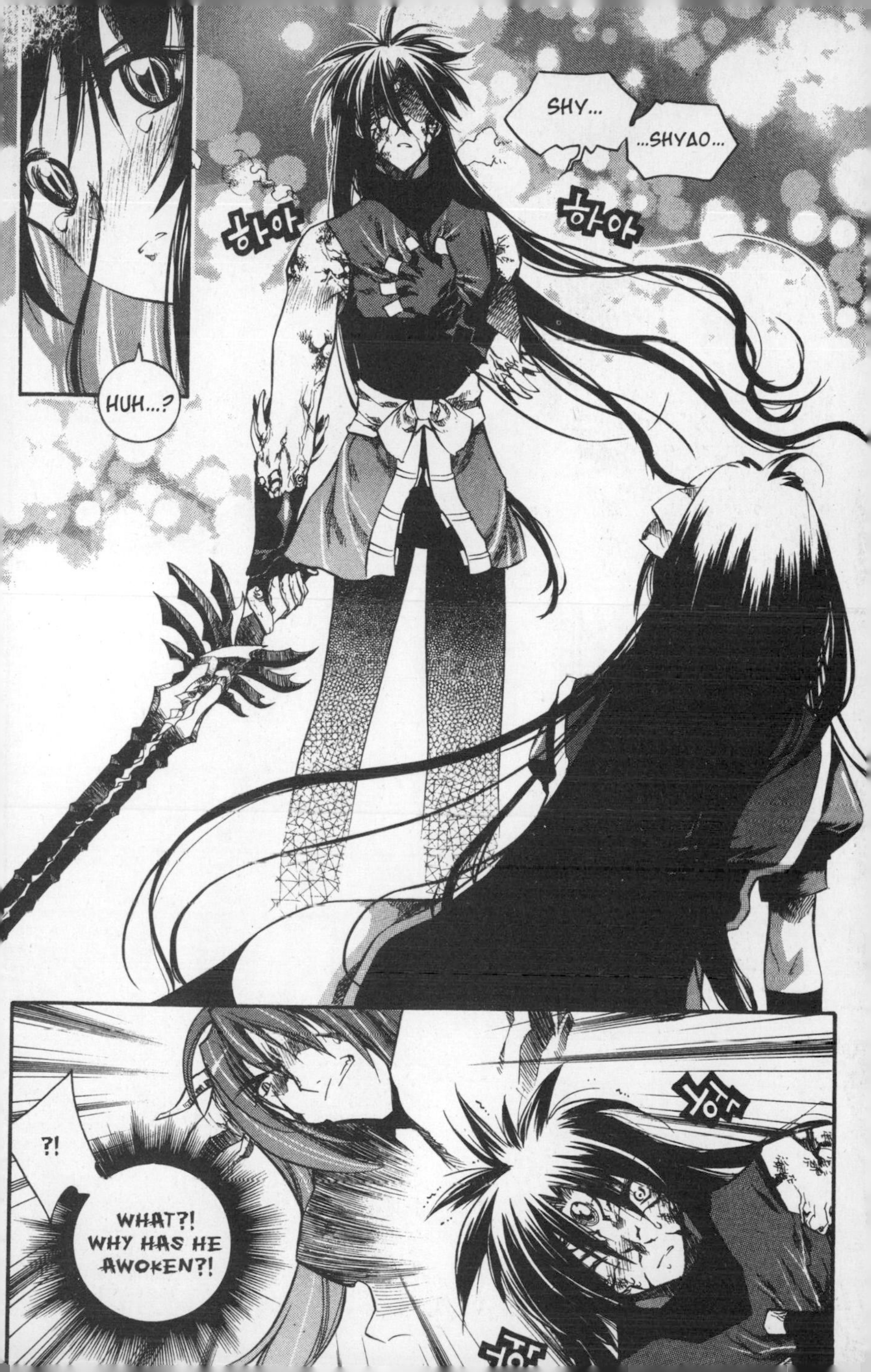
HUH...?
SHY...
...SHYAO...
하아
하아
?!
WHAT?! WHY HAS HE AWOKEN?!

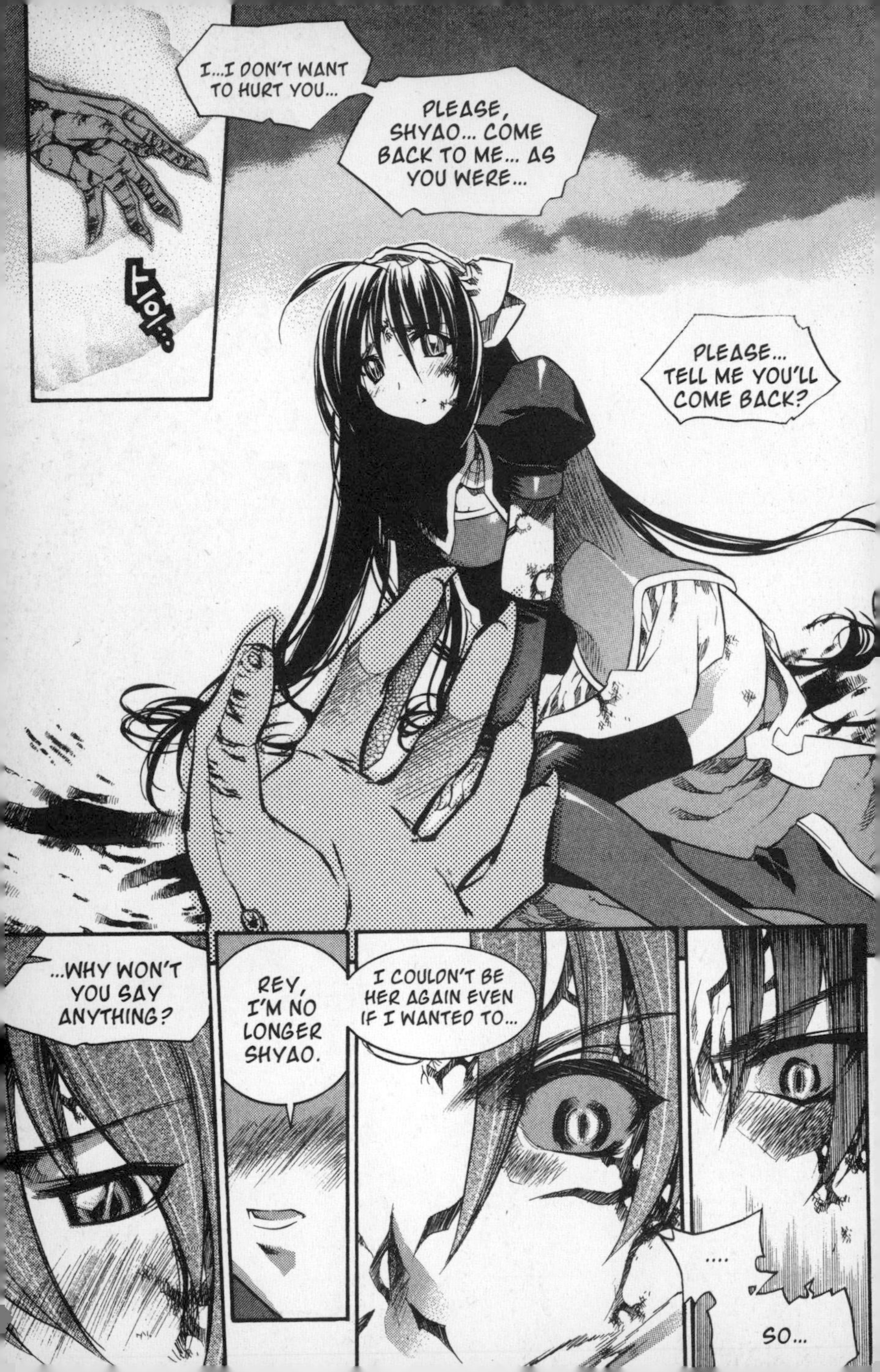
I...I DON'T WANT TO HURT YOU...
PLEASE, SHYAO... COME BACK TO ME... AS YOU WERE...
PLEASE... TELL ME YOU'LL COME BACK?
...WHY WON'T YOU SAY ANYTHING?
REY, I'M NO LONGER SHYAO.
I COULDN'T BE HER AGAIN EVEN IF I WANTED TO...
....
SO...

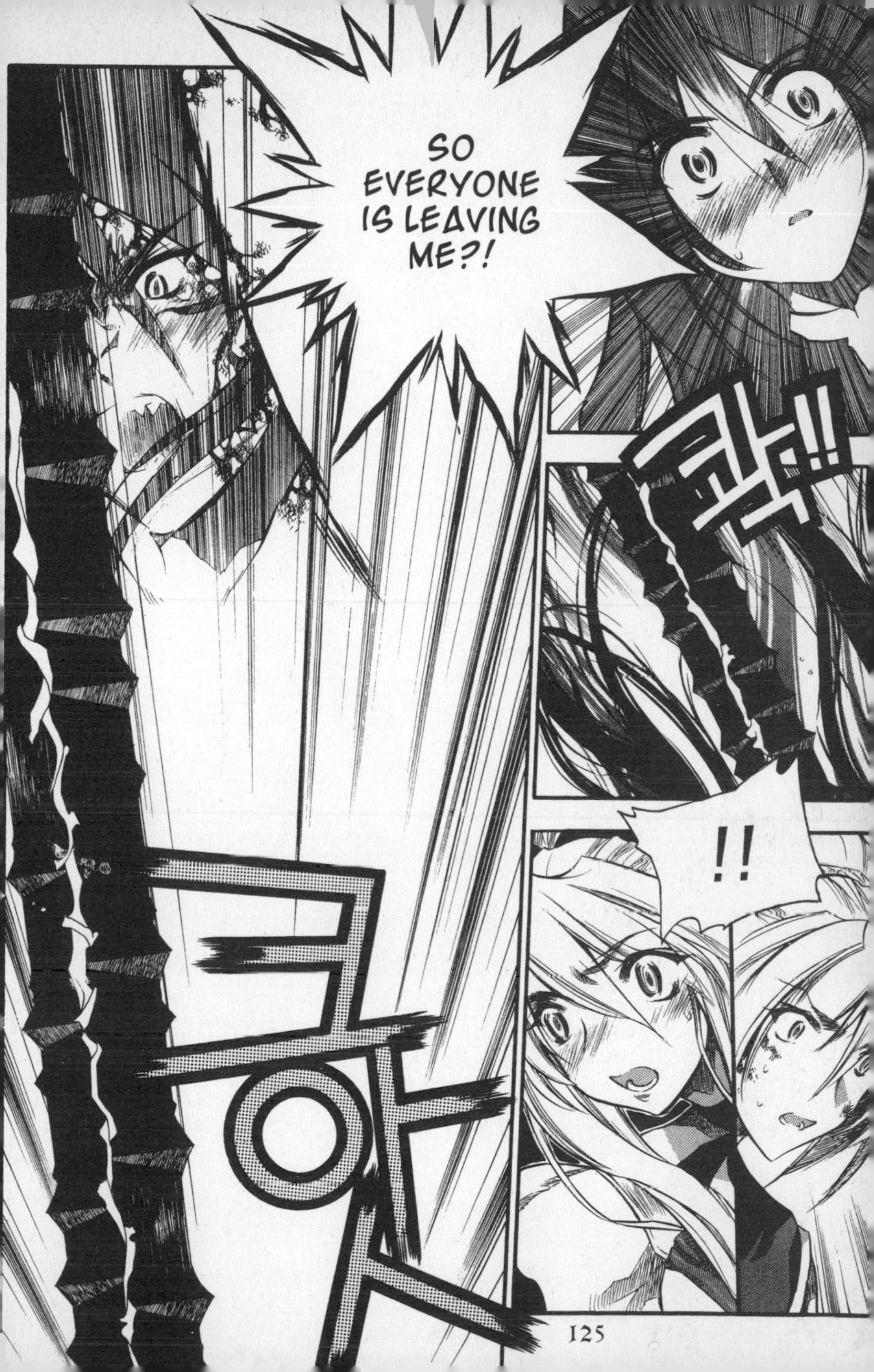
SO EVERYONE IS LEAVING ME?!
!!

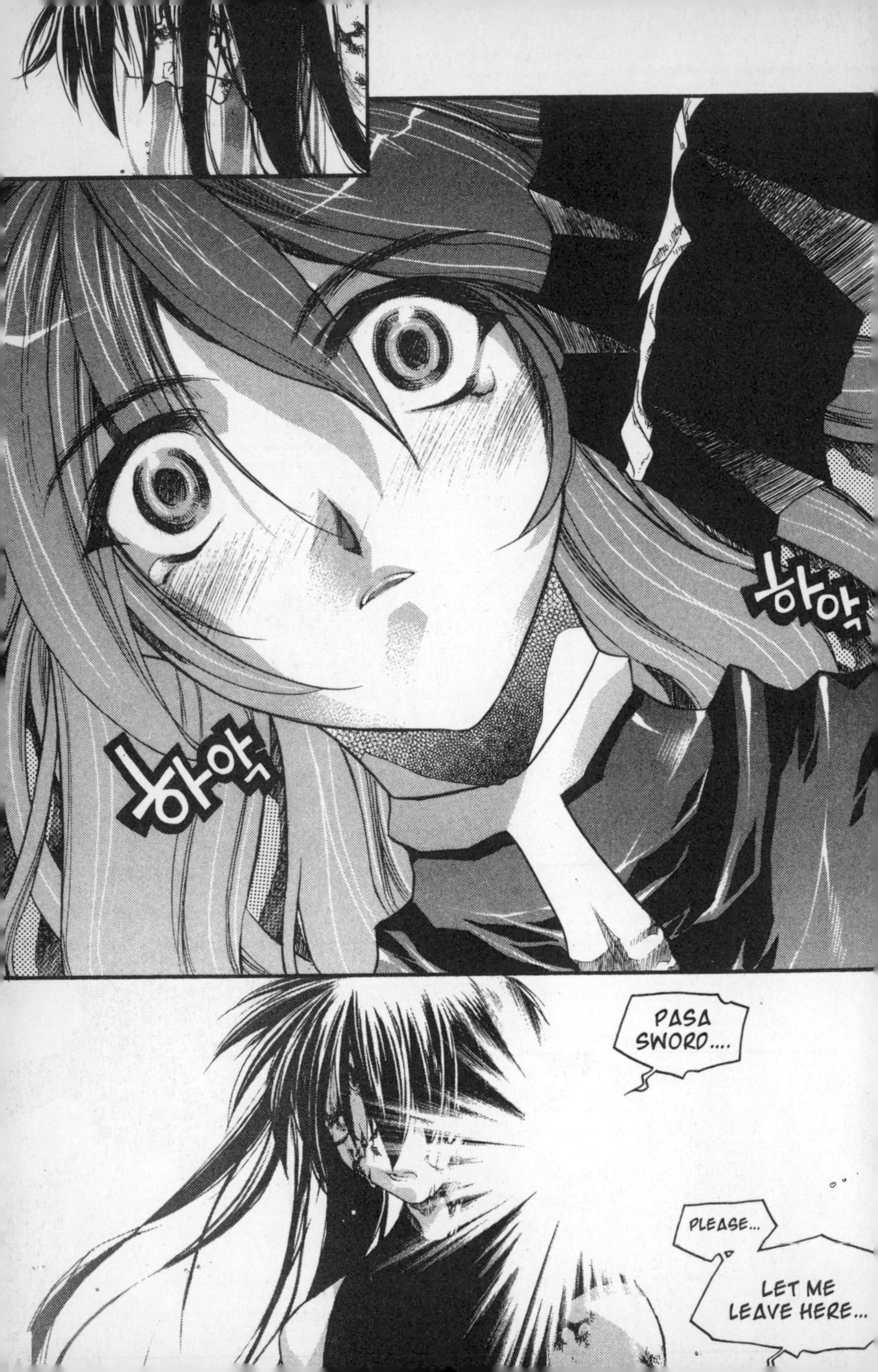
하악
하악
PASA SWORD....
PLEASE...
LET ME LEAVE HERE...

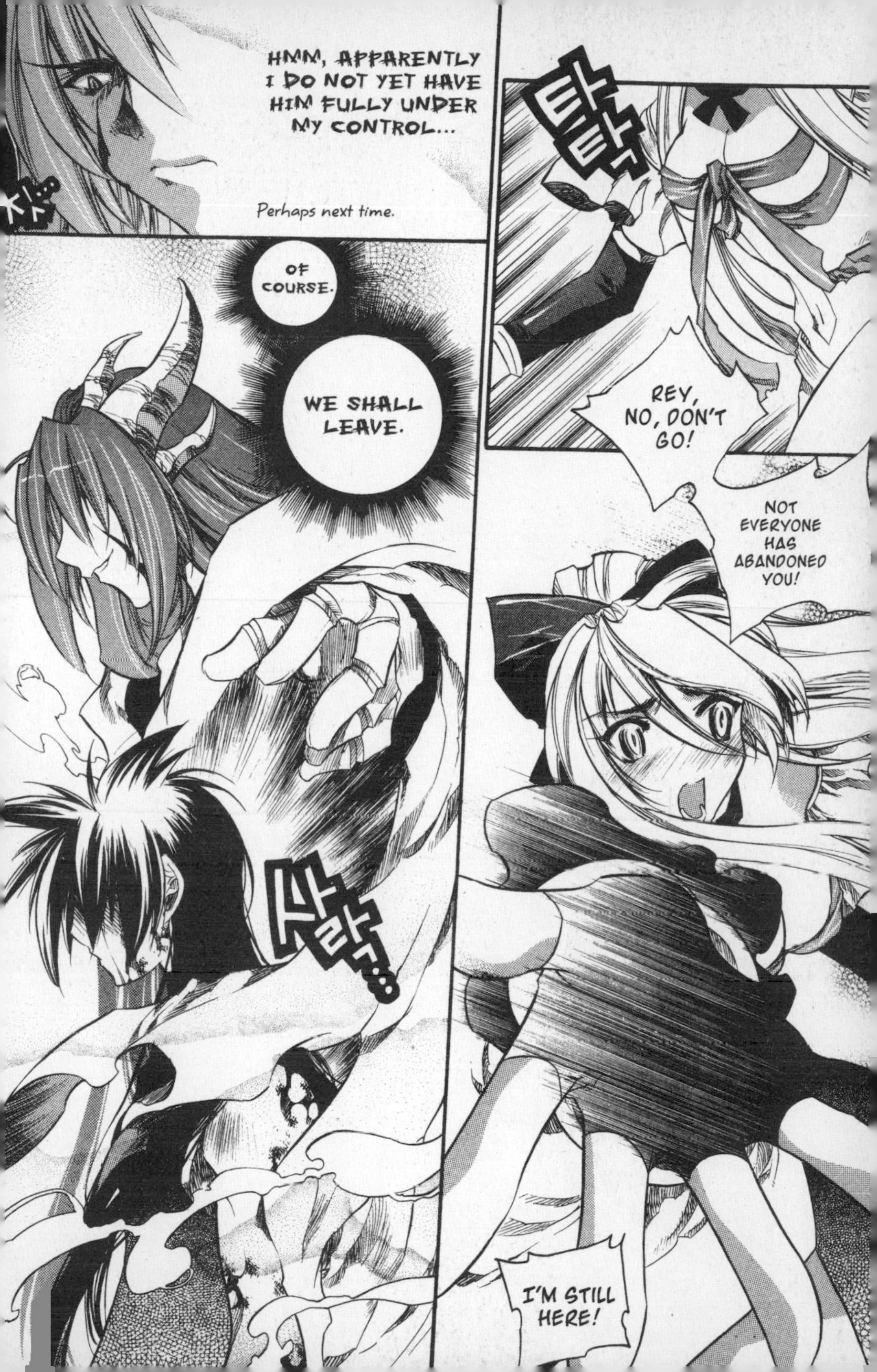
HMM, APPARENTLY I DO NOT YET HAVE HIM FULLY UNDER MY CONTROL...
Perhaps next time.
OF COURSE.
WE SHALL LEAVE.
REY, NO, DON'T GO!
NOT EVERYONE HAS ABANDONED YOU!
I'M STILL HERE!

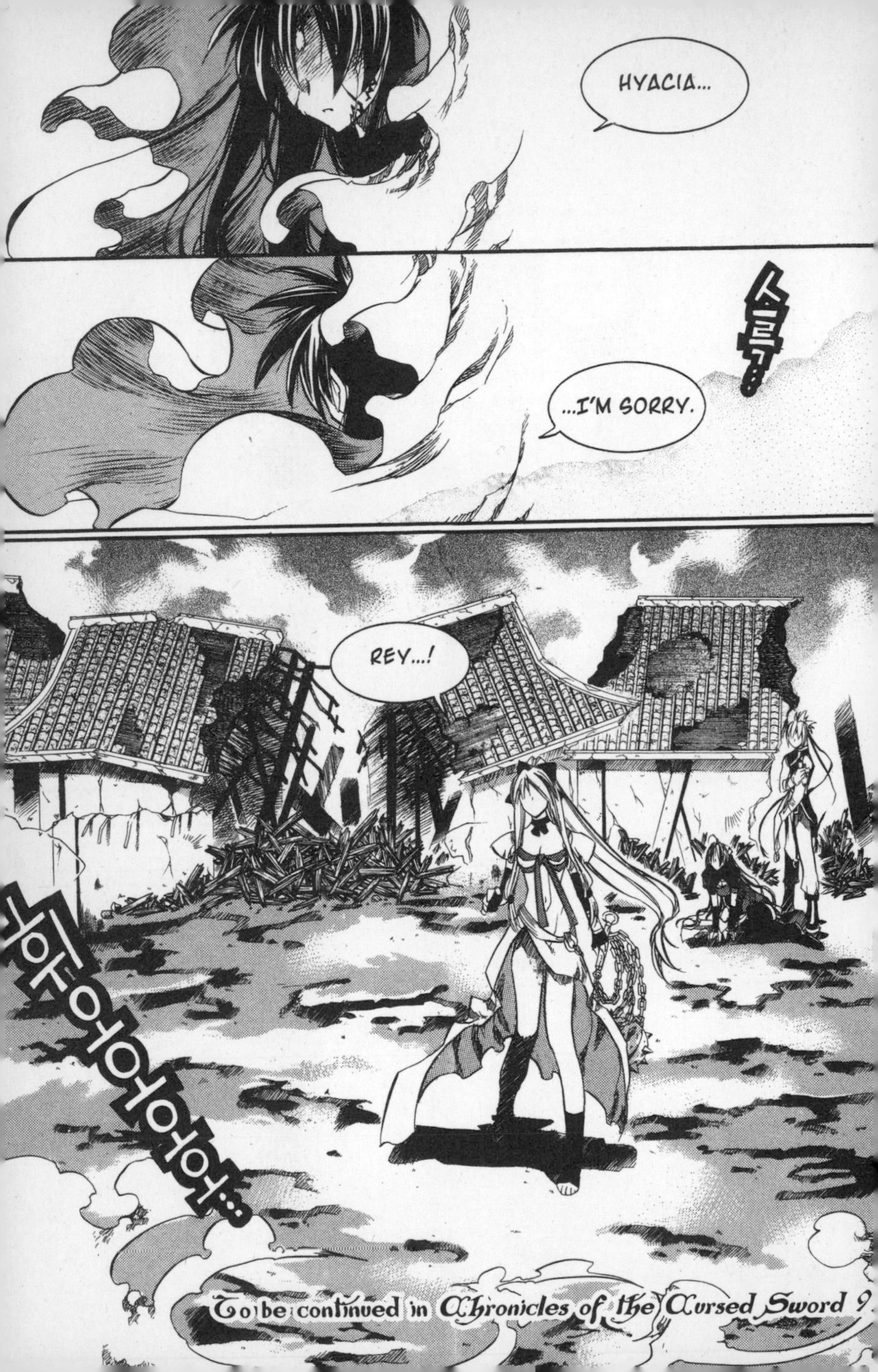
HYACIA...
...I'M SORRY.
REY...!
To be continued in Chronicles of the Cursed Sword 9

파검기 破劍記

RED MOON

赤月

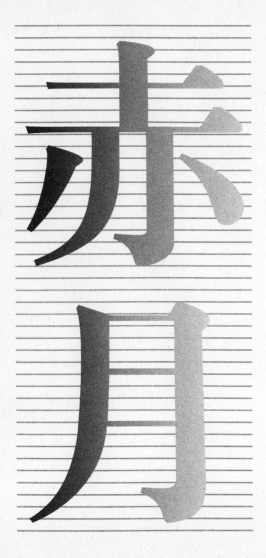

赤月

A Special Supplement:

INTRODUCING **Red Moon**, YEO BEOP-RYONG'S AND PARK HUI-JIN'S AWARD-WINNING ENTRY IN THE 16TH ANNUAL CHAMP COMIC BOOK COMPETITION...

STORY BY
YEO BEOP-RYONG
ART BY
PARK HUI-JIN

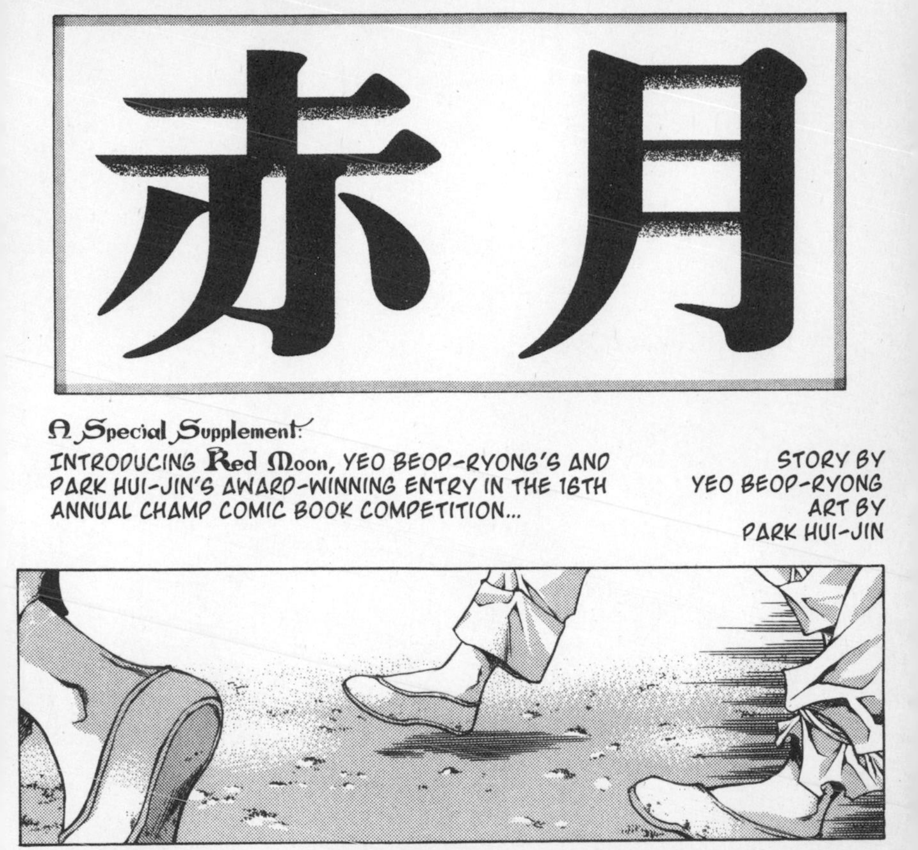

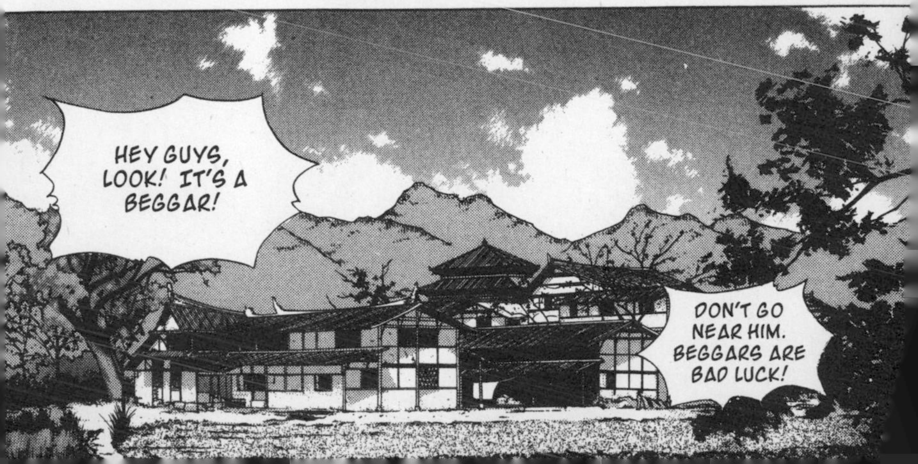
HEY GUYS, LOOK! IT'S A BEGGAR!
DON'T GO NEAR HIM. BEGGARS ARE BAD LUCK!

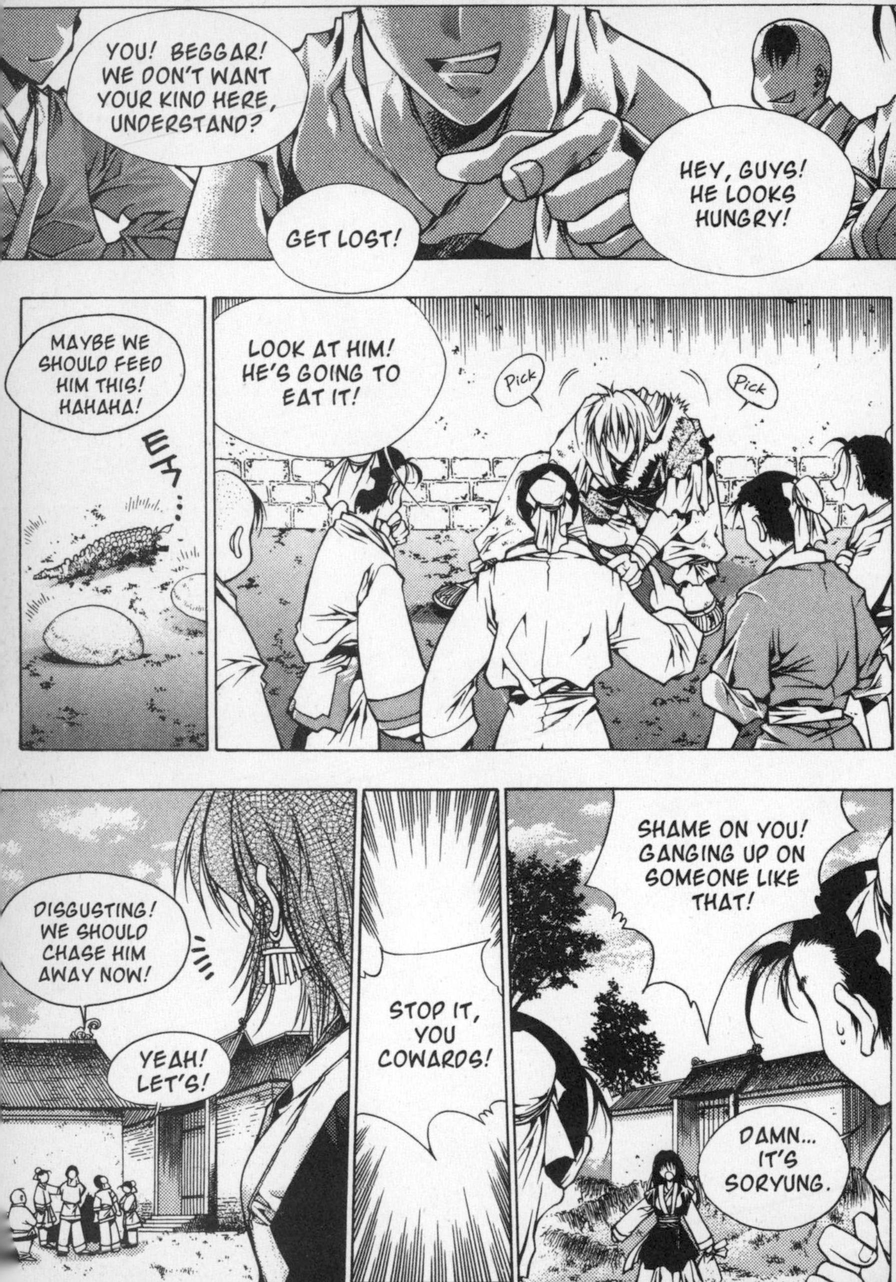
YOU! BEGGAR! WE DON'T WANT YOUR KIND HERE, UNDERSTAND?
GET LOST!
HEY, GUYS! HE LOOKS HUNGRY!
MAYBE WE SHOULD FEED HIM THIS! HAHAHA!
LOOK AT HIM! HE'S GOING TO EAT IT!
Pick
Pick
DISGUSTING! WE SHOULD CHASE HIM AWAY NOW!
YEAH! LET'S!
STOP IT, YOU COWARDS!
SHAME ON YOU! GANGING UP ON SOMEONE LIKE THAT!
DAMN... IT'S SORYUNG.

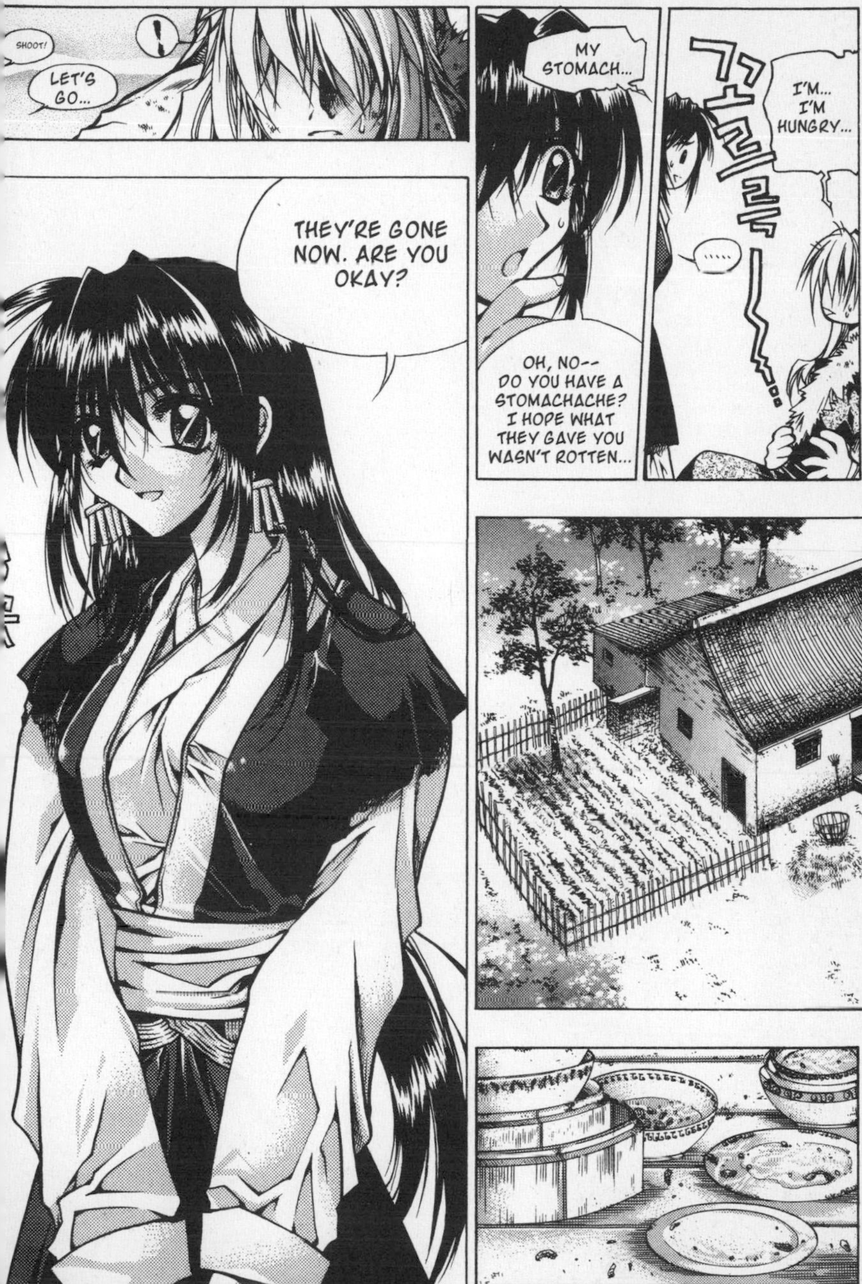
SHOOT!
!
LET'S GO...
THEY'RE GONE NOW. ARE YOU OKAY?
MY STOMACH...
OH, NO-- DO YOU HAVE A STOMACHACHE? I HOPE WHAT THEY GAVE YOU WASN'T ROTTEN...
I'M... I'M HUNGRY...
......

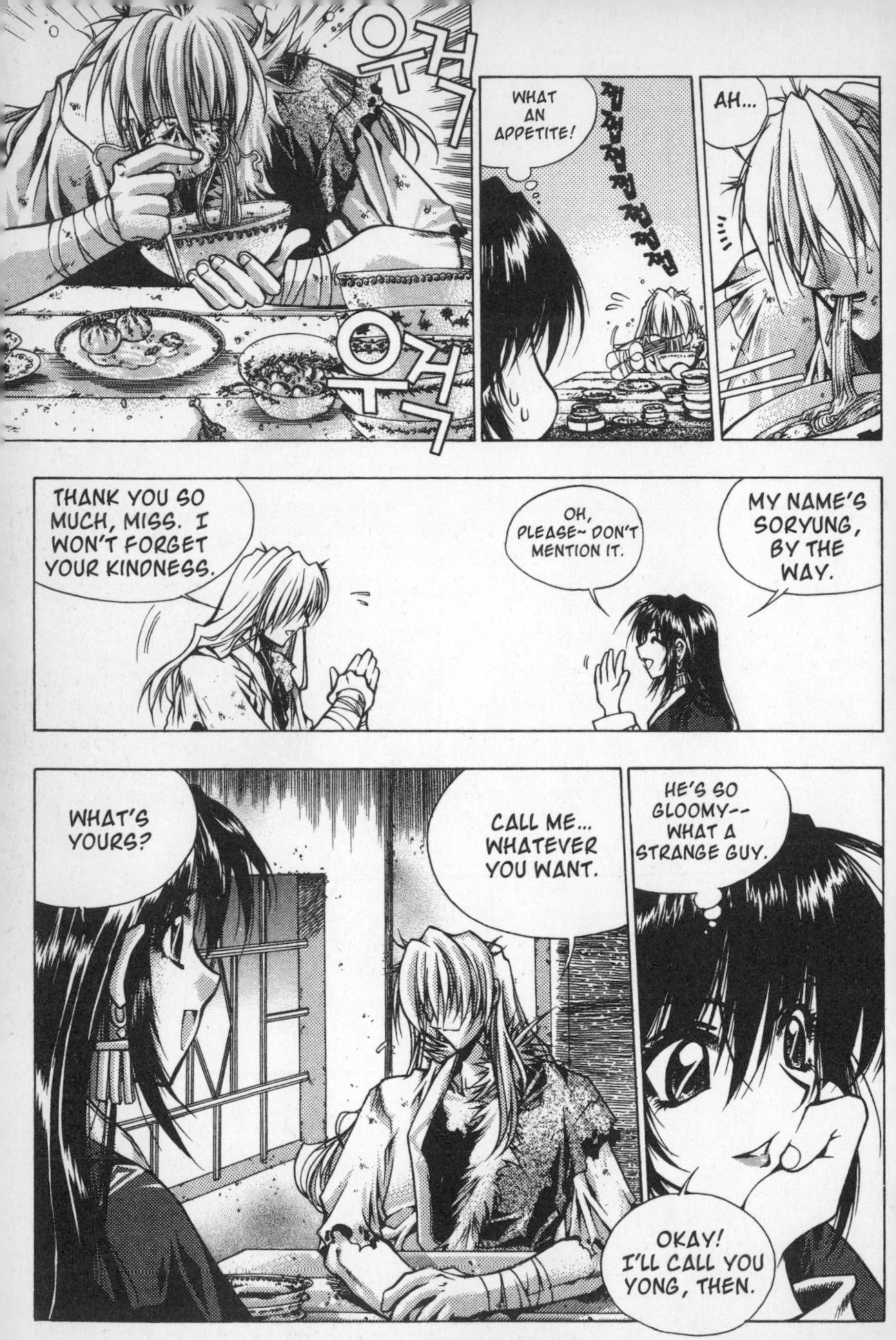
우걱
우걱
WHAT AN APPETITE!
AH...
THANK YOU SO MUCH, MISS. I WON'T FORGET YOUR KINDNESS.
OH, PLEASE~ DON'T MENTION IT.
MY NAME'S SORYUNG, BY THE WAY.
WHAT'S YOURS?
CALL ME... WHATEVER YOU WANT.
HE'S SO GLOOMY-- WHAT A STRANGE GUY.
OKAY! I'LL CALL YOU YONG, THEN.

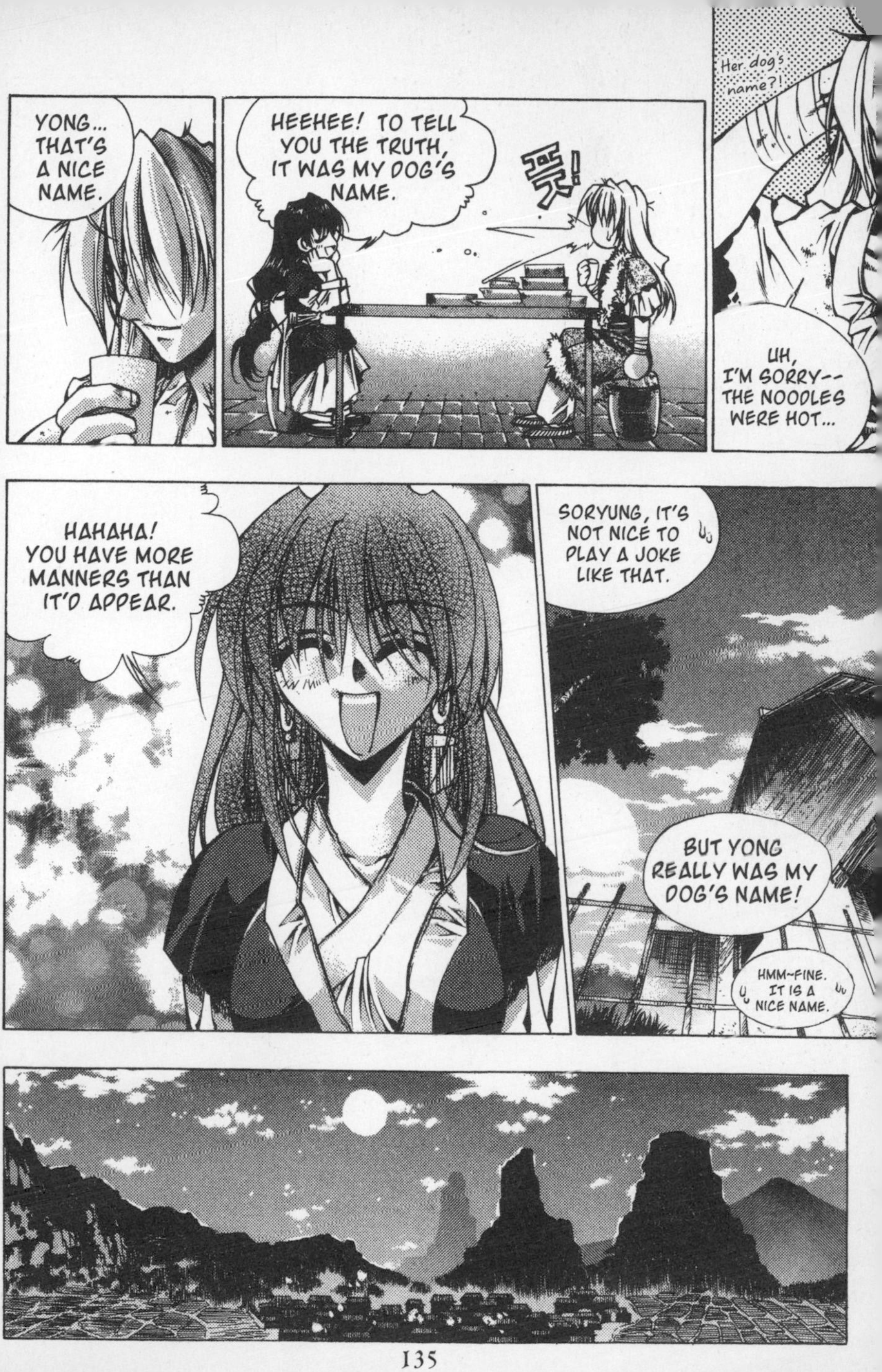
YONG... THAT'S A NICE NAME.
HEEHEE! TO TELL YOU THE TRUTH, IT WAS MY DOG'S NAME.
!
Her dog's name?!
UH, I'M SORRY-- THE NOODLES WERE HOT...
HAHAHA! YOU HAVE MORE MANNERS THAN IT'D APPEAR.
SORYUNG, IT'S NOT NICE TO PLAY A JOKE LIKE THAT.
BUT YONG REALLY WAS MY DOG'S NAME!
HMM~FINE. IT IS A NICE NAME.

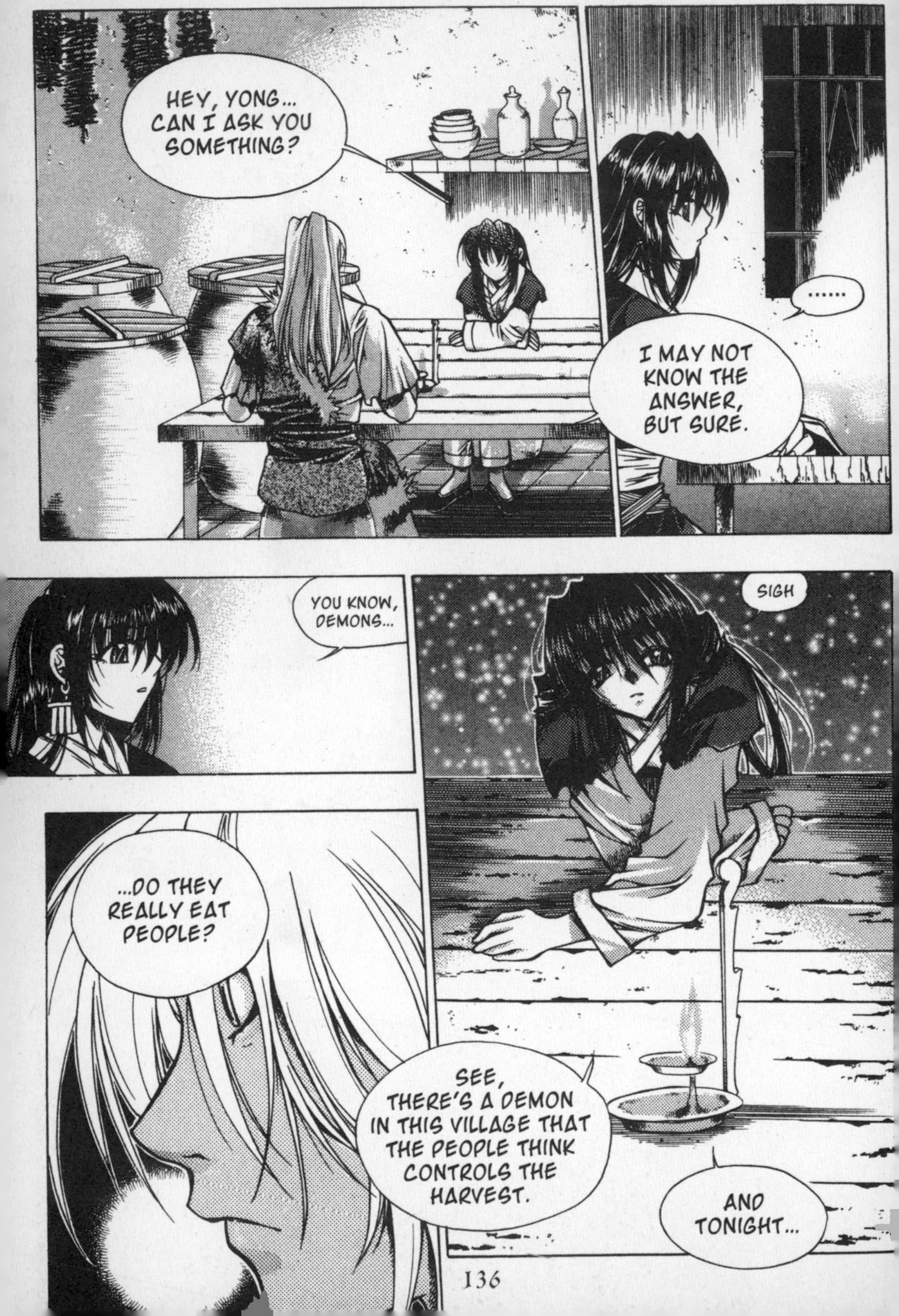
HEY, YONG... CAN I ASK YOU SOMETHING?
......
I MAY NOT KNOW THE ANSWER, BUT SURE.
YOU KNOW, DEMONS...
SIGH
...DO THEY REALLY EAT PEOPLE?
SEE, THERE'S A DEMON IN THIS VILLAGE THAT THE PEOPLE THINK CONTROLS THE HARVEST.
AND TONIGHT...

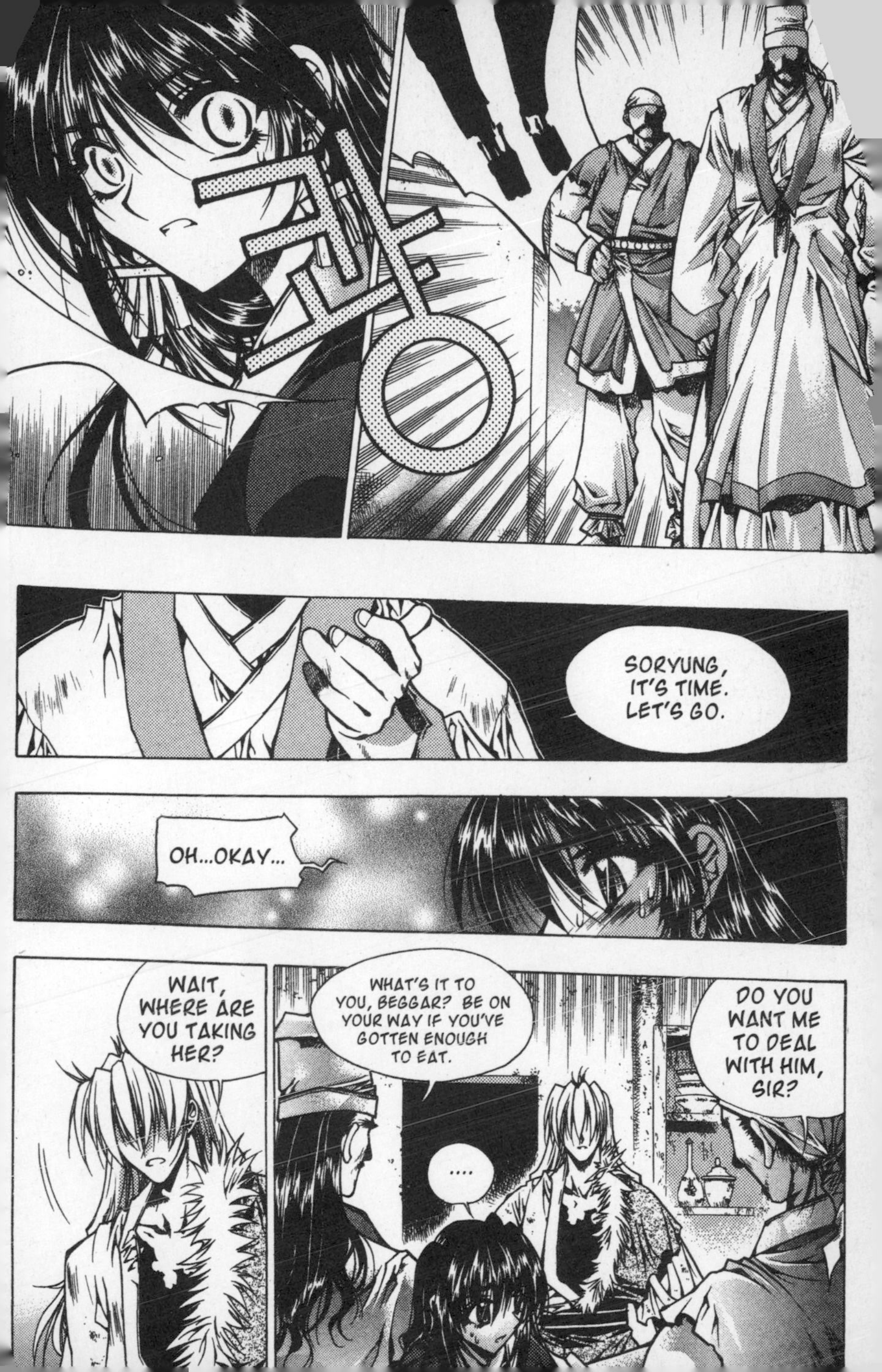
쾅
SORYUNG, IT'S TIME. LET'S GO.
OH...OKAY...
WAIT, WHERE ARE YOU TAKING HER?
WHAT'S IT TO YOU, BEGGAR? BE ON YOUR WAY IF YOU'VE GOTTEN ENOUGH TO EAT.
....
DO YOU WANT ME TO DEAL WITH HIM, SIR?

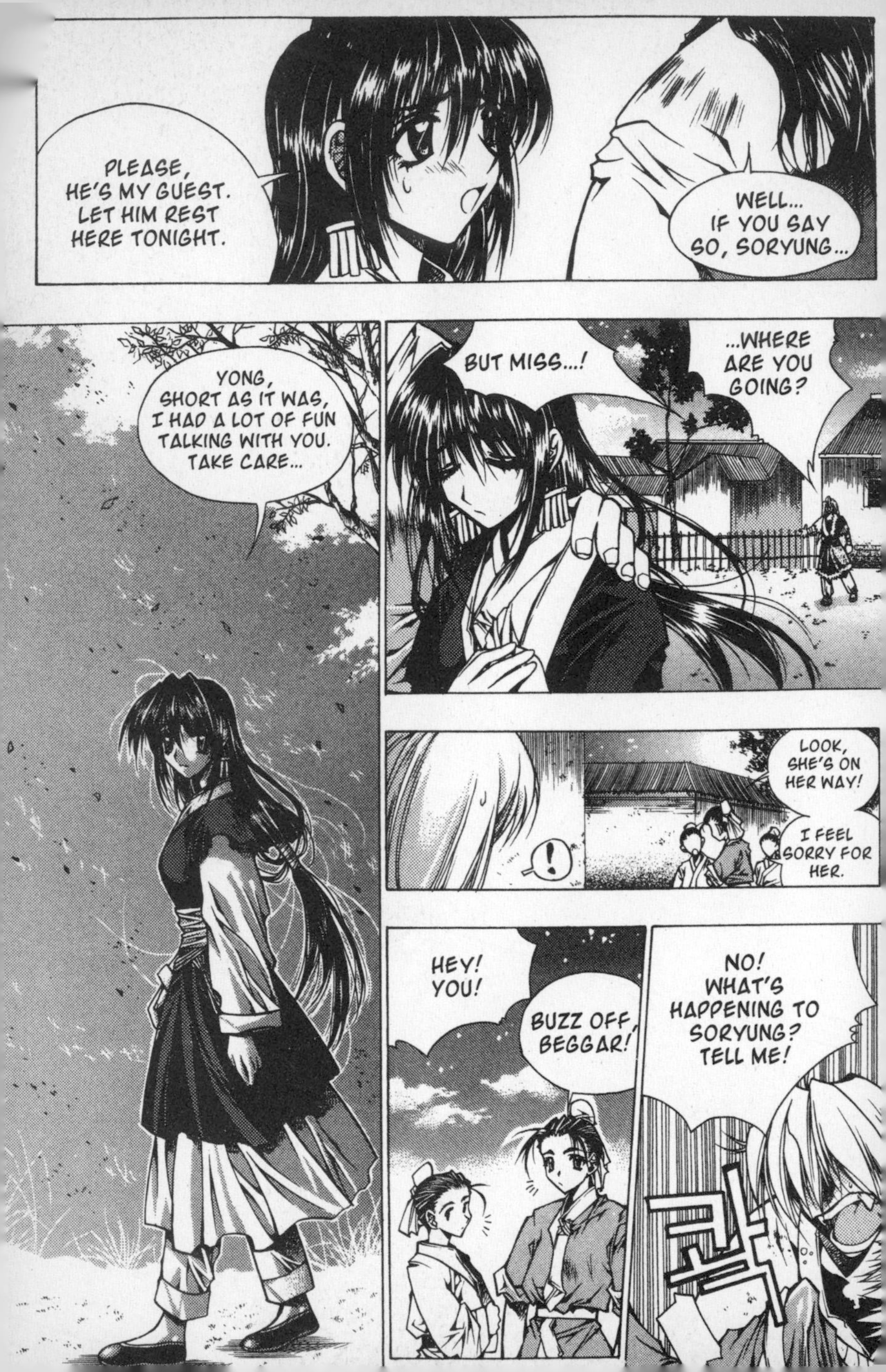
PLEASE, HE'S MY GUEST. LET HIM REST HERE TONIGHT.
WELL... IF YOU SAY SO, SORYUNG...
YONG, SHORT AS IT WAS, I HAD A LOT OF FUN TALKING WITH YOU. TAKE CARE...
BUT MISS...!
...WHERE ARE YOU GOING?
!
LOOK, SHE'S ON HER WAY!
I FEEL SORRY FOR HER.
HEY! YOU!
BUZZ OFF BEGGAR!
NO! WHAT'S HAPPENING TO SORYUNG? TELL ME!
꽉

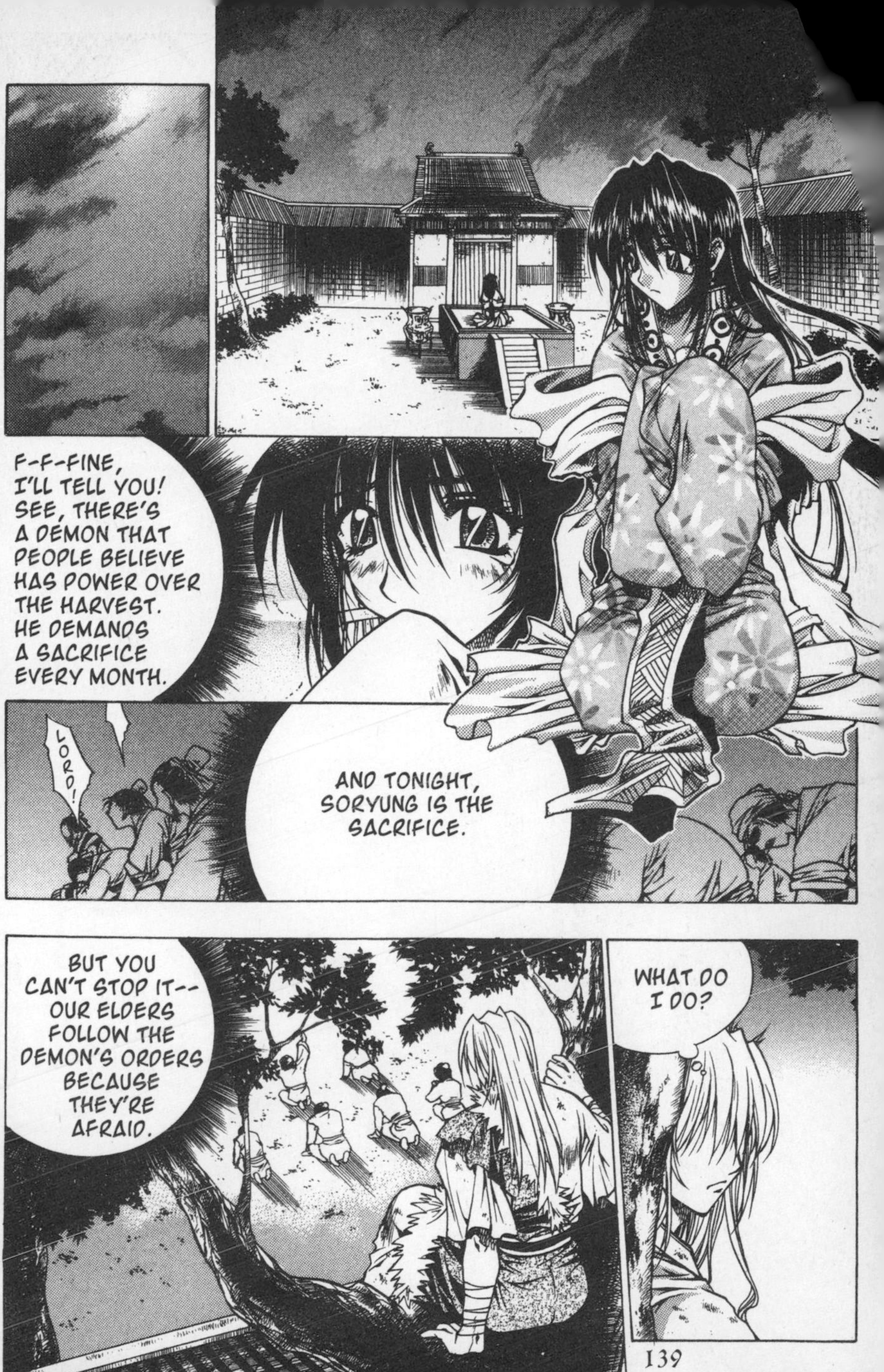
F-F-FINE, I'LL TELL YOU! SEE, THERE'S A DEMON THAT PEOPLE BELIEVE HAS POWER OVER THE HARVEST. HE DEMANDS A SACRIFICE EVERY MONTH.
LORD!
AND TONIGHT, SORYUNG IS THE SACRIFICE.
BUT YOU CAN'T STOP IT-- OUR ELDERS FOLLOW THE DEMON'S ORDERS BECAUSE THEY'RE AFRAID.
WHAT DO I DO?

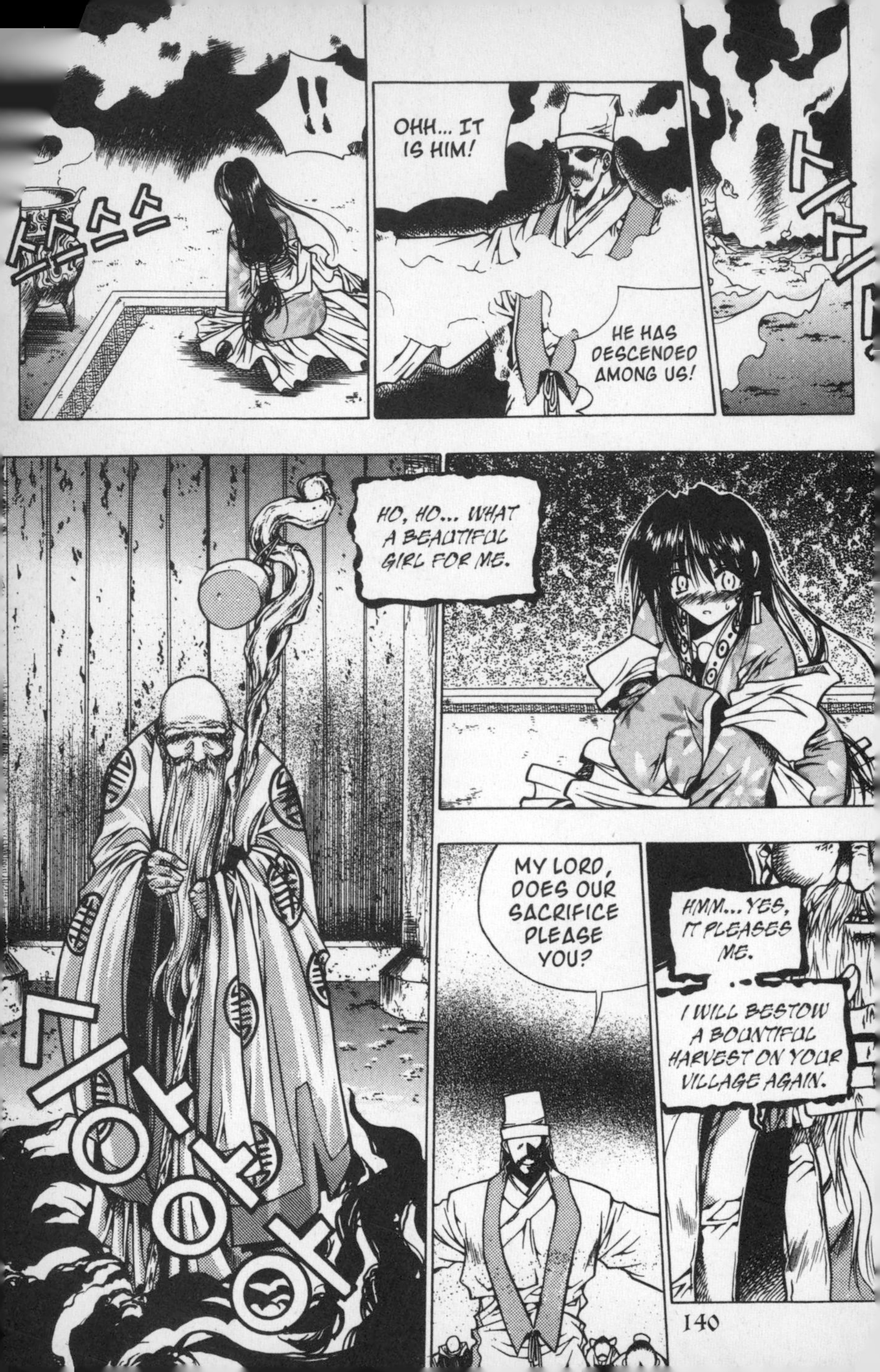
!!
OHH... IT IS HIM!
HE HAS DESCENDED AMONG US!
HO, HO... WHAT A BEAUTIFUL GIRL FOR ME.
MY LORD, DOES OUR SACRIFICE PLEASE YOU?
HMM... YES, IT PLEASES ME.
I WILL BESTOW A BOUNTIFUL HARVEST ON YOUR VILLAGE AGAIN.

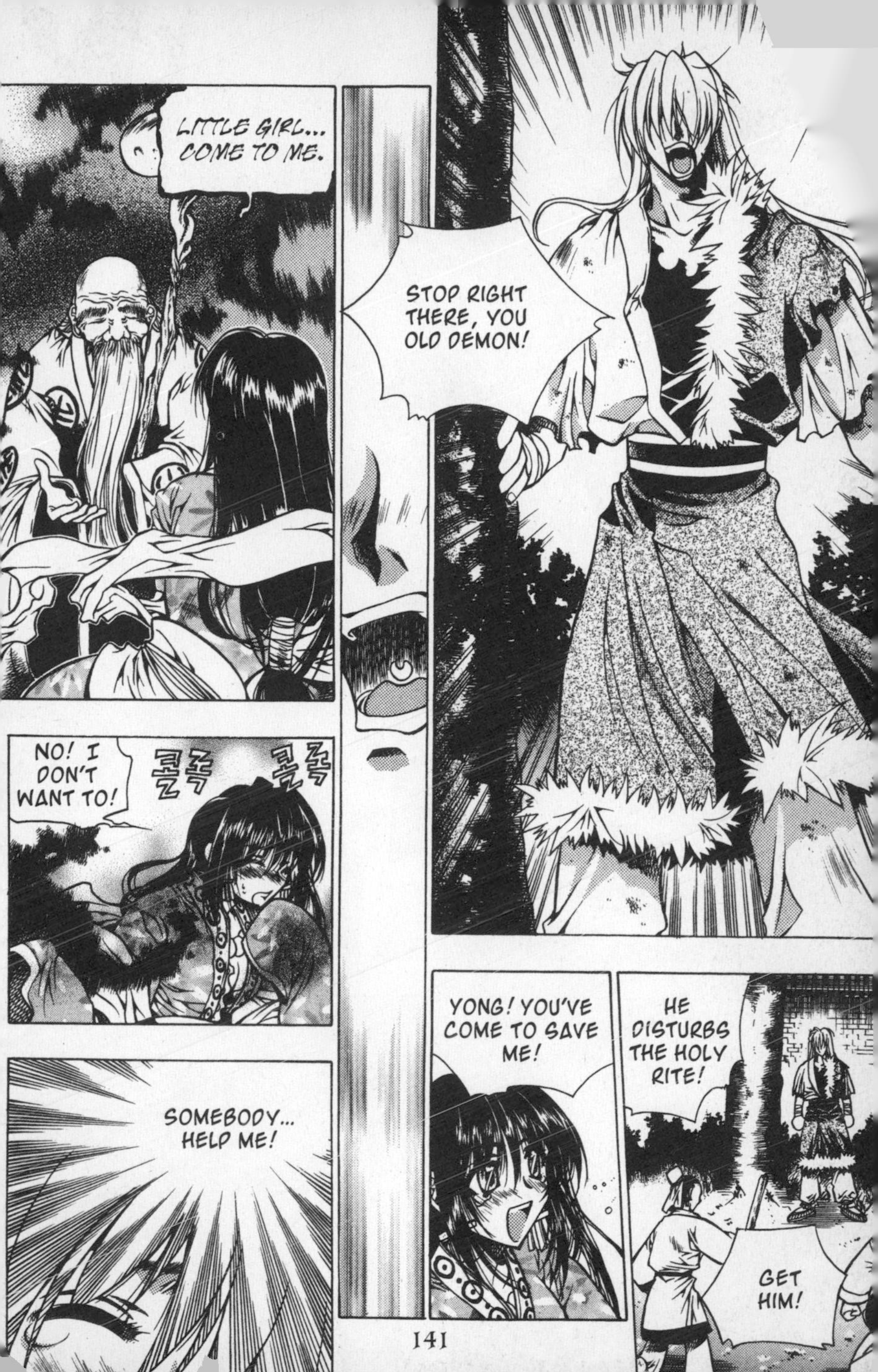
LITTLE GIRL... COME TO ME.
NO! I DON'T WANT TO!
SOMEBODY... HELP ME!
STOP RIGHT THERE, YOU OLD DEMON!
YONG! YOU'VE COME TO SAVE ME!
HE DISTURBS THE HOLY RITE!
GET HIM!

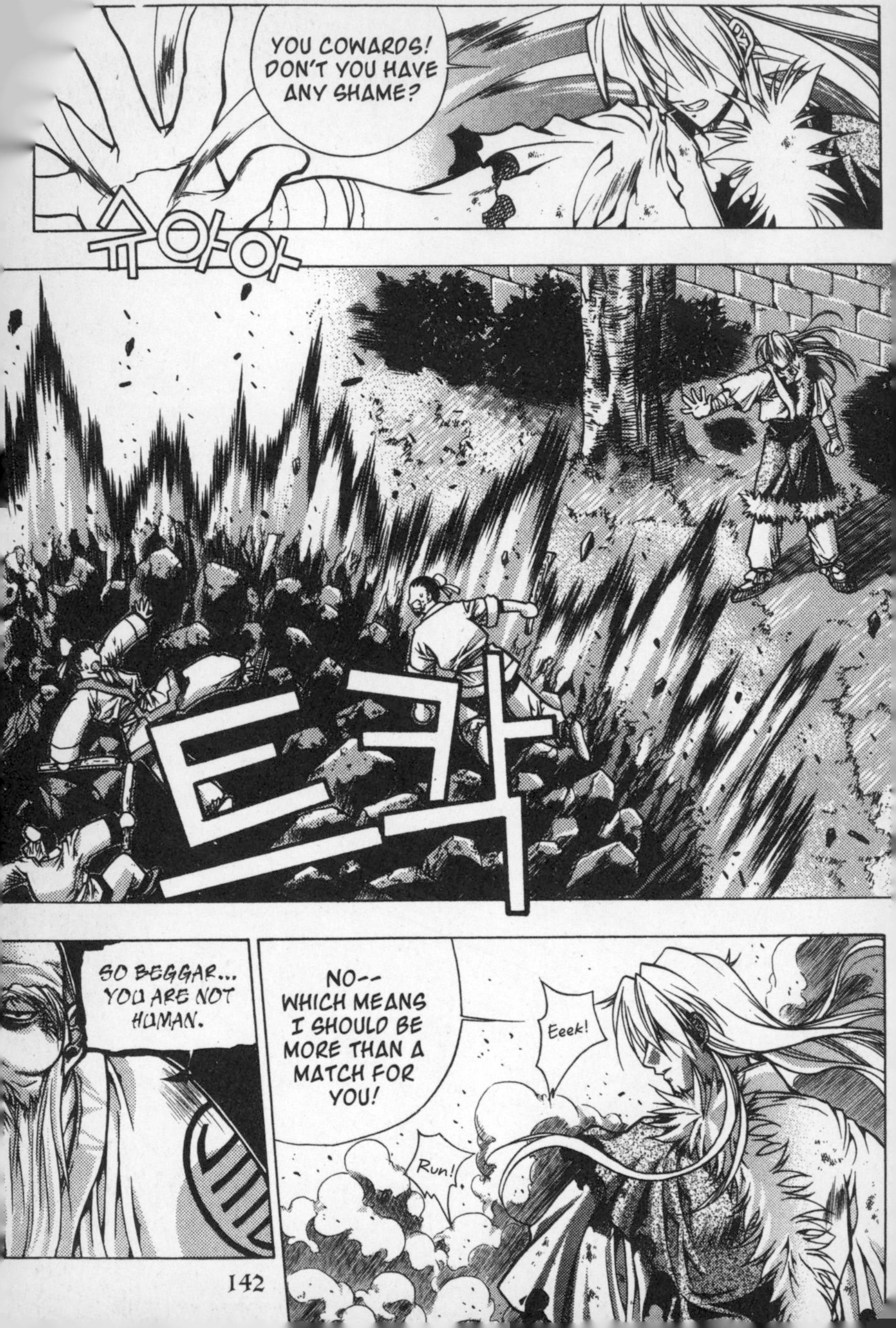
YOU COWARDS! DON'T YOU HAVE ANY SHAME?
SO BEGGAR... YOU ARE NOT HUMAN.
NO-- WHICH MEANS I SHOULD BE MORE THAN A MATCH FOR YOU!
Eeek!
Run!

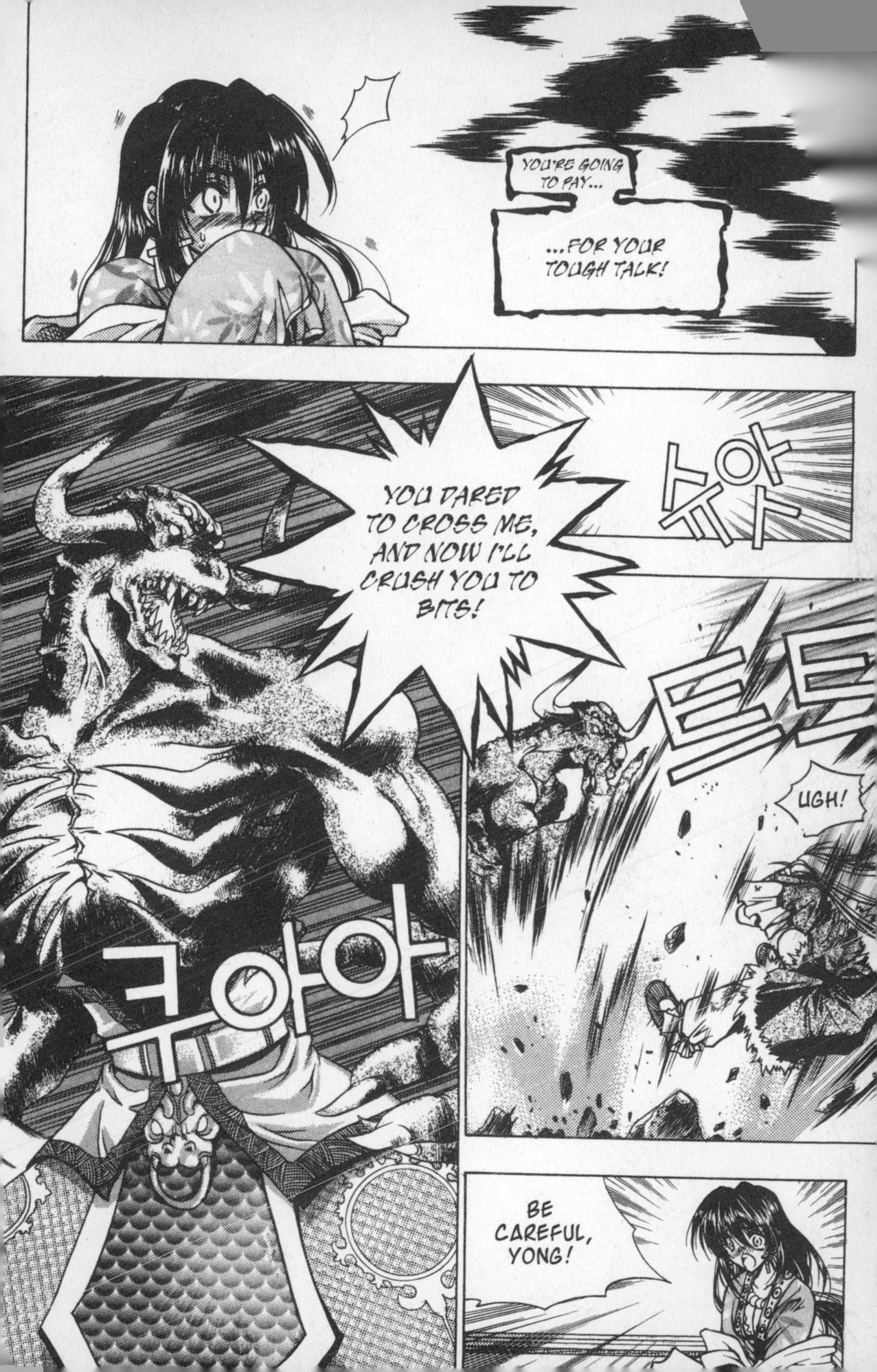
YOU'RE GOING TO PAY...
...FOR YOUR TOUGH TALK!
YOU DARED TO CROSS ME, AND NOW I'LL CRUSH YOU TO BITS!
크아아
UGH!
BE CAREFUL, YONG!

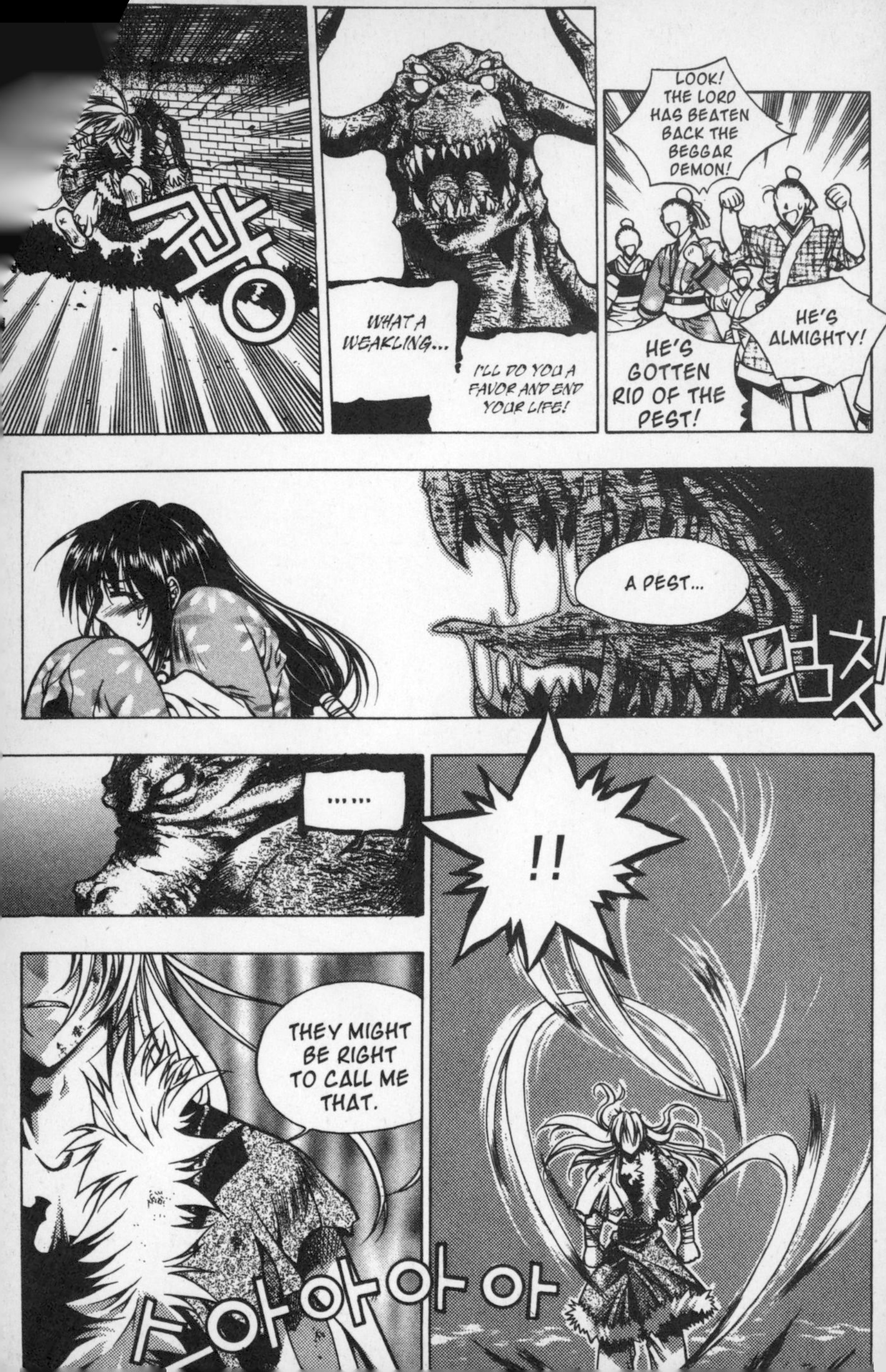
쾅
WHAT A WEAKLING...
I'LL DO YOU A FAVOR AND END YOUR LIFE!
LOOK! THE LORD HAS BEATEN BACK THE BEGGAR DEMON!
HE'S GOTTEN RID OF THE PEST!
HE'S ALMIGHTY!
A PEST...
멈칫!
......
!!
THEY MIGHT BE RIGHT TO CALL ME THAT.

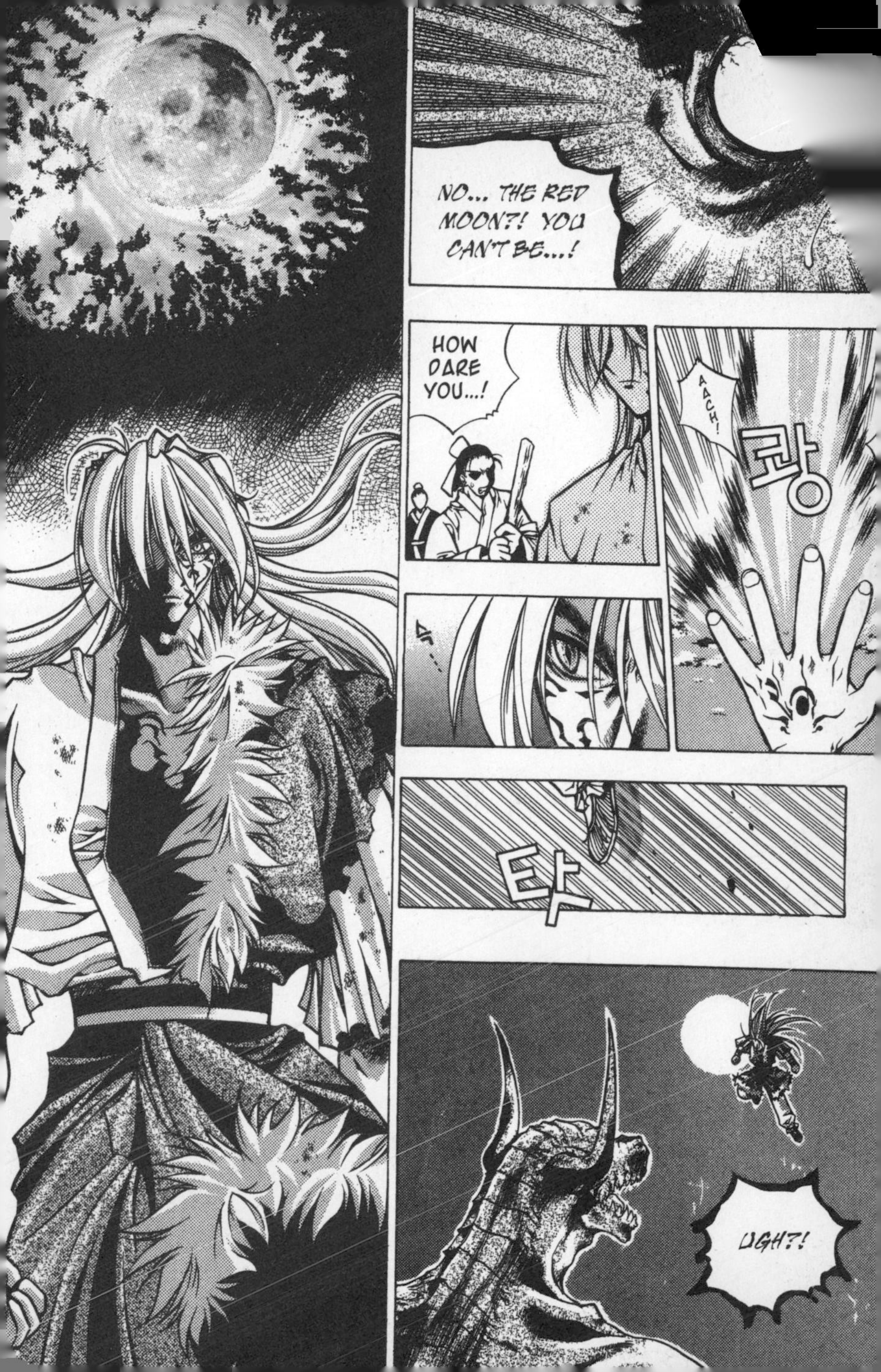
NO... THE RED MOON?! YOU CAN'T BE...!
HOW DARE YOU...!
AACH!
쾅
탁
UGH?!

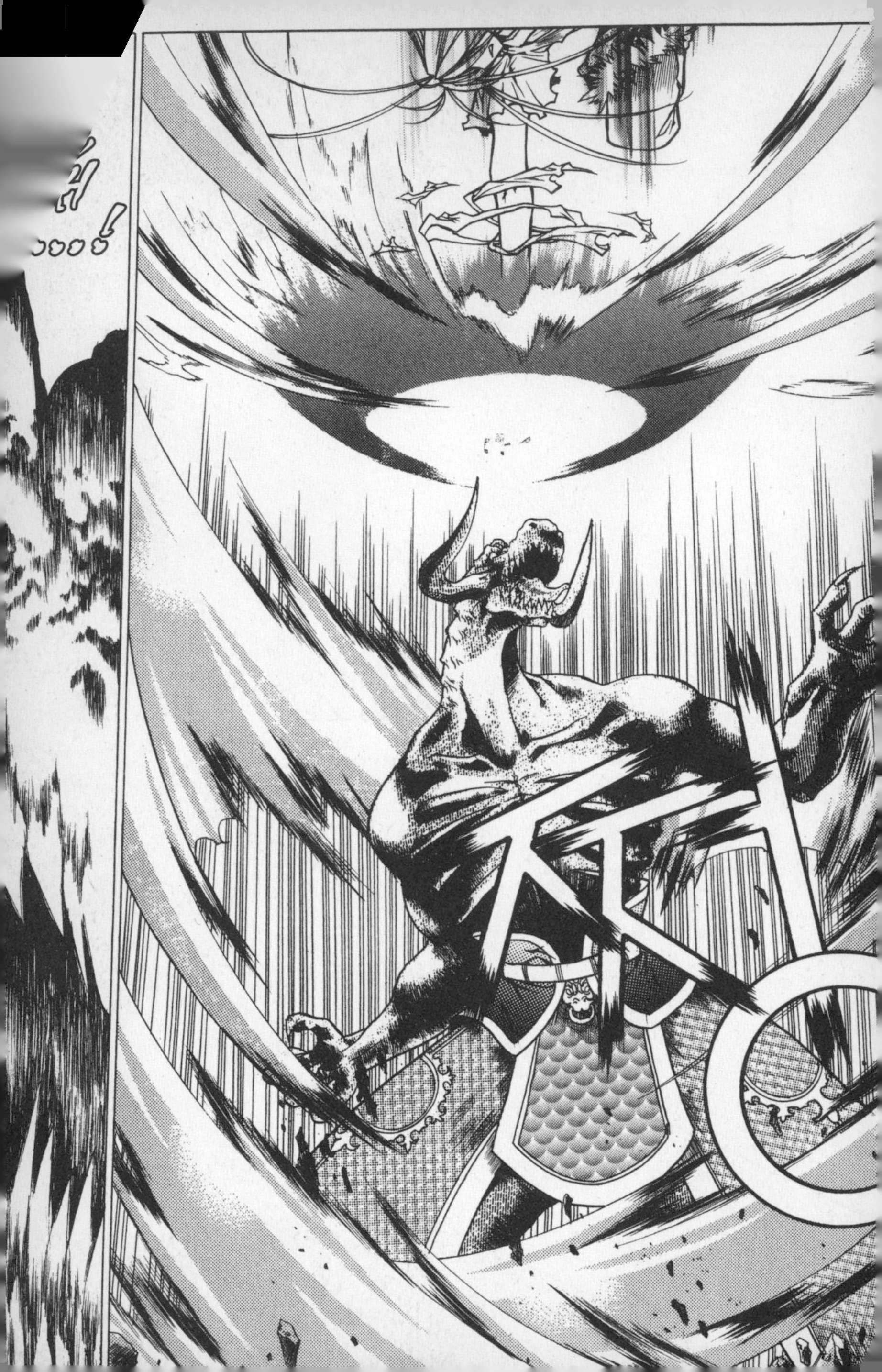

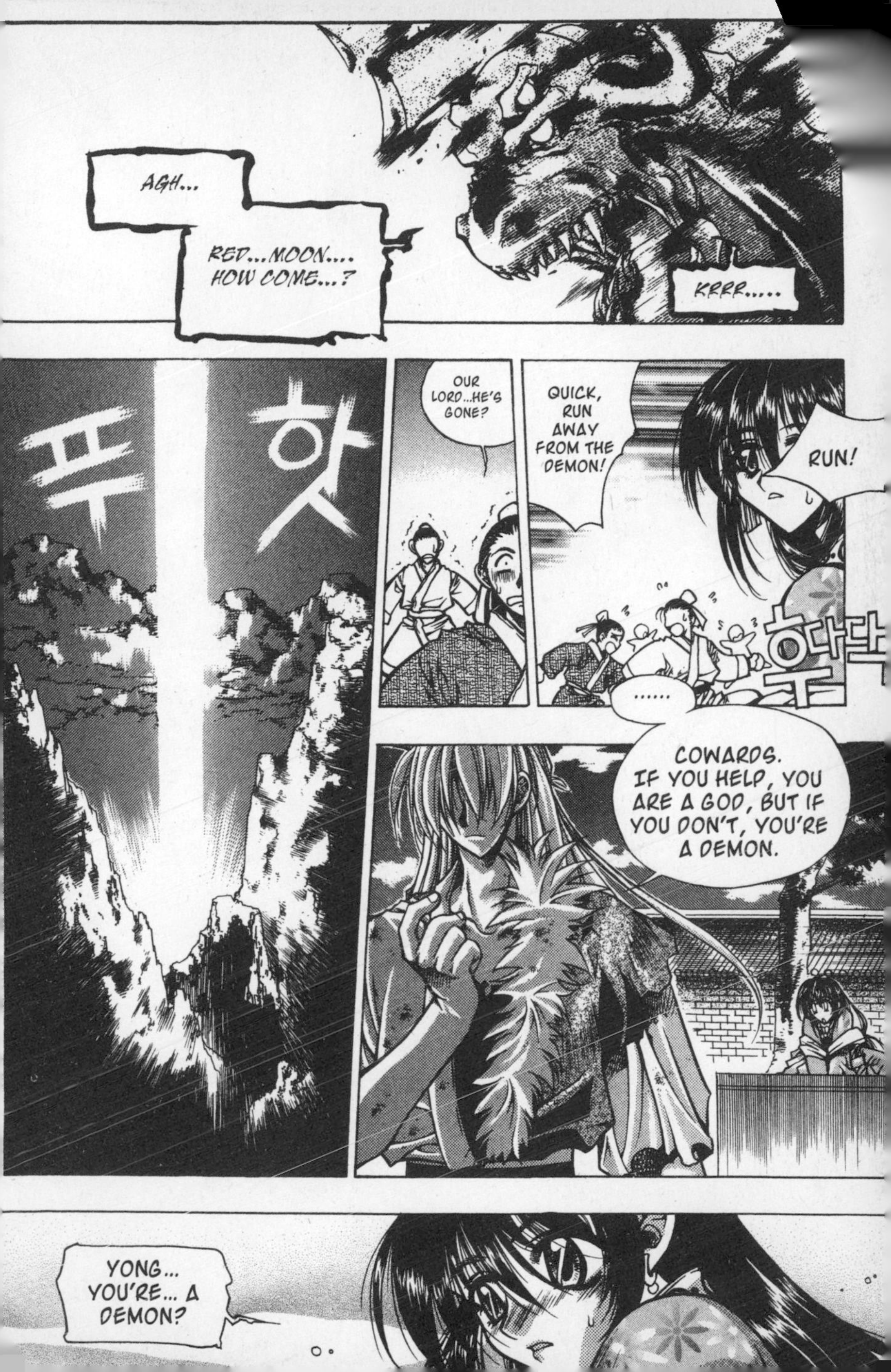

AGH...
RED...MOON.... HOW COME...?
KRRR.....
푸
핫
OUR LORD...HE'S GONE?
QUICK, RUN AWAY FROM THE DEMON!
RUN!
후다닥
......
COWARDS. IF YOU HELP, YOU ARE A GOD, BUT IF YOU DON'T, YOU'RE A DEMON.
YONG... YOU'RE... A DEMON?

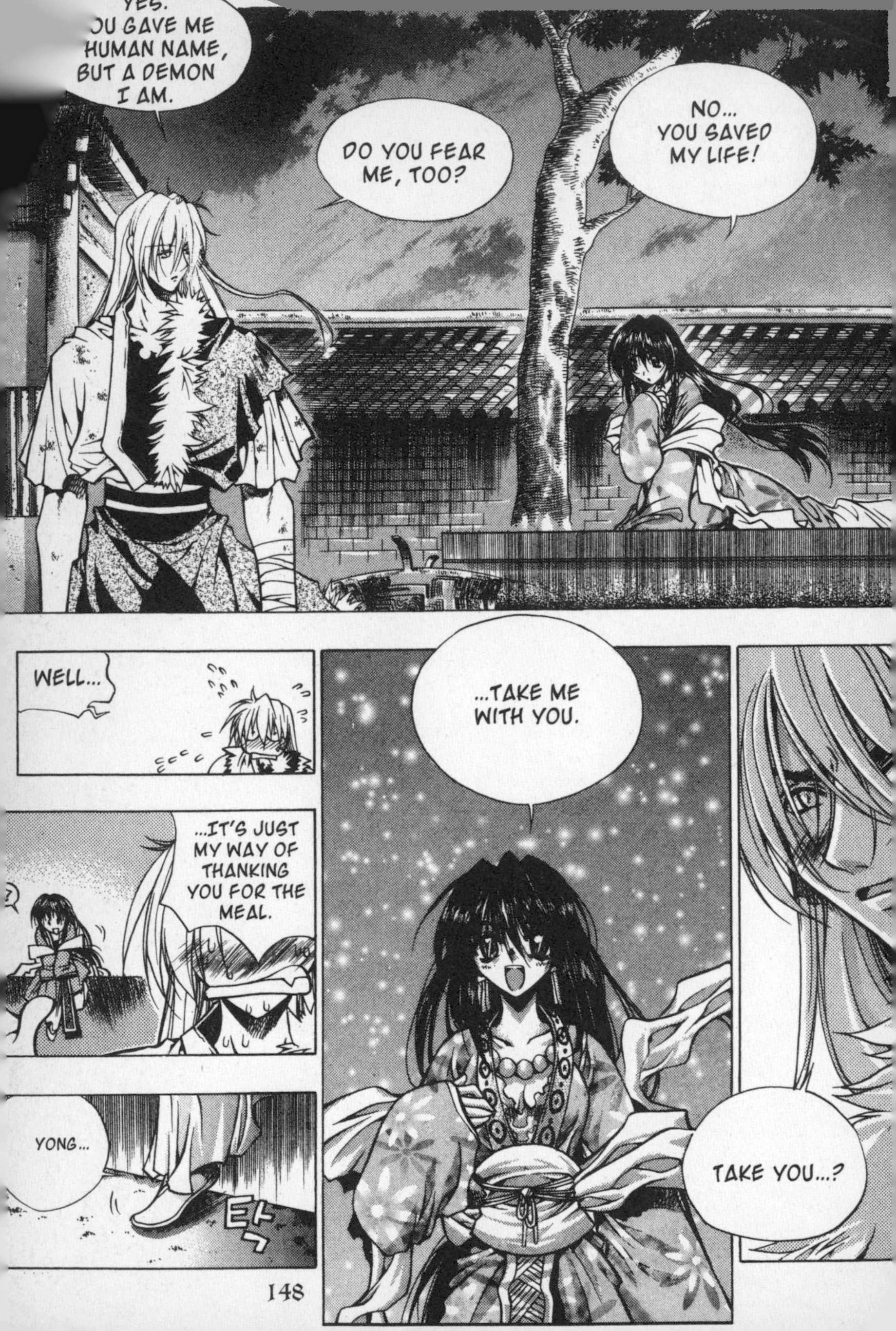
YES. OU GAVE ME HUMAN NAME, BUT A DEMON I AM.
DO YOU FEAR ME, TOO?
NO... YOU SAVED MY LIFE!
WELL...
...IT'S JUST MY WAY OF THANKING YOU FOR THE MEAL.
?
YONG...
탁
...TAKE ME WITH YOU.
TAKE YOU...?

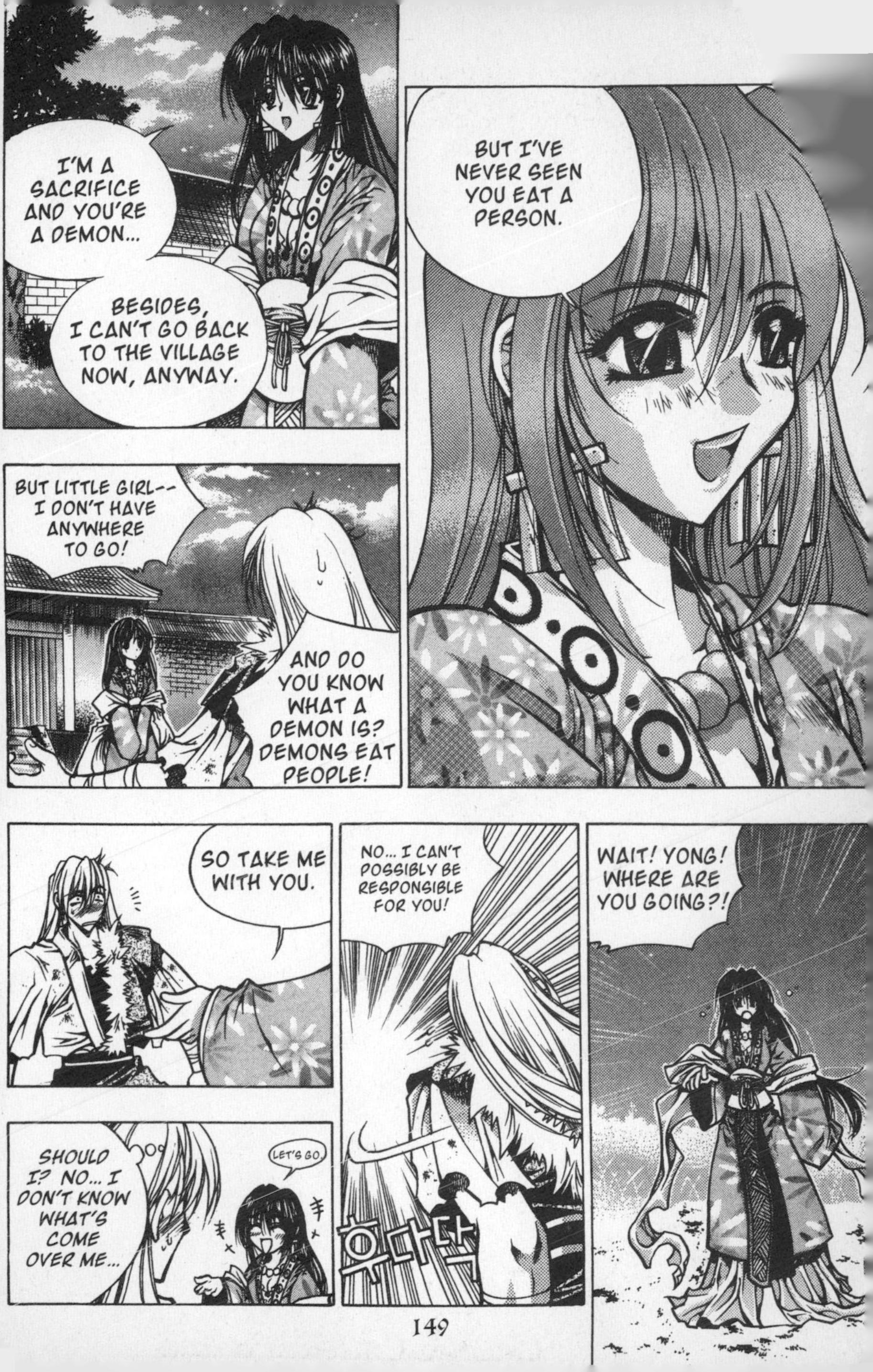
I'M A SACRIFICE AND YOU'RE A DEMON...
BESIDES, I CAN'T GO BACK TO THE VILLAGE NOW, ANYWAY.
BUT LITTLE GIRL-- I DON'T HAVE ANYWHERE TO GO!
AND DO YOU KNOW WHAT A DEMON IS? DEMONS EAT PEOPLE!
BUT I'VE NEVER SEEN YOU EAT A PERSON.
SO TAKE ME WITH YOU.
SHOULD I? NO... I DON'T KNOW WHAT'S COME OVER ME...
LET'S GO.
NO... I CAN'T POSSIBLY BE RESPONSIBLE FOR YOU!
후다닥
WAIT! YONG! WHERE ARE YOU GOING?!

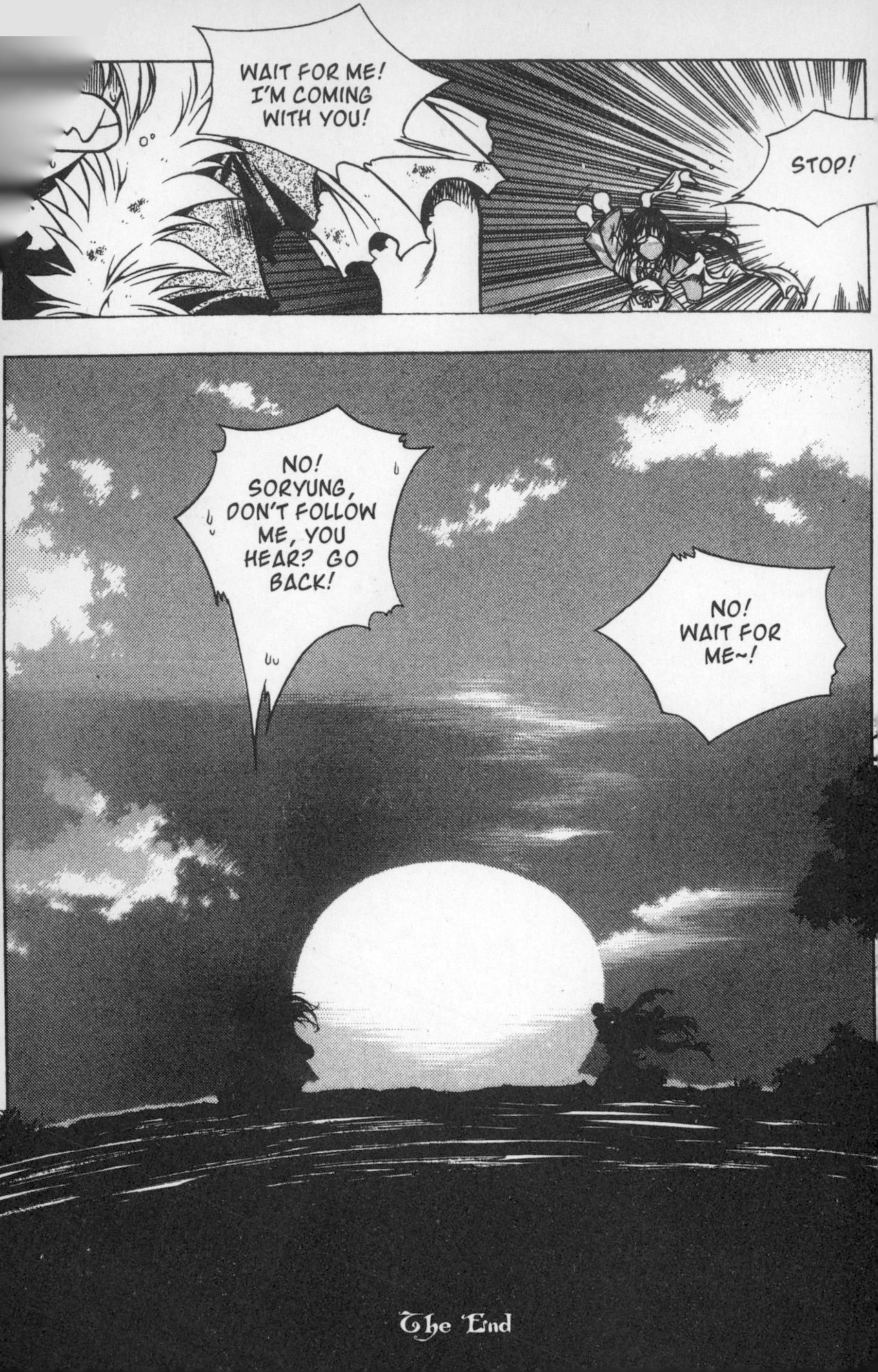
WAIT FOR ME! I'M COMING WITH YOU!
STOP!
NO! SORYUNG, DON'T FOLLOW ME, YOU HEAR? GO BACK!
NO! WAIT FOR ME~!
The End

Special Supplement: Celebrating Chronicles of the Cursed Sword

CHARACTER FILES

...and comments from
Hui-Jin and Beop-Ryong.

First, the major characters

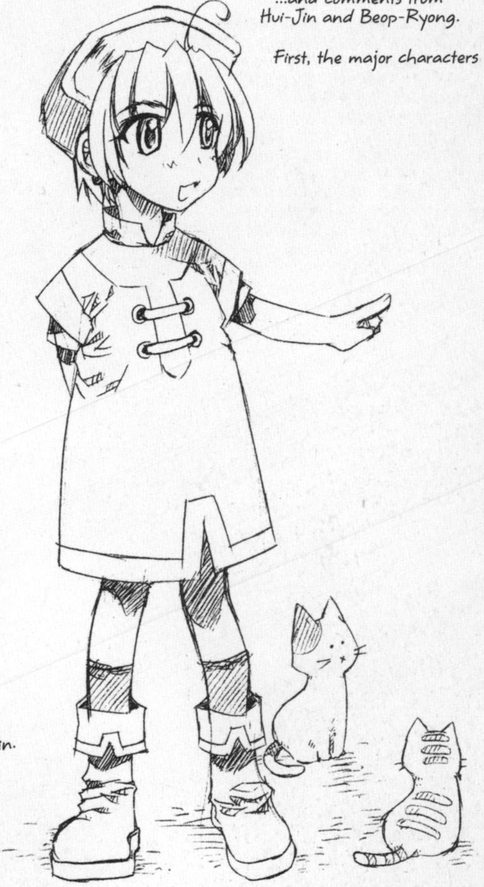

Art by Hui-Jin.

REY YAN

17 YEARS OLD. ORPHANED SEVEN YEARS AGO DURING AN EPIDEMIC, HE ROAMED THE COUNTRY FOR TWO YEARS WITH HIS YOUNGER SISTER, MAY, UNTIL HIS FATEFUL ENCOUNTER WITH SHIYAN. THE HARDSHIPS HE SUFFERED IN CHILDHOOD AND THE EXPERIMENTS SHIYAN SUBJECTED HIM TO HAVE LEFT HIM WITH A TOUGH, ALMOST TWISTED PERSONALITY, BUT REMNANTS OF HIS ORIGINAL UPSTANDING CHARACTER STILL SHINE THROUGH. HE IS QUICK TO ANGER, BUT DOESN'T HOLD GRUDGES. USING CHEN KAIHU'S CHASTITY TECHNIQUE AS HIS FOUNDATION, HE IS CURRENTLY IN THE PROCESS OF LEARNING THE TECHNIQUES ASSOCIATED WITH THE FIVE ELEMENTS (FIRE, WATER, WOOD, METAL, EARTH) FROM MASTER CHEN. WHEN THE SPIRIT OF THE PASA SWORD TAKES HIM OVER COMPLETELY, TATTOOS APPEAR ALL OVER HIS BODY AND HE FALLS PREY TO INTENSE RAGE.

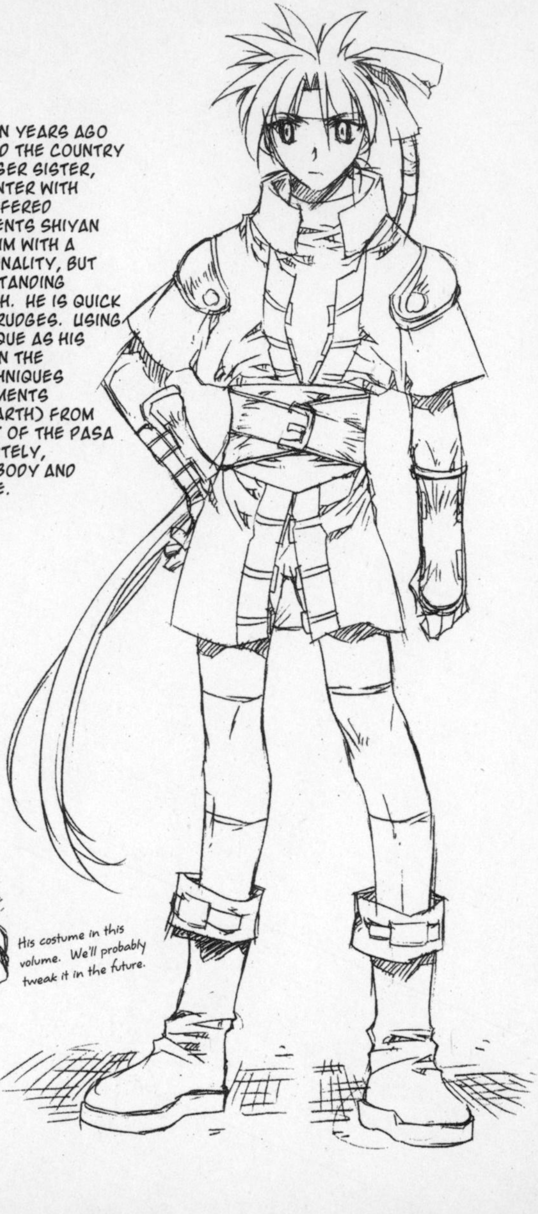

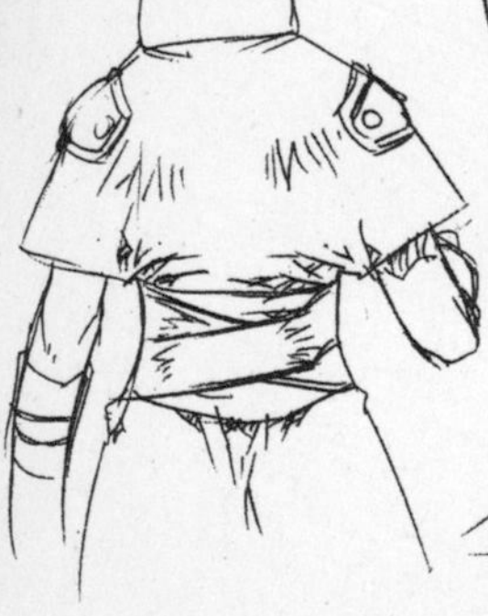

His costume in this volume. We'll probably tweak it in the future.

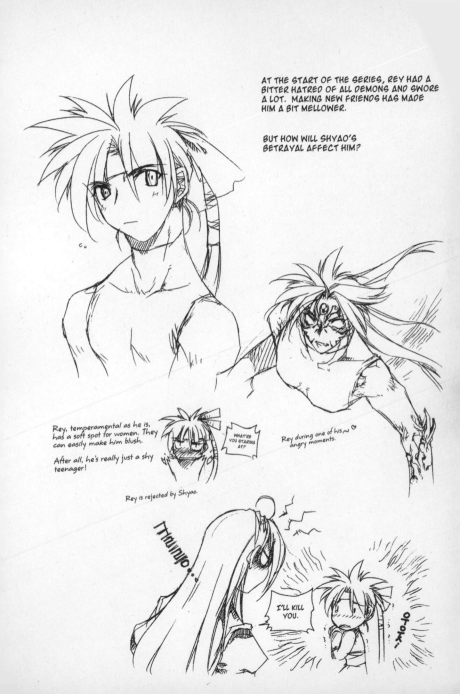

AT THE START OF THE SERIES, REY HAD A BITTER HATRED OF ALL DEMONS AND SWORE A LOT. MAKING NEW FRIENDS HAS MADE HIM A BIT MELLOWER.

BUT HOW WILL SHYAO'S BETRAYAL AFFECT HIM?

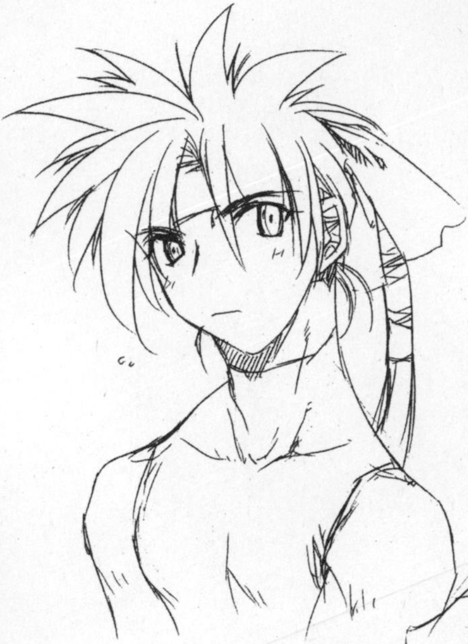

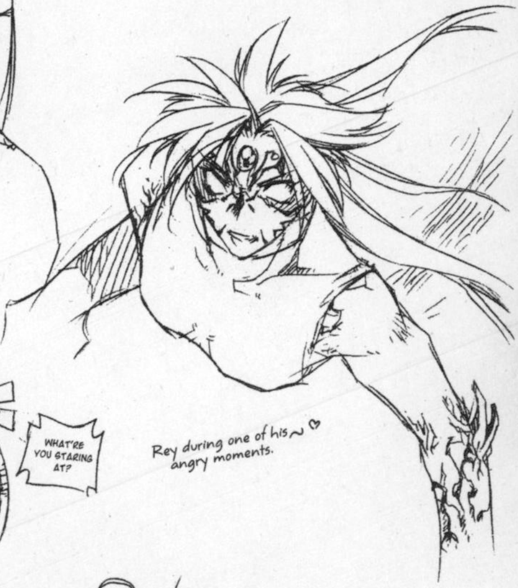

Rey during one of his angry moments.

Rey, temperamental as he is, has a soft spot for women. They can easily make him blush.

After all, he's really just a shy teenager!

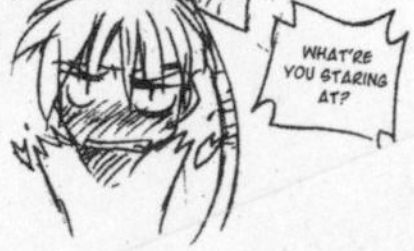
WHAT'RE YOU STARING AT?

Rey is rejected by Shyao.

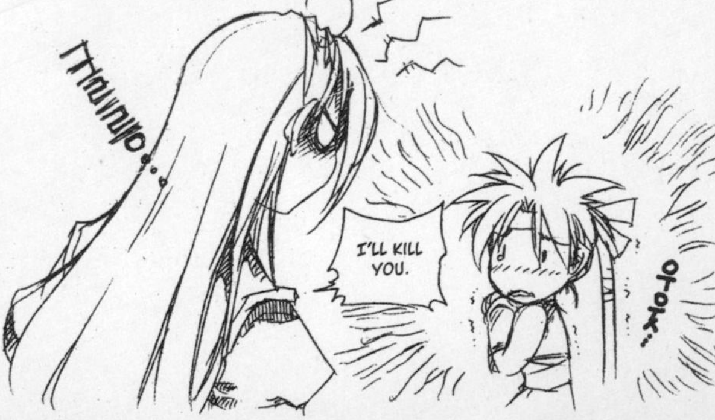
I'LL KILL YOU.

SHYAO LIN:

18 YEARS OLD. A LITTLE BIT NAIVE, SHE HAS BOTH REY AND JARYOON EATING OUT OF HER HAND AND DOESN'T SEEM TO KNOW IT. MASTER LORUAN TOOK HER UNDER HIS WING FIVE YEARS AGO, BEFORE HIS DEATH AT THE HANDS OF WHITE TIGER. AFTER MEETING REY, SHE BECAME A SELF-PROFESSED OLDER SISTER TO HIM. HER REAL IDENTITY, HOWEVER, IS RANA, THE LADY SOHWA, ONE OF THE EIGHT SAGES OF THE HEAVENLY REALM. THOUGH RANA WOULD HAVE ONCE BEEN CLASSIFIED AS AN "ICE PRINCESS" TYPE, HER EXPERIENCES AS SHYAO LIN HAVE BEGUN TO SLOWLY CHANGE HER PERSONALITY.

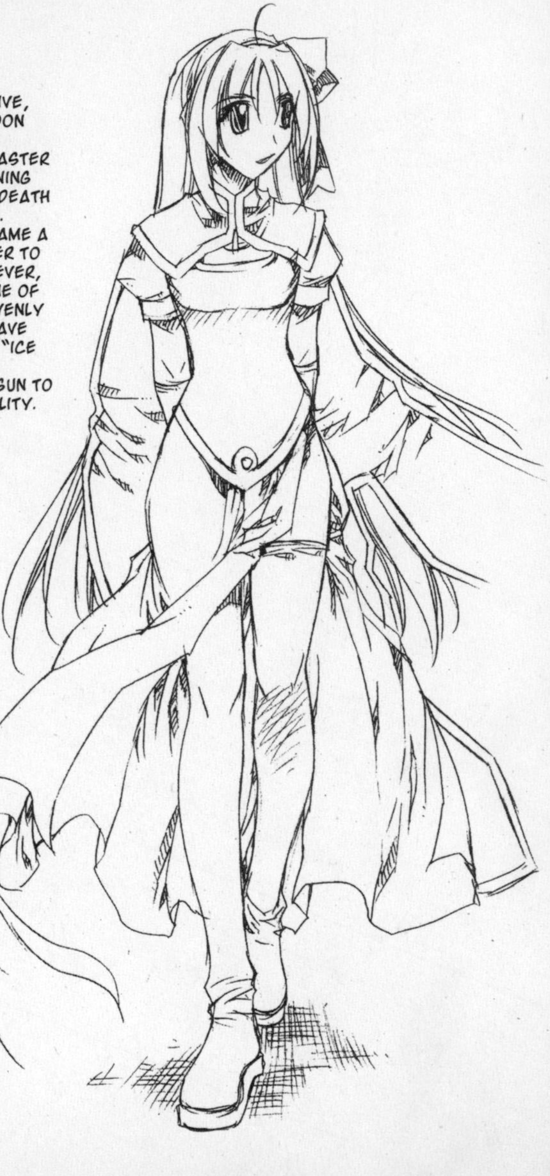

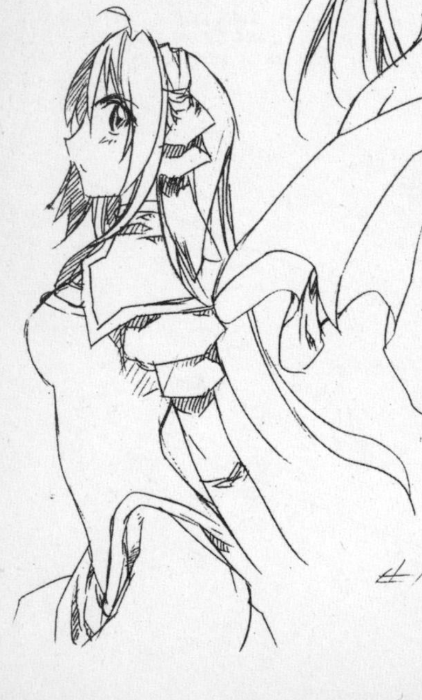

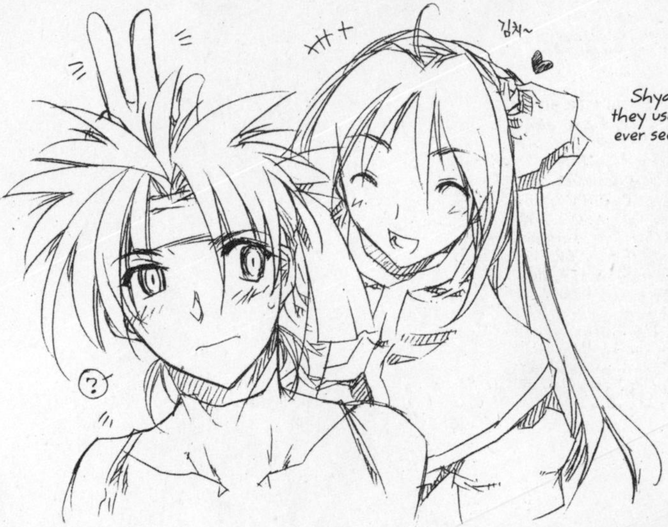
김치~

Shyao and Rey as they used to be. Will we ever see them this way again?

RANA STILL LOVES REY, BUT TRIES TO KILL HIM OUT OF A SENSE OF DUTY. THIS DECISION WILL LIKELY CAUSE HER INTENSE GUILT... EVEN MANY OF THE FANS ARE AGAINST HER NOW... BUT PLEASE, TRY TO BE A LITTLE MORE UNDERSTANDING!

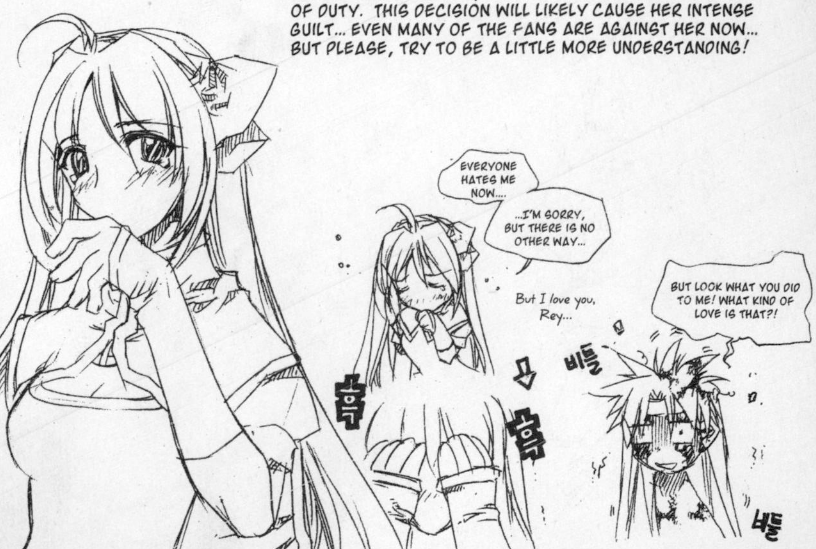
EVERYONE HATES ME NOW....
...I'M SORRY, BUT THERE IS NO OTHER WAY...
But I love you, Rey...
흑
흑
비틀
BUT LOOK WHAT YOU DID TO ME! WHAT KIND OF LOVE IS THAT?!
비틀

RYOON:

YEARS OLD. AS ZHOU ROYALTY, IS THE KING OF HAHYUN WHO RULES OVER SOME TERRITORIES IN THE SOUTH. HIS OLDER BROTHER IS THE EMPEROR, MOOSUNGJE.
HE MEETS REY AND SHYAO WHEN HE IS ABOUT TO BE KILLED AFTER BECOMING ENTANGLED IN SHIYAN'S PLOT. INTELLIGENT AND POSSESSING SUPERIOR MARTIAL ARTS ABILITY, HE IS NONETHELESS DUMBSTRUCK BY HIS LOVE FOR SHYAO. HOWEVER, AFTER SHIYAN PLANTS THE DEMON STONE IN HIM, JARYOON'S DARKEST DESIRES COME TO THE SURFACE. HE OBSESSES OVER SHYAO AND DEMOLISHES NEIGHBORING COUNTRIES IN HIS SEARCH FOR FULL DOMINATION. AT THE MOMENT, HE IS BUILDING UP HIS STRENGTH THROUGH THE HUMAN BLOOD THE PACHUN SWORD ABSORBS.

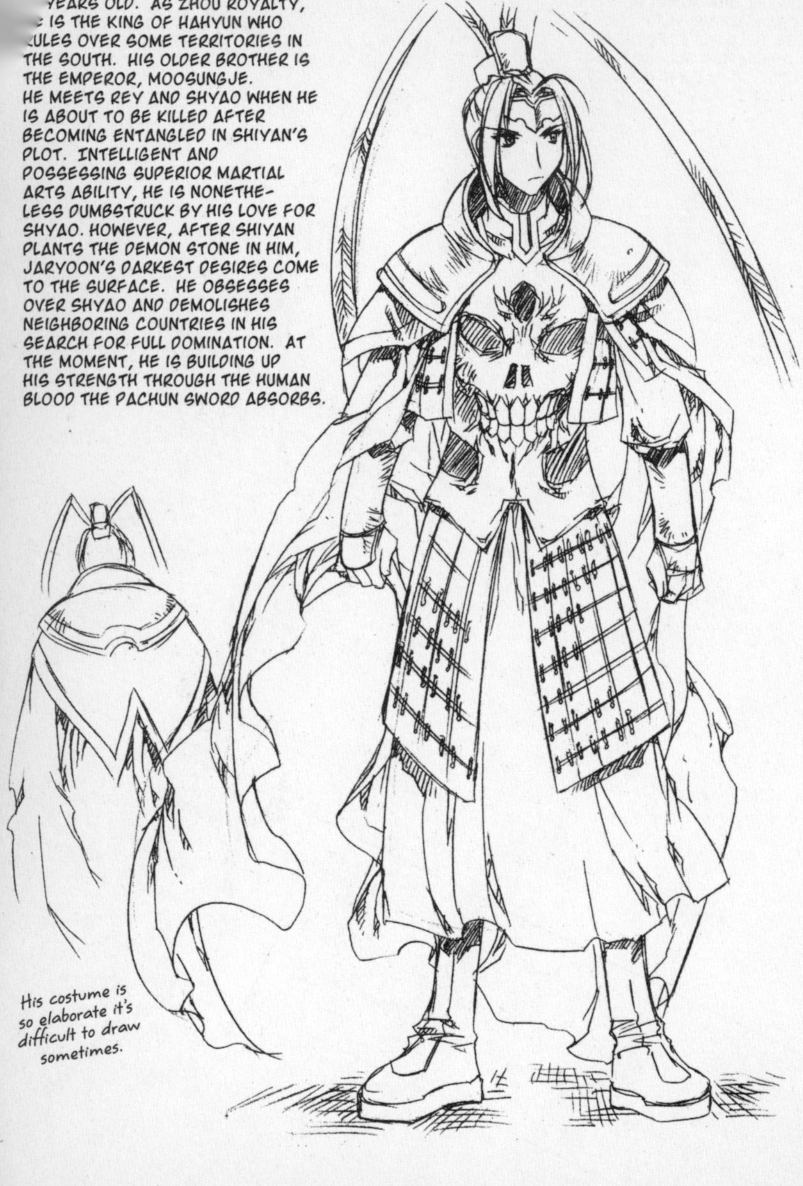

His costume is so elaborate it's difficult to draw sometimes.

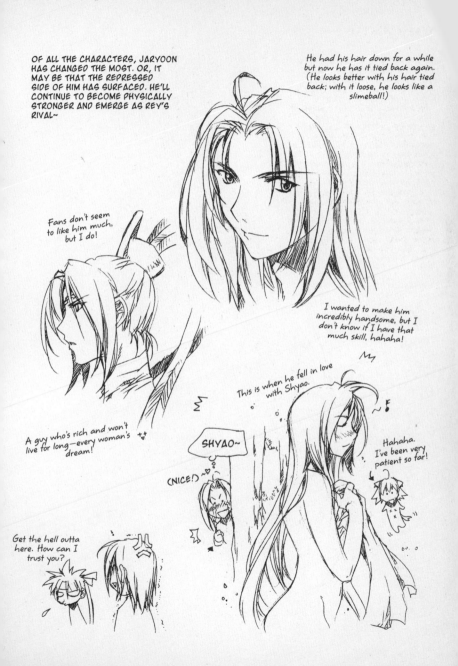

OF ALL THE CHARACTERS, JARYOON HAS CHANGED THE MOST. OR, IT MAY BE THAT THE REPRESSED SIDE OF HIM HAS SURFACED. HE'LL CONTINUE TO BECOME PHYSICALLY STRONGER AND EMERGE AS REY'S RIVAL~

He had his hair down for a while but now he has it tied back again. (He looks better with his hair tied back; with it loose, he looks like a slimeball!)

Fans don't seem to like him much, but I do!

I wanted to make him incredibly handsome, but I don't know if I have that much skill, hahaha!

This is when he fell in love with Shyao.

A guy who's rich and won't live for long—every woman's dream!

SHYAO~

(NICE!)

Hahaha. I've been very patient so far!

Get the hell outta here. How can I trust you?

HYACIA:

HER IDENTITY IS UNCONFIRMED, THOUGH SHE IS DEFINITELY A BEING OF IMMENSE POWER. HER INITIAL FORM DISINTEGRATED LONG AGO, AND SO SHE NOW LIVES IN ANOTHER HOST. HER STRENGTH IS ALMOST WITHOUT EQUAL IN THE DEMONIC AND HEAVENLY REALMS, BUT BECAUSE SHE DOESN'T HAVE A PHYSICAL BODY OF HER OWN, SHE IS WEAK AGAINST CERTAIN TECHNIQUES THAT MAKE HER SOUL LEAVE THE BODY SHE'S IN (SHOUREN FIGHTS WITH TECHNIQUES LIKE THIS, AS YOU SEE IN THIS VOLUME). HER SOUL IS NOT MUCH AFFECTED BY THESE ATTACKS, BUT SUCH TECHNIQUES FORCE HER TO LOOK FOR A NEW HOST. AT THE MOMENT, SHE IS WEARY OF HER LONG LIFE AND HER REFERENCES TO "DARKNESS," "FILTH," "CHAOS," AND "HATE" HINT AT A DARKER SIDE TO HER PERSONALITY. AND WHAT EXACTLY IS THE NATURE OF HER FEELINGS FOR REY...?

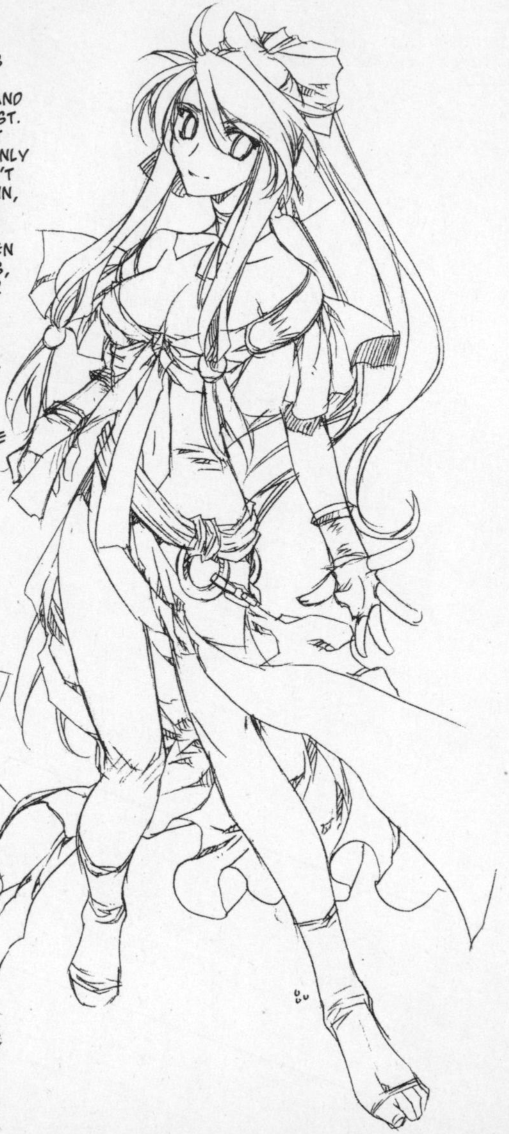

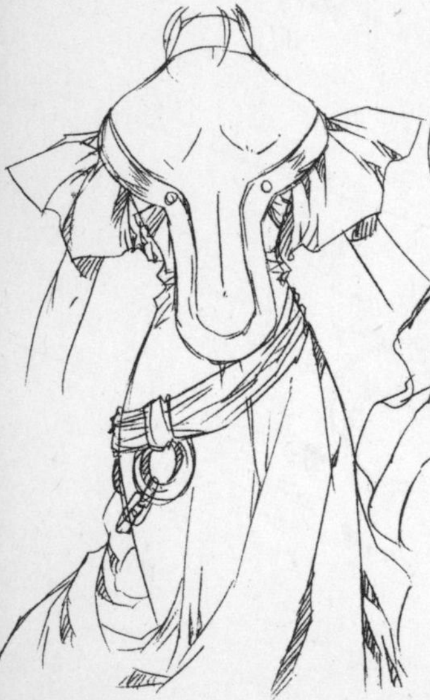

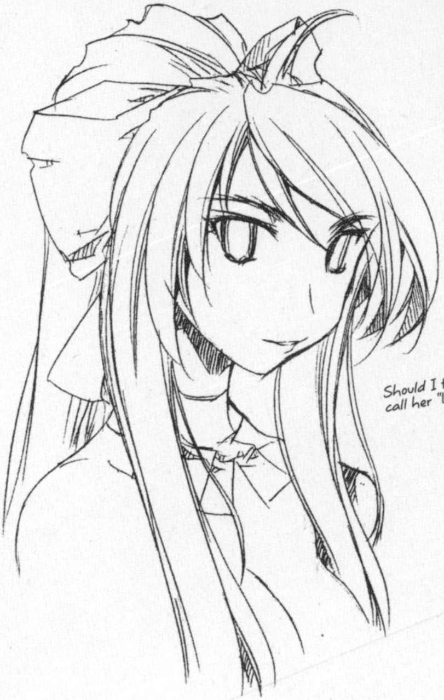

SHE APPEARS CHEERFUL ON THE OUTSIDE BUT HER INNER THOUGHTS REMAIN A MYSTERY. SHE KEEPS TO HERSELF, BUT DOES SHOW SOME TENDERNESS TOWARD REY. HYACIA IS ALSO THE FAVORITE FEMALE CHARACTER AMONG THE FANS. SOME FANS KEEP ASKING ME TO REVEAL HER TRUE IDENTITY, AND OTHERS ASK ME TO KEEP DEVOTING MORE TIME TO HER. MAYBE I WILL... I DON'T KNOW YET...

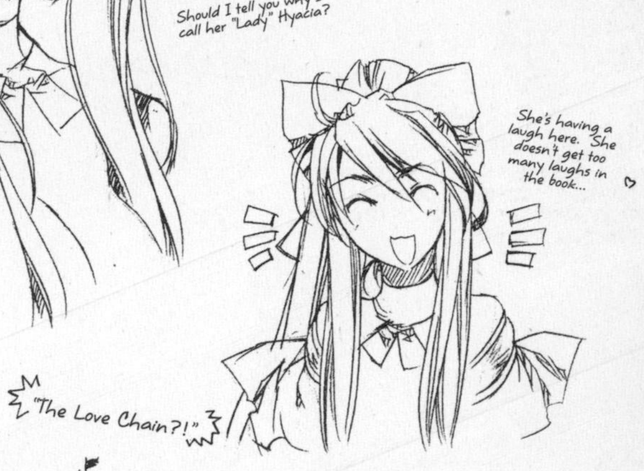
Should I tell you why I call her "Lady" Hyacia?
She's having a laugh here. She doesn't get too many laughs in the book... ♡
"The Love Chain?!"

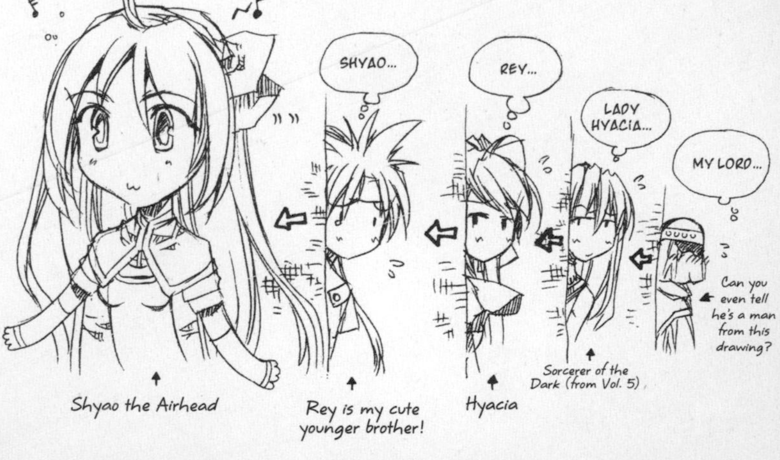
SHYAO...
REY...
LADY HYACIA...
MY LORD...
Can you even tell he's a man from this drawing?
Shyao the Airhead
Rey is my cute younger brother!
Hyacia
Sorcerer of the Dark (from Vol. 5)

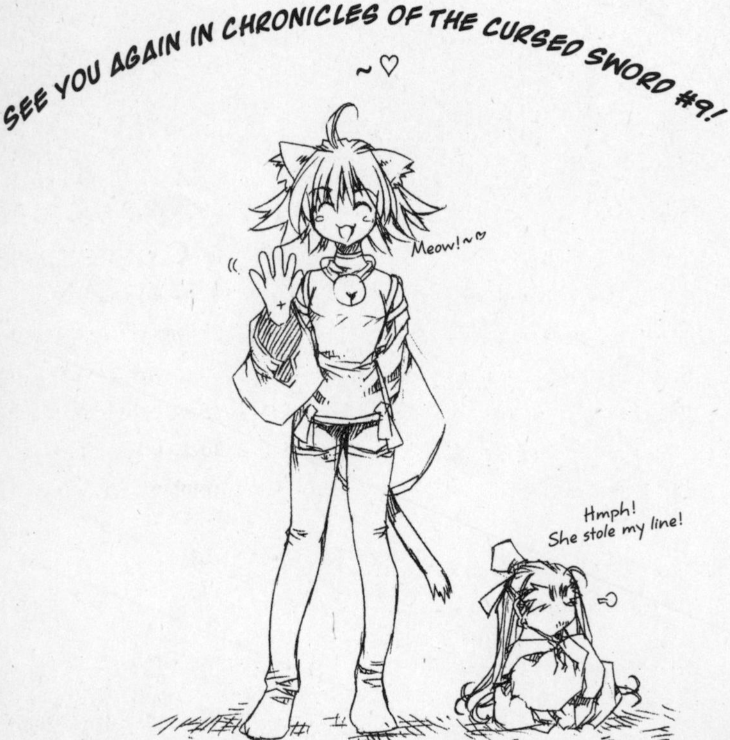
SEE YOU AGAIN IN CHRONICLES OF THE CURSED SWORD #9!
~♡
Meow!~♡
Hmph!
She stole my line!

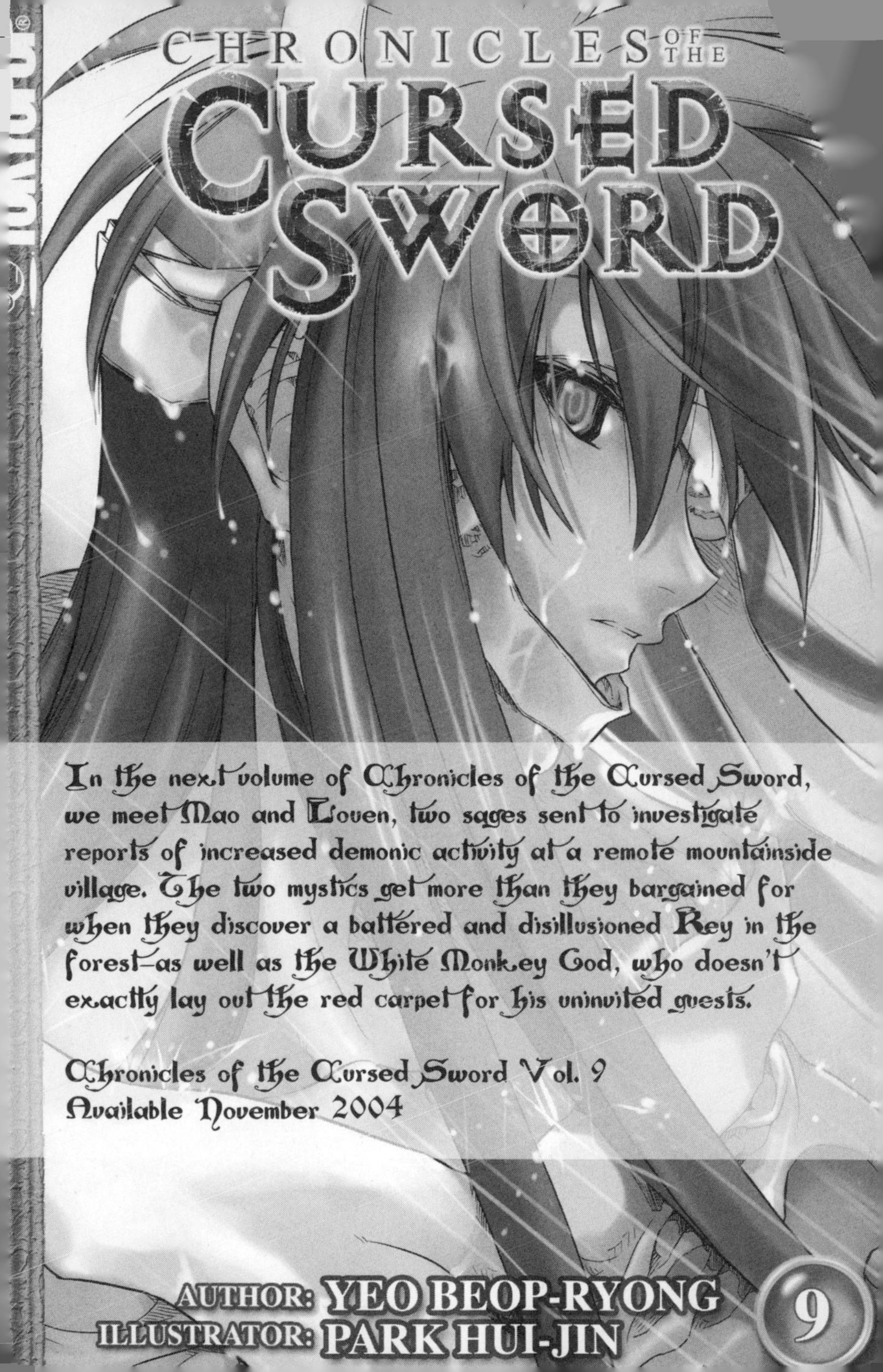

CHRONICLES OF THE CURSED SWORD

In the next volume of Chronicles of the Cursed Sword, we meet Mao and Loven, two sages sent to investigate reports of increased demonic activity at a remote mountainside village. The two mystics get more than they bargained for when they discover a battered and disillusioned Rey in the forest—as well as the White Monkey God, who doesn't exactly lay out the red carpet for his uninvited guests.

Chronicles of the Cursed Sword Vol. 9
Available November 2004

AUTHOR: YEO BEOP-RYONG
ILLUSTRATOR: PARK HUI-JIN

9

SO AVAILABLE FROM TOKYOPOP®

NGA

ACK//LEGEND OF THE TWILIGHT
LARGE
ABENOBASHI: MAGICAL SHOPPING ARCADE
A.I. LOVE YOU
AI YORI AOSHI
ANGELIC LAYER
ARM OF KANNON
BABY BIRTH
BATTLE ROYALE
BATTLE VIXENS
BRAIN POWERED
BRIGADOON
B'TX
CANDIDATE FOR GODDESS, THE
CARDCAPTOR SAKURA
CARDCAPTOR SAKURA - MASTER OF THE CLOW
CHOBITS
CHRONICLES OF THE CURSED SWORD
CLAMP SCHOOL DETECTIVES
CLOVER
COMIC PARTY
CONFIDENTIAL CONFESSIONS
CORRECTOR YUI
COWBOY BEBOP
COWBOY BEBOP: SHOOTING STAR
CRAZY LOVE STORY
CRESCENT MOON
CROSS
CULDCEPT
CYBORG 009
D•N•ANGEL
DEMON DIARY
DEMON ORORON, THE
DEUS VITAE
DIABOLO
DIGIMON
DIGIMON TAMERS
DIGIMON ZERO TWO
DOLL
DRAGON HUNTER
DRAGON KNIGHTS
DRAGON VOICE
DREAM SAGA
DUKLYON: CLAMP SCHOOL DEFENDERS
EERIE QUEERIE!
ERICA SAKURAZAWA: COLLECTED WORKS
ET CETERA
ETERNITY
EVIL'S RETURN
FAERIES' LANDING
FAKE
FLCL
FLOWER OF THE DEEP SLEEP
FORBIDDEN DANCE
FRUITS BASKET
G GUNDAM
GATEKEEPERS
GETBACKERS
GIRL GOT GAME
GIRLS EDUCATIONAL CHARTER
GRAVITATION
GTO
GUNDAM BLUE DESTINY
GUNDAM SEED ASTRAY
GUNDAM WING
GUNDAM WING: BATTLEFIELD OF PACIFISTS
GUNDAM WING: ENDLESS WALTZ
GUNDAM WING: THE LAST OUTPOST (G-UNIT)
GUYS' GUIDE TO GIRLS
HANDS OFF!
HAPPY MANIA
HARLEM BEAT
HYPER RUNE
I.N.V.U.
IMMORTAL RAIN
INITIAL D
INSTANT TEEN: JUST ADD NUTS
ISLAND
JING: KING OF BANDITS
JING: KING OF BANDITS - TWILIGHT TALES
JULINE
KARE KANO
KILL ME, KISS ME
KINDAICHI CASE FILES, THE
KING OF HELL
KODOCHA: SANA'S STAGE
LAMENT OF THE LAMB
LEGAL DRUG
LEGEND OF CHUN HYANG, THE
LES BIJOUX
LOVE HINA
LUPIN III
LUPIN III: WORLD'S MOST WANTED
MAGIC KNIGHT RAYEARTH I
MAGIC KNIGHT RAYEARTH II
MAHOROMATIC: AUTOMATIC MAIDEN
MAN OF MANY FACES
MARMALADE BOY
MARS
MARS: HORSE WITH NO NAME
MINK
MIRACLE GIRLS
MIYUKI-CHAN IN WONDERLAND
MODEL
MOURYOU KIDEN
MY LOVE
NECK AND NECK
ONE
ONE I LOVE, THE
PARADISE KISS
PARASYTE
PASSION FRUIT
PEACH GIRL
PEACH GIRL: CHANGE OF HEART

ALSO AVAILABLE FROM TOKYOPOP®

PET SHOP OF HORRORS
PITA-TEN
PLANET LADDER
PLANETES
PRIEST
PRINCESS AI
PSYCHIC ACADEMY
QUEEN'S KNIGHT, THE
RAGNAROK
RAVE MASTER
REALITY CHECK
REBIRTH
REBOUND
REMOTE
RISING STARS OF MANGA
SABER MARIONETTE J
SAILOR MOON
SAINT TAIL
SAIYUKI
SAMURAI DEEPER KYO
SAMURAI GIRL REAL BOUT HIGH SCHOOL
SCRYED
SEIKAI TRILOGY, THE
SGT. FROG
SHAOLIN SISTERS
SHIRAHIME-SYO: SNOW GODDESS TALES
SHUTTERBOX
SKULL MAN, THE
SNOW DROP
SORCERER HUNTERS
STONE
SUIKODEN III
SUKI
THREADS OF TIME
TOKYO BABYLON
TOKYO MEW MEW
TOKYO TRIBES
TRAMPS LIKE US
UNDER THE GLASS MOON
VAMPIRE GAME
VISION OF ESCAFLOWNE, THE
WARRIORS OF TAO
WILD ACT
WISH
WORLD OF HARTZ
X-DAY
ZODIAC P.I.

NOVELS

CLAMP SCHOOL PARANORMAL INVESTIGATORS
KARMA CLUB
SAILOR MOON
SLAYERS

ART BOOKS

ART OF CARDCAPTOR SAKURA
ART OF MAGIC KNIGHT RAYEARTH, THE
PEACH: MIWA UEDA ILLUSTRATIONS

ANIME GUIDES

COWBOY BEBOP
GUNDAM TECHNICAL MANUALS
SAILOR MOON SCOUT GUIDES

TOKYOPOP KIDS

STRAY SHEEP

CINE-MANGA™

ALADDIN
CARDCAPTORS
DUEL MASTERS
FAIRLY ODDPARENTS, THE
FAMILY GUY
FINDING NEMO
G.I. JOE SPY TROOPS
GREATEST STARS OF THE NBA
JACKIE CHAN ADVENTURES
JIMMY NEUTRON: BOY GENIUS, THE ADVENTURES OF
KIM POSSIBLE
LILO & STITCH: THE SERIES
LIZZIE MCGUIRE
LIZZIE MCGUIRE MOVIE, THE
MALCOLM IN THE MIDDLE
POWER RANGERS: DINO THUNDER
POWER RANGERS: NINJA STORM
PRINCESS DIARIES 2
RAVE MASTER
SHREK 2
SIMPLE LIFE, THE
SPONGEBOB SQUAREPANTS
SPY KIDS 2
SPY KIDS 3-D: GAME OVER
THAT'S SO RAVEN
TOTALLY SPIES
TRANSFORMERS: ARMADA
TRANSFORMERS: ENERGON
VAN HELSING

You want it? We got it!
A full range of TOKYOPOP
products are available now at:
www.TOKYOPOP.com/shop

05.26.04T

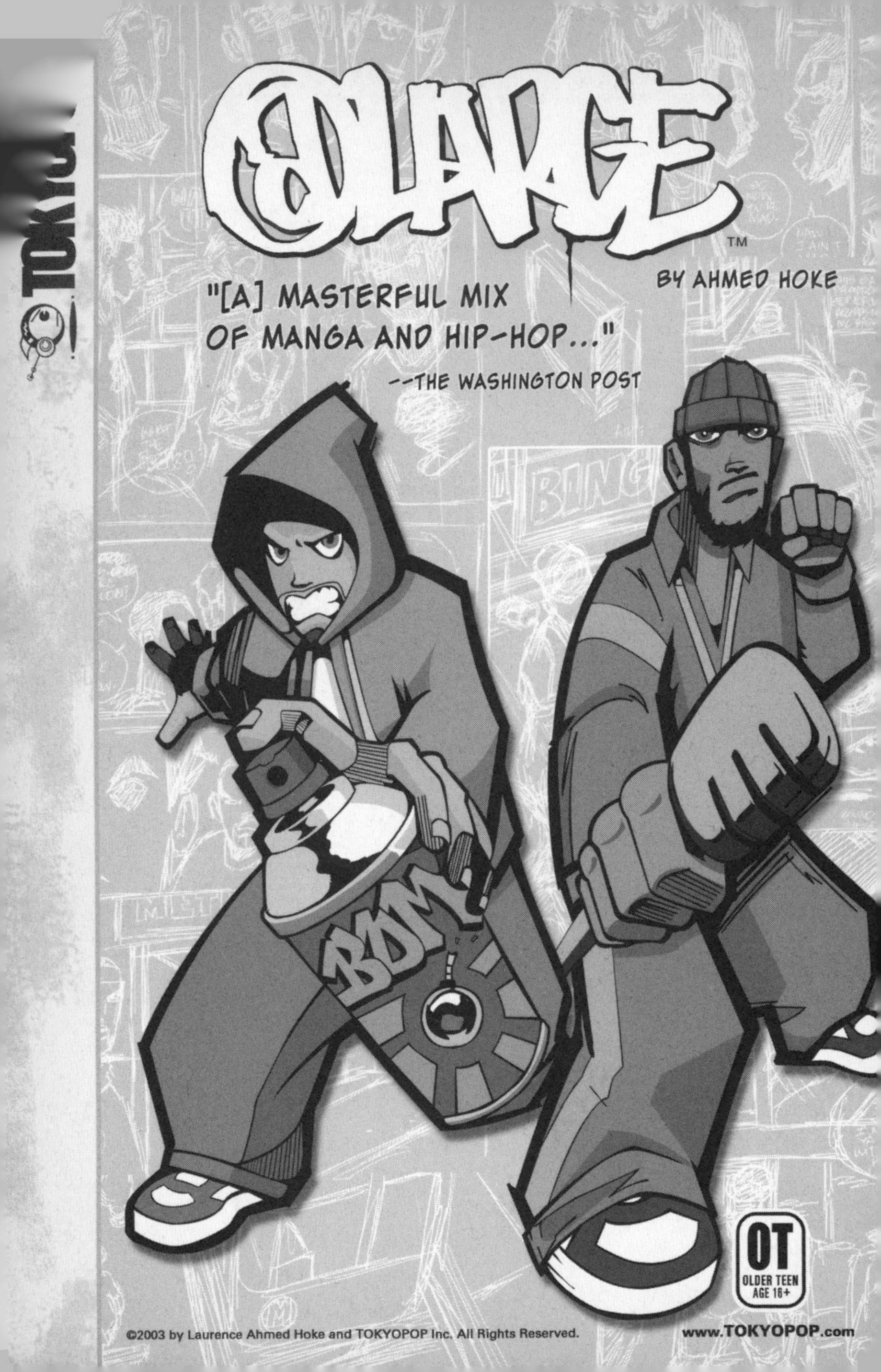
TOKYOPOP
™
BY AHMED HOKE
"[A] MASTERFUL MIX
OF MANGA AND HIP-HOP..."
--THE WASHINGTON POST
BING
BOM
OT
OLDER TEEN
AGE 16+
©2003 by Laurence Ahmed Hoke and TOKYOPOP Inc. All Rights Reserved.
www.TOKYOPOP.com

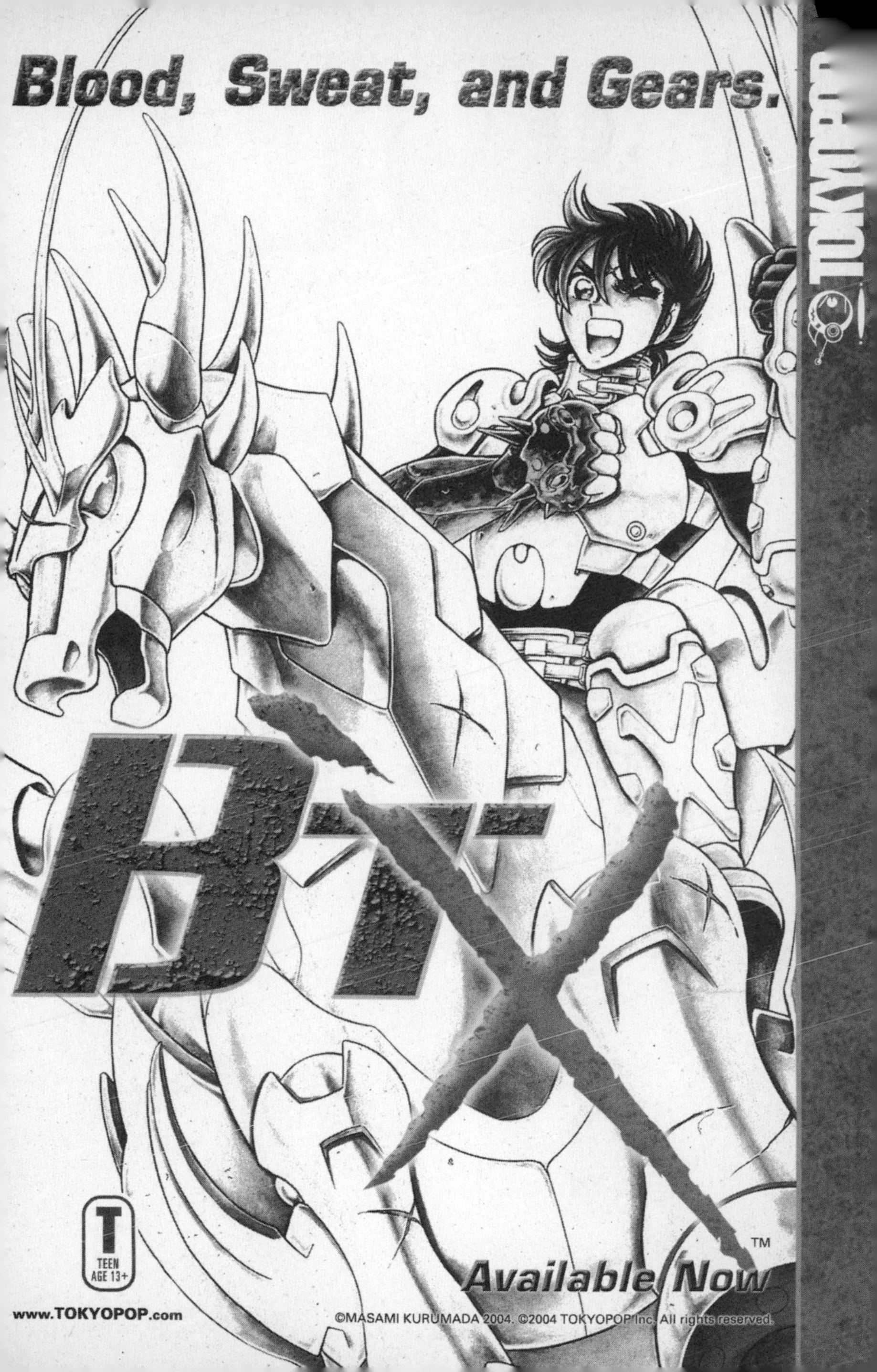

Blood, Sweat, and Gears.
TOKYOPOP
B'T X
TM
T
TEEN
AGE 13+
Available Now
www.TOKYOPOP.com
©MASAMI KURUMADA 2004. ©2004 TOKYOPOP Inc. All rights reserved.

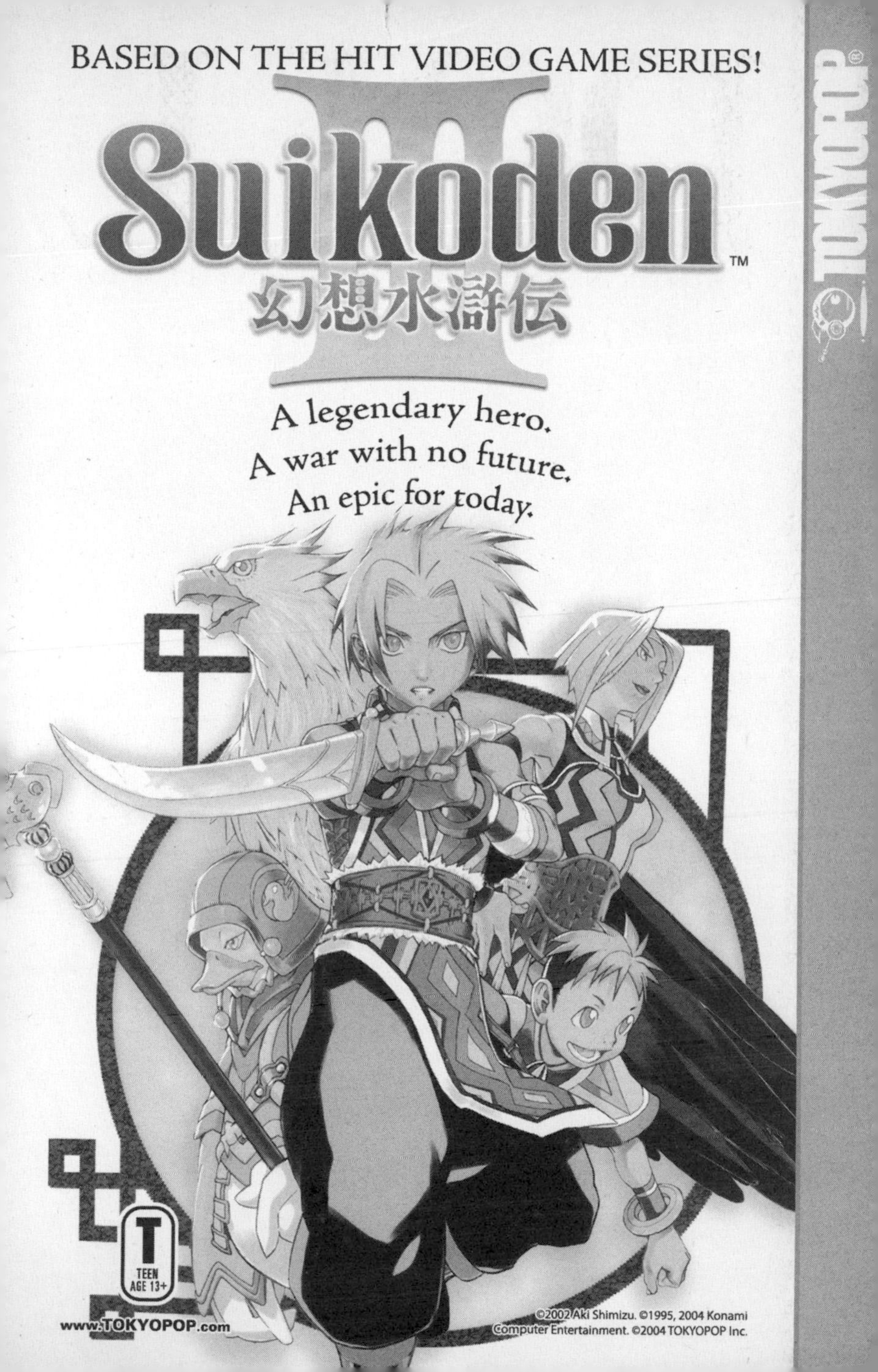
BASED ON THE HIT VIDEO GAME SERIES!
Suikoden III™
幻想水滸伝
A legendary hero.
A war with no future.
An epic for today.
T TEEN AGE 13+
www.TOKYOPOP.com
©2002 Aki Shimizu. ©1995, 2004 Konami Computer Entertainment. ©2004 TOKYOPOP Inc.
TOKYOPOP

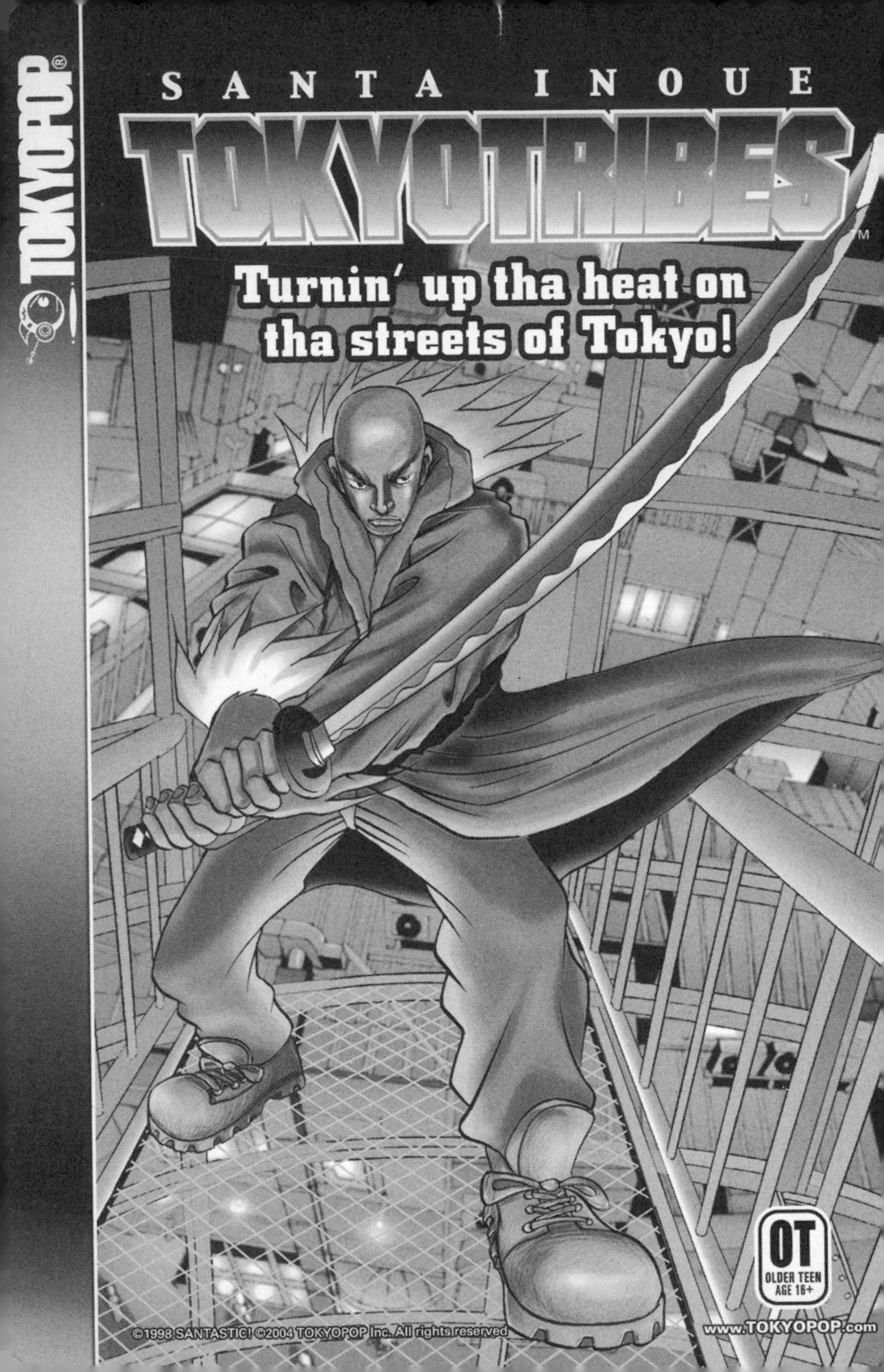
TOKYOPOP®
SANTA INOUE
TOKYO TRIBES™
Turnin' up tha heat on
tha streets of Tokyo!
OT
OLDER TEEN
AGE 16+
©1998 SANTASTIC! ©2004 TOKYOPOP Inc. All rights reserved
www.TOKYOPOP.com